SEPTEMBER'S TRILOGY

-Dew * Tell * Joy-

SEPTEMBER'S TRILOGY

-Dew * Tell * Joy-

ANOINTED ROSE PRESS™

ANOINTED ROSE PRESS™

The Anointed Rose Press name and logo are registered
Trademarks of ANOINTED ROSE PRESS™

SEPTEMBER'S TRILOGY©
Dew * Tell * Joy

SEPTEMBER SUMMER
E-mail: septembersummer09@gmail.com
Website: www.septembersummeronline.com

ISBN-13: 9780982684139
ISBN-10 0-9826841-3-4
© 2010 by September Summer

Anointed Rose Press
P.O. Box 21371
Philadelphia, PA 19141
E-mail: anointed.rose.press.@gmail.com

Library of Congress Control Number: 2010908057
Library of Congress Catalog-in-Publication Data

Summer, September

September's Trilogy / September Summer
p. cm.

ISBN 0-9826841-3-4 (trade pbk.: alk. paper)

1. Autobiography   2. Spirituality

Cover Design:
THE PRINTED WORD, INC.
Philadelphia, PA (215) 224-5500

Printed in the USA for worldwide distribution.
No part of this publication may be reproduced or transmitted for commercial purposes, except for brief quotations in printing, without written permission of the publisher.

...DEDICATION...

*I dedicate this publication
to my family, and to ALL families everywhere. My
prayer for you is that you will do whatever it takes to
keep your family's bond of unity.*

*You did not have the option to choose your family of
origin (or adoption), but now you do have the choice and
the power to love them, to forgive them for their failures
and to value them.*

They help to make us who we are.

...September

...ACKNOWLEDGEMENTS...

I give the utmost Praise and Honor to God my Heavenly Father, whom I love with all of my heart, and who is my Comforter, Provider, and Best Friend.

I thank my parents, my grandparents, my Nana and all who are the ones through whom I have come. They were used to make me who I am. I also thank my stepmother for her loving support. I thank my siblings who have their own victory stories of survival; with special mention to my sister/cheerleader, Felicia. We can celebrate together all of our yesterdays, today and tomorrows.

I thank my children, my grandchildren, my great-grandchildren and all of the "seed" who are coming after me for being the absolute blessings of God in my life.

Thank you to all of my friends, loved ones, prayerful supporters, and ministry colleagues.

Last, but certainly not least, I give special mention and appreciation to my spiritual mentors Apostle Bobby G. Duncan, Dr. William and Dr. Shirley C., and "Dr. M. Frances M. F."

Without "You" there would be no "Me". There are no words that can adequately say how I feel, so please accept this from my heart:

"Thank You" and "I Love You."

...... *September*

"In the Garden"

Author Unknown

I come to the garden alone,
while the dew is still on the roses,
and the voice I hear,
falling on my ear,
The Son of God discloses;

and He walks with me,
and He talks with me,
and He tells me that I am His own;
and the joy we share as we tarry there,
none other has ever known.

...Table of Contents...

Dedication... v
Acknowledgements................................. vi
"In The Garden"..................................... vii

Table of Contents................................... ix
Foreword.. x-xi
Preface.. xii

Book One... 1
    "While the Dew is Still on the Roses"
    A Victory Song

Book Two... 85
    "And He Tells Me I Am His Own"
    The Victory Song Continues

Book Three... 177
    "And the Joy We Share As We Tarry There"
    The Victory Song is Complete

Who Is September Summer?..................... 269

...Foreword...

"The Joy We Share As We Tarry There". has been one of the most exciting books that I have read yet. It will keep you on your toes; you just cannot put it down because the writer keeps you in suspense.

I would recommend that families and single men and women read this book because it will give everyone insight.

I would like to say to September Summer. "On your third book, keep writing to encourage the young as well as the old."

Apostle Bobby G. Duncan
Greater Deliverance Church
Coatesville, PA
www.greaterdeliverancechurch.com

...Foreword...

I met September Summer in 2006 through an organization headed by mutual friends of ours; it's an organization where we share and encourage one another in our prospective ministry assignments. My first impression of her was that she was a little shy, but always friendly and encouraging. As I discovered more about her, I knew that there was a heart connection being developed by God. I remember when September released her first book, *"While the Dew Is Still On the Roses"* at one of our gatherings. She was so excited to let us know about the book and praised God for how He had allowed her to accomplish this task on a low budget. She was printing the book herself and believing God that it would sell. I was so impressed with her enthusiasm, determination, and willingness to give God all of the credit. She expressed how hard it was for her to come to realize that her life would be of interest to anyone. As she told of some of the hills she had encountered in her life, the more I wanted to see what was in that book. Needless to say, I purchased the book right away.

September's first book was so emotionally moving, so real life, so down to earth, it took me back to the scenes where she described. She has such a gift for descriptive writing. She makes you relive the experience with her, feeling what she felt, seeing what she saw. When I got to the end of the book, it was a "cliff hanger." I thought to myself, she has got to write the next book! She cannot leave me hanging like this! What happened next?! Well, *"He Tells Me That I Am His Own"* is the answer. I have enjoyed the second book just as much as the first. The ability to express in writing that excitable, emotional, humorous wit in a way that only September can do is there in *"He Tells Me That I Am His Own."* She has found a way through the Grace of God to encourage others to press on to make a change, to hold fast to the promises of God, and to know the hope expressed in, *"He Tells Me That I Am His Own."* Sharing her life's experiences in such an open way gives hope to others who read about it. Can't wait to get the final book in the trilogy, *"And The Joy We Share As We Tarry There!"*

Prophetess Marilyn T. Carter, *Friend and Spiritual Sister in Christ*
Associate Pastor, Friends of God Worship Center and Bible Institute
Carroll & Marilyn Carter Worldwide Ministries, Inc.
www.cmcworldwideministries.org

...PREFACE...

For a long time, I had much bitterness in my heart towards my parents and grandmother. However, thanks be to God, I have come to peace with the fact that each one did "the best you could do, with who you were, what you had, and what you knew at that place in time." During the period of my life that the second book covers, I had much anger and bitterness in my heart towards my ex-husband, "Michael", but again, I have come to peace with the fact that he also did "the best he could do, with who he was, what he had, and what he knew at that place in time." The third book was, by far, the most challenging of the trilogy to complete. I had to reach waaaaaaaaaaaaay down deep to be able to share my vulnerabilities, as well as my triumphs with you. Thank God, I can honestly say that I have forgiven myself; and I did, "the best I could do, with who I was, what I had, and what I knew at that place in time. I now know that concerning my parents, Michael, and myself – that given a different set of circumstances, and with the knowledge of hindsight, we all may have made other choices."

There is a saying that "Truth is sometimes stranger than fiction", and that is surely true of my life's journey. However, as surely as the sun rises in the east, and sets in the west, these writings are true. As the vision to write and publish the story of my life's journey began to tease at my heart a few years ago, I had to ask myself, "What would be the purpose, and of what benefit would it be to anyone who reads it?" The answer that came back to my heart was, "It is a modern day true 'testimony' of how the Love and Mercy in God's hands will cover even a broken and bruised '**rose**' struggling to grow in the thorny Garden of Life, and how God's Grace can take even the fallen petals and put them back together again to make a victorious survivor who can still be beautiful and fragrant.

My brother once told me that I could make a movie of my life, and my response was, "It would require too many sequels to tell it all." Therefore, what I have written is truly a 'condensed version. Come along with me and let's laugh and cry together. ...***September***

*"For I know the plans that I have for you…
plans to prosper you and not to harm you…
plans to give you a hope and a future"*

…Jeremiah 29:11

Book One

"WHILE THE DEW IS STILL ON THE *ROSES*"

-A Victory Song -

by

September Summer

...The Beginning...

In the beginning, I was just a "loving thought" in the mind of my Heavenly Father. Then He spoke and said, *"**Let her be!**"* By His divine choice, in the process of time, I was born through the joining of my parents. The absolutely awesome and wonderful thing is that before I was even formed in my Mom's belly, God knew me, and had a plan for my life. My earliest childhood memories are of living in an apartment with my Mom and two older brothers, Pete and Dave. There were always a lot of people coming and going. I remember them laughing, talking, dancing, playing cards, and sometimes arguing and fighting. Adults think that children don't remember things from a very early age; let me share something with you to give you an idea of how young I was at the time of my very earliest vivid memory, as if it was yesterday.

"I am standing inside my crib leaning against the side rail, listening to people laughing and talking in another room. I am just standing there looking at Pete and Dave sleeping on the bed across the room. I have a diaper on and a milk bottle in my mouth. Suddenly the lights go out, everything becomes pitch black dark, and I hear people begin to talk loudly. At first I am surprised, and then a little scared but not crying. I am holding my bottle in my hand chewing on the nipple in my mouth, trying to see through the darkness. Then my hand hit the crib knocking the bottle out of my mouth. I am reaching around in the crib trying to find the bottle and I start whining softly for my Mom, as I hear people yelling and talking more loudly now. I am starting to get frantic while still reaching around trying to find my bottle. I start crying louder now for my Mom, but she doesn't come. I can't get over the side rail because it is too high, and I can't see anything. Okay, now is the time to panic, so I start screaming with the best piercing shriek I can get together. That works perfectly because here comes Mom

*with some kind of little light in her hand, and there is my bottle on the floor. Boy was I glad to see her. "What took you so long?" "... **I come to the garden alone..."***

Years later, when I was a teenager and told Mom that I remembered this incident, she was totally shocked. She said she could hardly believe I remembered it since I was less than two years old when it happened. As adults we don't realize just how much children see, hear and remember at extremely young ages. The source of the memory may be happy, sad or frightening and only fleeting, but the impression of it remains with us always; though we may not realize it. This is probably one of the reasons that I have been afraid of the dark for much of my life.

My parents were married when they were both very young, had my two older brothers, and separated before I was born. Mom later told me that she learned my Dad had been unfaithful, so she left him and went to live with her aunt. A few weeks later, she learned that she was several months pregnant with me. She made the decision to not reconcile with Dad. She later moved into the apartment with my two older brothers and me. It was from this apartment that I remember my Dad picking up Pete, Dave and me from time to time to take us out to do fun things like going to the movies, eating out at a restaurant or shopping for clothes.

His girlfriend, Ms. Lucy, would come with him for most of those days out; I really liked her. She liked going to church and would occasionally take us with her. I remember thinking that Dad and Ms. Lucy must be rich or something because they were always dressed in really fancy clothes and drove a nice car. I sometimes heard Dad talking to Ms. Lucy about what he thought of my Mom - complaining about how we children looked when they would come for us. Sometimes they would take us to Nana's house to bathe and redress us before taking us out.

Nana was Dad's grandmother, and I really loved that little lady. I was almost as tall as her by the time I was five years old. She hugged us when she saw us and told us how much she loved us. One of the things that I really liked about her was that she never had bad things to say around us about my Mom. Nana told me over and over how special I was because I was the first girl born into Dad's side of the family for about seventeen years. Needless to say, I was just a tad spoiled. Sometimes while we were at Nana's, Honey Gramms would be there too. Honey Gramms was Dad's mother; she was a tall and very beautiful woman who talked very proper. She also dressed in fancy clothes like Dad and Ms. Lucy. I liked Honey Gramms too, but didn't think she really liked me because she never told me that she did.

One day back home at the apartment, Mom brought a tall, really good looking man home with a soldier's uniform on. Mr. Texas quickly became one of my favorite people because he was so nice to us. Mom was really happy after he came; she stopped having so much company over all the time. Her mother and brother, Mom-Mom and Uncle T, visited a lot. They would play cards or just sit around and talk and laugh with Mr. Texas and Mom. After a while Mom had my baby brother, who was named after his Dad. Not too long after that, she had another baby boy, named Deacon. Things were really good for a long time, and we were happy. *...While the dew is still on the roses...*

...SCHOOL...

At age five, I started attending kindergarten at Carter Elementary School and I loved it. Pete and Dave were in the second and first grades; they were only thirty and fifteen months older than me, respectively. I had the best teacher in the whole world, Mrs. Robinson. I loved playing with the other kids, especially one little boy who liked to pull my hair. After lunch, we would take a nap on our little cots. The best part about the nap was the graham crackers and milk when it was time to get up.

When I close my eyes and think of it, it seems I can still taste and smell the cookies, and hear myself slurping the last drops of milk from the bottom of the cardboard carton. I can still see my classroom with all of the letters and numbers on the windows; and I can hear the laughter of my friends during recess out in the schoolyard. Some of my favorite memories of that time were my little plastic apron that I wore when I painted, and a really neat yellow raincoat and matching galoshes which I wore when it rained. *It's amazing how certain things stick out in our memories; it's a real blessing when the memories are good.*

Then one day when we came in from school, Mom was crying and Mr. Texas was telling us he had to leave to go somewhere else with the Army. He wanted us to go with him, but Mom said "No", she didn't want to move far away. Everything changed drastically after that. First of all, my little brother Deacon was sent to live with Mom's girlfriend and her family. The apartment starting filling up with people, day and night again. Things went back to how they were before Mr. Texas came. Pete, Dave and I were still going out with Dad and Ms. Lucy regularly; sometimes we would get to spend the day at Nana's house a few blocks from our apartment.

The following school year, at Mrs. Robinson's recommendation, I was skipped academically to the next school grade because of how quickly I learned. It was easy because I loved school so much, but Dave didn't care much for it since it caused me to catch up with him in school. The Christmas holidays came around and I remember Dad and Ms. Lucy taking Pete, Dave and me to a large department store in center city which had an extravagant Christmas pageant and lights show. People came from all over the world to see the show. Dad still loves to tell the story of how he gave each of us children the opportunity to have one toy of our own choosing. Since I was the "special" chosen female child of more than seventeen years, I thought I should get more than one. How do you spell "embarrassment"? Have a tantrum at the cash register; then have your Dad pull your coat up in front of everybody and spank your butt right there. I never tried that again, it wasn't worth it. What's more, I still only got one toy.

That was the same year that Dad was trying to take the boys to a football game without their little sister coming along. Just how did they think they could get away with that? What fun is a "football" anyway? I used my most efficient temper tantrum until Honey Gramms told them they had to take me; even Dad had to listen to her. After all, she was his mother. It was freezing cold out, so we got all bundled up, warm and snuggly, and went over to the old sports stadium. Everything was wonderful and exciting, with all of the music and pre-game show, people, balloons, *hot* chocolate, *hot* dogs, *hot* popcorn, and *hot* peanuts. Then, everything quieted down and people sat down to watch these guys kicking some stupid ball and knocking each other down. Not to mention the fact that all of my "hot" stuff was gone, and I started to feel a little cold.

"Okay Dad, the fun is over, can we go home now" - I cannot even begin to describe the strange look on my Dad's face as he looked like he was about to choke or something. He informed me the game was just starting and that I would just have to wait until it was over. I lasted all of about 5 minutes before my fingers, toes, and face, which was wet with tears, were almost frozen. Then I went into a world class temper tantrum, with the loudest

most piercing shriek I could muster up. This caused the people near us to get angry with my Dad. The final outcome – my Dad refused to take me home, took me to the back of the bleachers, spanked my little legs, and zipped me up inside his coat with him. I cried myself to sleep while they finished watching the game. I have never ever been to another live football game, and don't even particularly want to watch it on television.

    As I think about my Dad in those early years, I think of one of the most aristocratic and handsome men that I have known in my whole life. Although he was away from us just about as much of the time that he was with my brothers and me, he was still "my hero". I just knew that when Dad was around, everything was okay. I used to always have a sense of "waiting" for him until he would come home; though sometimes it would be weeks or months in between. I remember that even the sound of his voice would make me feel happy. He would often take us around his friends and brag on us as his children. He wasn't mean like Honey Gramms; he could tell you what to do, and you would just do it because he said so. He would hug me and tell me that he loved me when he was around. *...And the voice I hear, falling on my ear...*

....MAJOR CHANGES........

Early in the fall of following school year, Mom became ill and had to be hospitalized; leaving Mom-Mom and Uncle T at the house to babysit us children. The truth is, there should have been someone babysitting them. One day we kids were in the living room playing; and Mom-Mom and Uncle T were playing cards. An argument broke out between the two of them; and suddenly, Mom-Mom threw a jar of Dixie Peach hair pomade at Uncle T. The jar missed him, but flew across the room and hit Dave directly in the head. He screamed as blood started running from where the jar had struck him. Mom-Mom and Uncle T were still arguing, oblivious to us; so Pete grabbed a towel and wrapped Dave's head in it.

There was no phone in our home at the time, so Pete told Dave and me to come with him. We ran the six or so blocks to Nana's house. I don't even believe Mom-Mom and Uncle T realized we had left until after we were gone. Just imagine the sight of a seven year old, a six year old and a five year old running through the streets like wild banshees; with a blood soaked towel wrapped around Dave's head and me screaming hysterically like a maniac. When we arrived at Nana's, she telephoned Dad. Within what seemed like a few minutes, the house was filled with people – Dad and Ms. Lucy, Honey Gramms and her boyfriend Sugar Pops, Nana's brother and the neighbors. Dave was taken to the hospital and had his "first" in a long line of boyhood experiences requiring sutures. Pete went with them but I was bathed and put to bed, with the smell of Dixie Peach hair pomade still fresh in my mind. Even now, as I am writing this, I still remember the light blue and yellow label on the jar, and smell the poignant fragrance of the yellowish-white hair pomade.

I went to sleep that night crying for my Mom, not knowing if my brother was dying; and not knowing that my life was never to be the same again. I woke up in the middle of the night, hearing the voices of adults talking and arguing in hushed voices. When I got up to see what was going on, I was reassured that everything was all right and that I should go back to bed. I found Pete and Dave asleep in the next bedroom, so I went and got in the bed with them. We never had a chance to see the apartment again that I remember so well with mixed emotions. The next day, we were kept home from school. Later in the day, Dad and Ms. Lucy came in the house with our clothes from the apartment. We stayed at Nana's and went to school from there.

Report card time came and lo and behold, I did not have all A's this time. Oh my God! There was a "B" on my report card. I was horrified and thought for sure that I was going to get "murderized" by my Dad or Honey Gramms. I ran home, waving at Nana as I ran pass her standing at her girlfriend's store around the corner. I flew into the house, changed my clothes, stopped long enough to make me a couple slices of mayonnaise and sugar toast and rushed out the door before anyone else could get home. *By the way, you haven't lived until you have eaten mayonnaise and sugar toast, with extra mayonnaise sprinkled with sugar and toasted under the broiler. Umm Umm*!

"Where could I run that Dad and Honey Gramms couldn't find me? Where could a five year old go by herself, when she is scared to cross any big streets alone?" The farthest places I had been allowed to go by myself off the block was to school and to my girlfriend's house around the corner. So, I went to Miriam's house around the corner. I told her Mom that Nana said I could come to their house for dinner and to spend some time with Miriam. After dinner, as it was coming up on time to go to bed, Mrs. Brown asked me if I shouldn't be going home now. I told her that Nana had given me permission to spend the night. She didn't say anything, but a few minutes later, I heard her on the phone telling Nana she thought it was strange that they would let me stay out after dark, especially on a school night. *Oops! Time to go!*

Out the door I went running as fast as I could, down the street and around the corner. Suddenly, it dawned on me that it was dark out! At least it was the spring of the year and kind of warm. Being afraid of the dark, I decided to hang out in the alleyway at the corner from our house. I could see the house but they couldn't see me. *Maybe I could sleep on Ms. Alice's porch across the street.* Wow! There was a lot of activity going on at our house. There were two red and white police cars out there and people going in and out; and Nana is in the door crying. Oh my God, they must be looking for me! *Boy, I am in some real trouble now.* My mind is racing, "Maybe I can run away, get a job and take care of myself until I finish school. Then I'll get married and run off with my husband. But, first I have to find a way to get over to Ms. Alice's porch across the street, without them seeing me."

I was so focused on trying to figure out how to sneak across the street, and watching all the activity in front of the house; that I did not notice a yellow taxicab pull up near me. By the time I did notice the cab, the door opened and I saw my Mom getting out. *Hey, Mom is here to save me!* I started running towards her, but my Dad's car pulled up behind the cab; and he caught up with me. By that time, someone near the house saw us. The next thing I knew, I was swarmed with all kinds of hugs and kisses from everybody. Dad and Honey Gramms were crying. Everybody else was telling me they were so glad to see me, and crying and laughing. *Okay, maybe they won't "murderize" me for the "B' on my report card.*

I don't know why my Mom didn't take me with her that night. After she left, Honey Gramms told me that if I ever did that again, she would kill me. I believed her, and never tried it again. A few nights later, in the middle of the night, we were taken out in our pajamas and placed under blankets in Dad's car. Dad and Ms. Lucy told us we were going on a fun trip. All I remember before falling back to sleep is that it was still dark. The next day when I awoke to daylight, we were in the city of Rose Tree, New York. From that time, my Mom did not know how to find us for the next nine years, (*I want my Mom!!*). **...The Son of God discloses...**

...Rose Tree...

Our childhood years in Rose Tree were turbulent to say the least, with intermittent periods of returning to our hometown. My first memory of Rose Tree was Dad pulling up in front of a barbershop, and telling us to come in to meet a friend of his. We went inside, and the first wall that I saw took my breath away and made me stand completely still. It was a ceiling to floor hand painted mural with multiple scenes of Niagara Falls, Indians, buffalo, tents, villages and mountains. It must have been how that area had looked hundreds of years before. It was so lifelike that it seemed as if I should be able to hear the pounding of the thousands of tons of water rushing over the falls. I was so amazed that I stood there for a long time looking at that mural, until Dad took me by the hand to introduce me to his friend, Mr. Cunningham. This gentleman and his family turned out to be some of the nicest people. They quickly became our adopted family, and my brothers and his son became the best of friends.

Dad, Ms. Lucy, Dave, Pete and I moved into an apartment up the street from the barbershop; and life settled down for a bit. We quickly made new friends, and loved our new neighbors and the newness of the neighborhood – I remember the streets being the hugest streets that I had ever seen. As I think back, I realize that it was as much a commercial area as a residential area. There were huge stores, factories and other commercial properties intermingled with homes. That's probably why the area seemed so gigantic to me; having come from a residential area of tightly joined row homes. We kids were a novelty to the other kids on the block because of our different accent; and the words that we used, like taffy or lollipop instead of "sucker", and soda instead of "pop". We were like mini-celebrities, for all of a hot minute. We began attending School Number 8 immediately, which was one of the greatest joys of my life since I loved school. Of course, being the new kids on the block, and coming from another whole state, we went through a period of being teased about our dress style.

For me, what was even worse was that I had begun to sprout up like a "weed", as Honey Gramms was fond of saying. My long skinny legs in those horrible brown square-toed orthopedic shoes I was forced to wear did not help. My feet were very long and narrow, and my pediatrician felt that I should have the extra support of "Buster Brown" orthopedic shoes!! How horrible can life get to be when you are already the tallest, skinniest girl in the whole class for your age? Not to mention the fact that you have been skipped in school, so that your classmates are already looking more like teenagers to you; and are more cool than you to begin with? Here you come in the middle of the school year, with these huge boats on your feet, at the end of the twigs you have for legs. This, on top of the fact that your hair is long, down midway your back, but you are made to wear it up in three plaits. No - not "French Braids"; but plaits, like a toddler. All of the other girls in your class are wearing cute little shoes, with stocking-like leotards, and their hair with a bang and ponytails; and then....there is you. You, whose nickname the kids have "lovingly" deemed the *"black tree"*; because not only are you tall with all this long hair, but you are almost "see through" skinny. My brothers fought many a fight protecting me from the teasers. *Does anyone know how I can get back to my Mom's house or even where she is? How far away is she, and how long would it take me to get there?*

All-in-all, things went smoothly for a while. At least, as smoothly as things can for a six year old who likes the new apartment, but who would sure love to see, or at least talk to her Mom. We were introduced to Dad's stepfather who also lived in Rose Tree, with his mother. They were nice enough people, but Grand-Pop's mother was very old. Her house was kind of moldy smelling and spooky to me. We used to visit once in a while, but I didn't like the place, so didn't enjoy the visits. The good thing about Grand-Pop's mother was that she would take us to Sunday School with her sometimes. I really enjoyed it, but the boys didn't like going.

One of the most truly traumatic things about life in Rose Tree was the snow. I had never seen so much snow at one time in all my young life. I cried every morning when it was time to go to school until Pete would feel sorry for me and pull me on his sled to school; after helping me put on my big old one piece snowsuit. I still shiver remembering those days. Dave was horrible about it. He would put little snowballs down my back and then fall out on the ground laughing. *Jerk!*

It didn't take long for me to realize that we were not in heaven. For one thing, Dad and Ms. Lucy began to argue often; and Dad would stay out all night at times. I began having nightmares, and created a hole in the wall next to my bed because I would bang my head on the wall in my sleep. Dave began sucking his thumb and wetting the bed; and Pete started getting into trouble by fighting in school. Ms. Lucy was a very pretty woman and initially kind and soft-spoken; gradually she became mean and eventually cruel. She was a refined and educated woman, who was a school teacher. I was told later she had come from a well to do family. I heard rumors her family disowned her when she left town with Dad; to move in with a man she was not married to, and his children. I don't know if that is true or not; but I know all of us lost something, because of Dad's decision to "rescue" his children by kidnapping us...***And He walks with me...***

....To the Rescue...

It was the early 1950s, during the winter of "Hurricane Hazel" and the "Asiatic Flu". By the grace of God, we managed to survive our first winters in Rose Tree. Then, finally things came to a head at home. One day when we kids came in from school, no one was home. Ms. Lucy had left town, and Dad followed after her; leaving us children there alone for days. Of course, at that time, we didn't know where either of them was, and we had no phone. What we did have was Dad's standing credit account with the small grocery store next door to us. We would go over there to get food for sandwiches and snacks. We continued going to school, while waiting for Dad to come home. After a few days, Dad called Honey Gramms at home, and told her that we were in Rose Tree alone. She called us on the next door grocer's phone; and a few days later, she arrived in Rose Tree.

Needless to say, she was not a happy camper; and it was not difficult for my brothers and me to know it. Our friends just thought it was the coolest thing that this young looking woman was actually our grandmother. That took us up a couple notches on the popularity chain. At least, now we had some real home cooked food. To sidebar for a bit, my Honey Gramms was an enigma to me. As I look back, I believe she actually did love us in her own way, but I never once in my life remember hearing her say it. I don't remember her ever hugging us or showing us any outward demonstration of love. I guess she felt that it was enough that she showed us her love by helping to provide the best in clothes, food and provisions for us.

I believe she had the making of a millionaire, had she been given the right opportunity and resources. She was an extremely intelligent and creative woman, who was also a perfectionist with a capital "P". Unfortunately, she was also a bitter and angry person, who was saddled periodically with three young grandchildren to rear. We were also the offspring of a woman whom she despised. It was not a situation that she was able to handle well. Many years later, I also learned a few things about Honey Gramms' own hurtful past that helped to explain a lot of her bitterness. She was a true "noble" woman in every way, from her speech to her dress style, to how she carried herself with distinction. She was a woman of high ideals and determination, with a powerful work ethic and an inner drive to achieve something in life. She studied many things in life through reading, radio and television and was powerfully self educated concerning the arts and other 'higher' arenas of life.

By profession, she was a seamstress. I remember her being hired one time by a company over the phone, only to have them reject her when she got there. It turns out, they thought she was Caucasian because of how she spoke. I've seen her amazingly take a used piece of cloth and make a beautiful dress for me to wear to a party; or cut out cardboard inserts for her worn shoes while shining them until they glistened like glass, so that we could have new school shoes; or turn a dirty old partially broken crystal chandelier from the second hand store into a beautiful and gleaming masterpiece. She made tailored living room drapes from used pieces of cloth; and made a slumped over, gawky and clumsy young girl walk with books on her head until she would stand up straight.

Honey Gramms worked diligently trying to instill the best of all of those things, along with her powerful character, into my two brothers and me; in spite of the dysfunctional situations that we were experiencing. The one thing that was so lacking in her, that we would rather have had, was a warm and loving grandmother whose lap we could sit on, and who we could go to for comfort when something hurt, without fear. In her quest to make us 'better', she would have qualified for the term 'abusive parent' in today's vernacular – physically, mentally and verbally. Sad to say, I believe I was one of Honey Gramms' greatest disappointments in life. She worked very earnestly to make me into a charming young "lady"; teaching me to crochet and knit, and how to sew starting with doll clothes. For many years, all of my school and dress clothes were tailor made and wonderfully designed by Honey Gramms, even down to the little labels that she made to go on the inside. She taught me to speak with proper diction, and made me study books on proper etiquette. She even had her heart set on me becoming a medical doctor.

Unfortunately, to me all of her training felt like torture. I wanted to wear store bought clothes like my friends; and would have preferred to be out running with my brothers instead of learning how to make lace. Plus, those stiff crinoline slips scratched the backs of my legs when I tried to sneak and ride my brothers' bikes around the corner from the house. I am very sure it was a vindictive man who created those slips for the purpose of torturing women and young girls. Then there were times when she said she thought I was purposely trying to drive her out of her mind. I really wasn't; I was just "adventurous."

For example, one Easter she made me the most beautiful yellow lacy suit. I wore it to church, and when I came home, I asked if I could change my clothes to go outside. Honey Gramms said "No, I want you to look like a little girl all day today." *Now really! Whose mistake was that?* With my suit still on, I asked if I could go out to play. She gave me permission with a threat. I went out and sat on a pillow on the step…walked up and down…stood up and spun around in circles…played hop scotch, and did everything that I could think to do without getting my dress dirty. Finally, after being bored out of my mind, I decided to just take a short ride on my brother's bike…just a short one. *Hello!* How was I to know that there was a little pool of black motor oil in the street waiting just for me? Just as I reached the corner and made a U-turn, the unthinkable happened; and I slid into the pool of oil. My whole backside was soaked with black motor oil. I don't even have the heart to describe how my Honey Gramms looked that day when I stood on the steps and rang the bell. All I will say is that God was so good to her, to keep her from having a heart attack on so many occasions when she could have.

Now, in hindsight, I can see that Honey Gramms tried to give my brothers and me the very best that she had in her. In light of all of our other experiences, we never quite met her expectations. I remember the conversations we had when she would tell me to strive for the better things in life. She would say "Reach for the moon and even if you don't quite make it; at least you'll land in the stars." The problem was that I felt like such a klutz, I couldn't even imagine getting off the ground, much less to the sky.

...CHRISTMAS...

Shortly after Honey Gramms had come to Rose Tree to rescue us, while Dad was off trying to bring Ms. Lucy back, the Christmas Holidays came. Dad had not come back, and it turned out that Honey Gramms had taken a leave of absence from her job to come stay with us. The decision was made for her to bring us back to our hometown for the Christmas Holiday Season, as Dad had already planned. We never saw that apartment again.

Honey Gramms, Sugar Pops and Nana made sure that we had the best Christmas ever that year. They had been planning and working on it for several months. Of course, they thought we would have all come back together. My brothers and I stayed at Nana's house. On Christmas Day woke to a huge Christmas tree, as tall as the ceiling; and my Dad's awesome Lionel electric train set. That set would have been worth a fortune by now. That was the year Honey Gramms tailor-made my favorite coat, a navy blue six-button Benny dress coat, with a matching hand muff and ear muffs. There is also another reason why my clothes that year were significant to me. It was the year that the tall walking dolls had come out; and the one they bought for me could actually wear my same sized clothes. It was like having a little sister.

Let me share with you what one "sweet" little girl did when her brothers, Pete and Dave, wouldn't share their 100^+ metal railroad worker figurines with her (we won't mention any name). She got up early the next morning, took half of the figurines and buried them in little holes she dug in the backyard, a few at a time. She then returned to bed before anyone else got up. If it hadn't been for that stupid mud on the bottom of her shoes, and on her pajamas, she would have probably gotten away with it. Some of the buried figurines were never found, and the report is that for years after that, whenever there was an extremely hard rain, one or more of the figurines would wash up in the mud. *Screeeeeam!*

In retaliation, Pete felt it was his brotherly responsibility to let me know that Santa Claus was not real. No amount of railroad figurines was worth the pain that I felt in my heart. *"How could this be??"* If that was true, who had been eating all those cookies and drinking the milk that I had been leaving all of these years? If I could have, I would have drunk one of Honey Gramms' "highballs" that night; they always seemed to help her feel better. It was a wonderful time, but in spite of the festivities; what I really missed that first Christmas away from my Mom was "my Mom, Texas and Dallas." However, based on the looks that we got from Honey Gramms whenever we asked about them; we had quickly learned to not ask any more. *Does anyone know where my Mom is? One day while we were supposed to be outside playing, Pete, Dave and I snuck over to the apartment to look for them, but they didn't live there anymore. Now what?* **"...And He tells me that I am His own..."**

Shortly after Christmas we were sent back to Dad and Ms. Lucy in Rose Tree on our first ever airplane ride. I wore my navy blue six-button Benny dress coat, and "walked' my doll-sister up the runway with me, dressed in a set of my clothes. My brothers were in full dress suits. All of the staff and other passengers just 'oooh-ed' and 'aaah-ed'; and treated us children and my "doll-sister" like celebrities. Maybe a fare was paid for her because she was permitted to sit in her own seat right next to me. I hugged her and slept until we got there.

Back in Rose Tree, Dad and Ms Lucy set up another apartment real nice. Everything was "normal" again for a while, with the two of them acting like lovebirds. The rest of the school year was unchanged with me still having nightmares, Dave still sucking his thumb and wetting the bed, and Pete still fighting and acting out at school. Unfortunately, that had become the norm for us. As the spring of the year came in, there were some truly fun times, like the time I begged Pete and Dave to let me follow behind them and their friends. I screamed and threw a tantrum out in the street until they conceded. Sure enough, they took me tree climbing with them, and were very helpful. They "helped" me up into a humongous crab apple tree in the yard of a woman who had a very large dog. Then those guys were more helpful by leaving me up there alone, scared to come down because the tree was too high, and it was starting to get dark.

They actually went home and sat down for dinner, until my Dad asked them where I was. Did they really think that my presence would not be missed at the table? That was the end of my very short tree climbing days. Who needed to hang out with the boys anyway? There was another time that they "helped" me to go swimming with them; and then wouldn't allow me to tell people I was their sister because I would only go in the toddler pool. It didn't seem to matter to them that I was quite happy with the water not coming any higher than my knees.

Finally, there was the time that Pete "helped" me so much that he tickled me until I barfed all over the place; finally passing out because I couldn't breathe. We all got in trouble that night because I was so messed up that I couldn't stop giggling even when it was time to go to bed; and Pete kept sticking his hand in my door wiggling his "tickling" finger at me. After we were given multiple threats to be quiet and go to sleep or else; I was still giggling and snickering out of control. We all ended up with a whipping; with me simultaneously crying and laughing myself hysterically to sleep. My brothers were the most "helpful" brothers that any sister could possibly hope for, and still survive. *... **And He talks with me...***

...Home Again....

At the end of that school year, we were brought back to our hometown to spend the summer with Nana, Honey Gramms and Sugar Pops. My Sugar Pops quickly became my next most favorite person in the whole world other than my parents; Nana was number one. I was Sugar Pop's, "baby girl" and he treated my brothers and me like he was our own loving granddad. He was actually just Honey Gramms' boyfriend. For part of the summer, we stayed at Nana's house; where we had another whole set of friends, and did things that kids do. I remember using Ajax or Comet powder cleanser and a scrub brush to scrub many of our neighbors' beautiful white marble steps on Saturday morning, to make movie theatre money. Not far from where we lived was a theatre that only cost ten cents. Later that summer, they had the nerve to go up to a quarter. Plus, there was Mr. Max's grocery store at the corner. He gave us an extra piece of candy when we went to the store for Nana; and would take our returned glass soda bottles and give us money (five cents for the small bottles and a quarter for the large ones).

One of our favorite neighbors was Mrs. Bishop who was originally from the Virgin Islands, and who had the greatest accent. She had the most beautiful and unique knickknacks in her house; and she and her daughter, Ms. Sheila, usually had snacks for the block kids. We also had a real celebrity who lived right on our block; Mr. Gee, who was a real true blooded American Indian who had acted in a few cowboy movies. He had several famous friends who would visit him, like Chuck Connors from the television show "Rifleman", the guy who played the "Lone Ranger", Sally Starr, and Roy and Dale Rogers. Can you imagine that? Right in our neighborhood we had movie stars.

Everybody in the block and around each corner knew everybody else, and it was great. I loved jumping double-dutch, playing hopscotch, playing the "hand clap games" like "Who Stole the Cookie Jar?", and playing jacks with the little ball. I still have a couple little scars inside my hands from the jack points. Those were truly some "good old days." Every Friday Nana would take us to the seafood take-out restaurant a few blocks away to buy fried flounder and French fries. Every Saturday evening we had hotdogs and baked beans. On Sunday mornings, we were sent to Sunday School at Jones Tabernacle AME church, or I would go to the little storefront church around the corner from us. I really liked the little storefront church best because I was invited to join the children's choir.

    Two of my funniest relatives who would visit us from time to time were Nana's adopted niece, Aunt Marsha and her husband whose name was Uncle Reese. He was a "huckster" who would drive through the block with an old rickety truck selling all kinds of fruit and vegetables, and huge blocks of ice. A lot of people still had ice boxes instead of electric refrigerators. I used to love hearing him yell up the street as he came, "waaaaaaaaaatermelon, peeeaches, - get 'em 'fore they gone". Pete, Dave and I were three very energetic kids, hanging out with our little short Nana. I was looking eye to eye with her by then because I was so tall. She would beat us with a feather duster when we misbehaved - the handle part, not the feathers. *Ouch, that really hurt!!*

    We also had another relative who lived across the street from Nana, Aunt Debra, who had one of the first televisions in the neighborhood. She didn't have the money to pay outright for it, so the store put a meter box on the back. A quarter had to be put in the meter box for each hour of TV viewing; and a collector came out each week to collect the money. Hah! It only took about ten minutes for her sons to figure out how to jimmy the box with a knife; we would watch for hours at no cost. Finally, the collectors realized that they were being duped, and took the TV back.

...Training or Abuse?...

For the second part of that summer, we stayed at Honey Gramms' apartment, which was totally awesome because it was on the third floor and we had access to a fenced in roof. We had a rooftop flower garden and used to sleep out on the roof on hot nights. We were close to one of the main streets in the town so we would sit and watch the people coming and going. By now, I was old enough so my training began for doing laundry and learning to cook simple things. I wouldn't have minded doing the laundry except that my perfectionist grandmother would make me iron the same shirts over and over and over again trying to get some little wrinkles out that I could hardly see, which she called "cat faces". I thought to myself that since cats are so cute, why is it such a problem to have their faces, which I couldn't see, on the shirts?

I had to soak the white clothes in a dark liquid named 'bluing'. I never understood how that dark stuff would make those clothes sparkling white. Then I would scrub them in the tub on a scrub board. Some of my knuckles are still smooth and have cut marks from that scrub board. Then, after I had them perfectly white enough, I had to hang them up on the line in a concise order with all of the matching socks together, then the t-shirts, then the underpants, then the dress shirts, and so on…hung in order and tightly, with no sags as they hung on the line. One time, I found a t-shirt left in the bottom of the basket after I had hung up everything else, and decided to hang it at the end of the line, out of order. I didn't see where it made a difference, but Honey Gramms didn't agree with me. She pulled all the clothes off the line, and dropped them into the dirt (not cement). One of her favorite sayings was, "There is a right way, a wrong way, and my way. We do it my way." I think Uncle Sam borrowed that from her.

I had to take everything down, wash the dirtied ones again and hang them back up in order, to put that one stinking little t-shirt in the right place. "Oh well, guess I won't get outside to play *again* today." Not to mention getting my arm caught one time in the wringer part of the washing machine, while trying to keep my whole body from being sucked into that monster. *What maniac could have invented such a thing?* None of this may seem significant to you, but if you knew how days and weeks and months of compulsive training felt like punishment to a young girl; you would understand why by the time I got married and had my own family, I could not – absolutely, could not - hang clothes on the line out of proper order. I was thoroughly brain-washed. To make my point, years later, after watching me hang up the laundry, my mother-in-law suggested that I try to hang them out of order just to free myself from the completely "anal" need to be a perfectionist about hanging up clothes. I tried it. Then I went in the house and all the way up to the third floor where we lived. I looked out the windows at the clothes, broke out in a cold sweat, became nauseous and finally went downstairs and re-hung those clothes. That, my friend, is truly a psychotic reaction to hanging up the laundry. It is not God's will for us to be bound by any such compulsion, especially if it is not a life and death issue; and especially not from a tender age. *It was not that important!!*

It was challenging, but living there with Honey Gramms wasn't all bad. In fact, I have many happy memories including our friends, and the picnics out in the park which Honey Gramms and Sugar Pops would take us to. You have not really lived until you take blankets and everything that you need for a picnic to the park on a public bus. The return bus trips at the end of the day were even better, when no one in their right mind wanted to sit next to you because you looked and stank like a mud pie. Sugar Pops loved you enough though to let all of us sit with him. He was so cool!!

From Honey Gramms' place, my brothers and I were sent to the church around the corner to attend Sunday School, while all the adults slept in. In fact, after a while Dave and Pete usually just dropped me off and disappeared until Sunday School was over. I never knew where they went, but I truly loved being in church and learning about the Bible stories and God. I pictured God as a "little old man with a long white beard who took care of the whole world; and to whom people would pray and ask for help." It was during those days that I began to really develop my own concept of who God was. I figured He sat on a throne and was sweet, kind and loving like my Sugar Pops, just older. *(I started asking God to let me see my Mom, Texas and Deacon because by now I was thinking that I might not even be able to remember what they looked like any more. Plus, I overheard Honey Gramms say Mom had another little baby girl, named Felicia. How did they know that if they didn't know where my Mom was? I thought about it, but knew better than to ask.)*

    Meanwhile, I still had to wear the biggest and ugliest orthopedic shoes, and those stinking three plaits. At least now I was permitted to wear bangs (which should have been in the books for being the biggest bangs in history) on the front of my forehead. They even covered my eyebrows. Honey Gramms didn't want to cut my hair - her pride and joy - short enough in the front for "real" bangs. I kept begging because I was tired of all the teasing from the other kids. Finally, Honey Gramms agreed that she would cut the bangs and curl them for me with the hot curlers to go to church on Easter Sunday. The big weekend came; and that Saturday night I was so ecstatic that I could hardly sleep. Sunday morning came and I was anxiously waiting for her to get up. I kept watching the clock as it was getting to be time to go to Sunday School.

    I decided to take matters into my own hands. Shucks, I had seen her heat up the curling irons on the stove enough times that I figured I could do it myself. How hard could it be? So, I turned the stove on (which I was not supposed to touch without supervision), and I put the curling irons in the fire. I waited a couple minutes, and took them out but realized I didn't know how to tell if they were hot enough. They were still black so I figured they weren't hot enough yet. I put them back in the fire and waited another few minutes. By this time, they were starting to look a little pink, so I figured they were just about ready. I would give them one more heat-up. This time when I took them out of the fire they were glowing red hot, and I figured they were ready. I took hold of my super long bangs and held them out in front of my face. As I bringing my hand towards them with the red glowing curlers, I heard Honey Gramms' blood curdling scream behind me. I was startled and before I could do anything else, the curlers touched my bangs; which promptly caught on fire, going up in smoke. Suddenly, I felt a yank at the back of my neck, and soon found my head and half of my body in the sink under running cold water. I was wondering what was wrong with this woman. She was screaming, "I'm going to break your neck". I was thinking, "She's already doing that, and drowning me too." She was screaming at me and crying at the same time; and I was trying to catch my breath under the cold water for what seemed like an eternity.

Finally she turned the water off and grabbed the tea towel to dry me off a little, still telling me that she was going to break my neck. She stopped screaming long enough to look at my face good. Then she started screaming again, while this time beating me with the wet tea towel. She dragged me into the bathroom while I was still trying to catch my breath, and lifted me up to the medicine cabinet mirror. Wow! My bangs were finally short like I wanted them!! *But, what was that brown fuzzy looking stuff at the end of them?* Then as I look a little closer, my eyebrows and eyelashes were the same brown fuzzy color like the ends of my bangs. I think I got twenty-five whippings - not spankings - whippings over the next couple days; and smelled like smoke for a week. *Thank God that He woke her up just at the right time.*

I decided later that all of the whippings were worth it just to get the short bangs. By the time the brown fuzzies fell off, mine was even shorter than my girlfriends'. Hooray!! Way to go!! Of course, I looked a little weird for a while until my eyebrows and eyelashes grew back in*...And He tells me I am His own...*

...Surprise, Surprise...

Sometime later, I received one of the biggest surprises of my life. One day out of the clear blue, Honey Gramms took us to an apartment about four blocks from where we lived, which turned out to be Mom-Mom's apartment!! She lived there with her boyfriend, Uncle Jakes. Wow! I didn't even know that Mom-Mom knew Honey Gramms like that! *Maybe we were getting ready to see my Mom too.* We had been given enough warnings about "butting in when grown folks are talking", that we knew we had better wait until they finished talking and would call us into the living room to say anything. I near about wet my pants trying to wait until they finally called us in to visit with Mom-Mom; who hugged us and cried saying she was so glad to see us, and how good we looked. Finally the big moment came, when Pete asked if Mom was coming over too. Everything went quiet, and I thought he was going to get a real licking.

Then Mom-Mom told us that no one knew where my Mom was; that she had left Felicia and Texas with some friends who brought them to Mom-Mom over a year earlier. Mom-Mom said she couldn't take care of the two of them, so her boyfriend, Uncle Jay's sister in New York had agreed to take them. Texas was missing because he had run away from Mom-Mom when they were getting in the car to be moved to New York. No one knew where he went, but somebody later said they had seen him hanging around the old apartment where we had all lived together. No one had been able to catch him. He was only about seven years old. How could he just disappear? As we were leaving, Mom-Mom and Uncle Jake said they were going to bring Felicia and Dallas to see us. They never did. *(Can somebody please help me to understand; where my Mom is; and how can my little Texas take care of himself at night? Who is going to feed him, and how will he stay warm when the weather gets cold again? Is the part of New York where my Felicia lives close to Rose Tree, N.Y. where we live with Dad and Ms Lucy? Can we walk there?)*

Troublesome times for Pete, Dave and I were also far from over. When it was time for us to go back to Rose Tree to return to school; we were told instead by an angry Honey Gramms that we would have to stay with her for a while longer. She registered us in school in our hometown. The "little while longer" turned into two school years. For the first year, Honey Gramms returned me to my beloved Carter Elementary School, but my brothers were sent to another school. It seems that their behavior records from Rose Tree weren't good, and the school board actually wanted to put Pete into some school for really bad boys. Honey Gramms fought that in court and somehow, he ended up going to the same school with Dave. Good for them, but who was going to protect me while I went to school by myself?

I began walking to school alone for the first time in my life. As if that was not bad enough, I had to walk about one half hour one way to get there, across the biggest street I had ever tried to cross alone. Then, to add insult to injury, I was supposed to walk about fifteen minutes on the other side of the school and back at lunchtime to go to Nana's house three times a week to make sure she ate her lunch because she was sick. I was absolutely petrified.

Thank God for Sugar Pops who walked with me for the first couple weeks. He gradually weaned me by walking on the other side of the street – first so I could still see him— and then not see him at all for a little bit because he would hide behind cars, and then let me see him again. Finally, I was able to do it by myself without standing at the light and letting it turn green three to four times before I would finally cross. For a couple weeks, I used my lunch money to bribe a girlfriend at school to walk with me to Nana's. I eventually gave up on that when the girl didn't want to walk with me anymore; I figured Nana was strong enough by now. I loved her, but it was too hard to run all the way to her house and back eating a sandwich while running, in order not to be late for the afternoon class.

Then one day, when I was supposed to go to Nana's, I didn't. I spent my money and bought me some brand new candy named Pez which had just come out in the stores, in the coolest animal shaped dispensers. That same day, the bottom dropped out. While I was in class, Honey Gramms showed up during school hours and spoke to my teacher in private. Then she took me home with her and I was whipped severely. Nana had become real sick again and couldn't get herself out of the bed. So she had thrown something through her bedroom window to get someone's attention. It worked, and the next door neighbor went inside, found her there sick, and called Honey Gramms at work. Nana was in the hospital, and I was treated like I was Public Enemy Number One who had tried to kill my Nana. Why couldn't they understand that I really loved Nana, but was still uncomfortable with walking through the streets all by myself; especially during lunch while all the other kids were in school? *Can I go back to my Mom now? Does anybody know where she is yet; and has anyone found my little Texas? How can you lose a whole kid?* "

For the second year with Honey Gramms, I was transferred (again) to an elementary school closer to the apartment. Now, at least I just had to walk about ten minutes to come home for lunch. Lunch was supposed to be at home with my two brothers, but never was because they just hung out in the street. I was on my own until they knew it was time for Honey Gramms to come home. It was at this new school that I fell in "like" with a boy for the first time in my life. His name was Jeremy Griffith, and I thought he was just the cutest boy in the world. He smiled at me all the time, and took his life into his hands by telling my brother Dave that he liked me. That was the end of that. I think Dave must have threatened him or something, but at any rate, after that he practically ran every time he saw me. I thought it was because I was so skinny and still had on those cursed orthopedic shoes. It wasn't until years later that I connected his reaction to his talk with my brother…my hero.

I had one of my most traumatic challenges at my new school. It was a requirement at this school that each student had to take swimming lessons once a week at a nearby college's pool. On top of that, my homeroom teacher was one whom I thought sure was straight from the pit of hell, there to scare the kids into behaving themselves. First of all, she had a "sixth finger" on each hand (for real); secondly, she looked like a witch and thirdly, she was physically abusive and would beat your hands with her yardstick in a "New York hurry." On one of her hands, the sixth finger was actually more like a little nub on the side of her pinky. However, on the other hand, the "nub" had actually grown to the size of a small finger, but it flapped with no bone in it. My greatest terror was that she would touch me with that boneless finger. *Ugh!*

    I finally worked up enough nerve to go to Ms. Ghoul as politely as I could to ask if I could be excused from swimming. I had almost drowned when I was younger (true story), and I was petrified of water above my knees in a swimming pool. I asked if I could do something else to make up the work. My grandmother also wrote her a note. True to her witch-like look, Ms. Ghoul curtly refused to excuse me. She escorted me with the rest of the class to the swimming pool, with me crying hysterically. The swim instructor would not listen to my pleas for mercy either. He insisted that I allow him to teach me how to float. He assured me that he would hold his hand under me and would not let me go. *He promised!!*

    Just about the time that I began to feel really comfortable floating with his hand supporting me, he moved his hand! There is no way that I should have been held responsible for what happened next. I felt his hand move, and my body went a little lower in the water. I began to grab frantically for the closest thing to me to help save my life. After all, I was in danger of drowning!! I was nearly out of my mind with terror, and really should not have been held accountable for anything that I did to save myself. Unfortunately for the instructor, the closest "tangible" thing that I could grab hold of was the long thick forest of hair on his chest. That man screamed louder than any human I had ever heard before. Prior to that, I didn't know that men could scream with a piercing scream like a woman. *Wow!!* He later even accused me of almost drowning him, when all I was trying to do was hold on until some more help came. Shucks, I was going under. *Anyone in their right mind would have done the same thing.*

I apologized as profusely as I could, but he wouldn't accept my apology. Miraculously, the next week, I was excused and given work to do in school while the rest of the class went to swim class. I was even allowed to sit right outside of the school office to do it. What a difference one swim class can make!!

My two favorite subjects in school were English and spelling, and I was on the school's spelling team. Our team won several spelling bee competitions, and there was only about two months from the upcoming citywide competition. I worked really hard to become one of the top spellers in our school; and I was also scheduled to graduate that year to go on to junior high school. Well, the next shoe dropped, and for reasons that I don't understand and will never know, the powers that be decided it was time for me to move back to Rose Tree. With just a few weeks left before the graduation and the spelling bee, Dave and I were sent back to Rose Tree, and Pete was transferred to the school for disobedient boys. *What the heck?????????????* ***...And the joy we share as we tarry there...***

...Rose Tree Again....

It was not bad enough that I missed my chance for the citywide spelling bee, but I was transferred to a new school in the spring of a school year, when the year was almost over. Dad and Ms. Lucy had moved to a completely new neighborhood while we were away, so I was back at square one all over again. The problem for me was this time I was angry and bitter because I had been made to miss the competition. *I was really sick of moving!!* We were moved so often that I missed all but one graduation while in school as a child; and didn't walk down the aisle until many years later as an adult, when I graduated from Bible School. *Where is my Mom? I am sick and tired of never knowing who I am and who I can trust. I have no real friends, and I don't even really know most of my family except Pete and Dave. Now, you have not only taken Pete away from my same school, but he's more than 8 hours of drive time away.*

I refused to make any friends in the new school for the rest of that school year; and later learned from a friend in my hometown school that my team lost the spelling bee by a word that I had studied for weeks, "antidisestablishmentarianism". Who cares?????? I became an angry child and began to stay to myself most of the time.

Finally, at the invitation of a neighbor, I decided to spend a lot of time upstairs from where we lived. Miss Mags had a beautiful little baby girl named Suzy who I would babysit to make extra money. In between I hooked up very briefly with a couple of "not so nice" girls, and ended up getting picked up for shoplifting at the mall. The security guards told my Dad they knew I was an amateur following behind someone else because the other girls had valuable jewelry, and all I had was some stupid leotards. *Stupid-o!!*

Dave and I were left home alone a lot because Pete hadn't come yet, and Dad and Ms. Lucy worked a lot. It was during that time that Dave started running away from home. He told me he was going to try to find his way back to our hometown to find Mom. Then he would be missing for a few days. Sometimes he would call me on the phone when he thought no one was home with me, or he would leave something on our front patio to let me know he was okay. Dad would report him as missing to the police. One time they found him walking along some train tracks and brought him home. He told them he was walking to get back to our hometown, but they said he was unknowingly going north towards Canada instead of south where he thought he was going. *After all, he was only a kid.*

Over the following summer months, Pete did come home to Rose Tree, but by then he was very different. He was smoking now and he would sneak and drink some of Dad's stuff in the liquor cabinet. He and Dave would get into really horrible arguments about stupid stuff. Pete started hanging out with one of our neighbors across the street who was a little older, named Drew McKnight. Drew had a sister, Anna, who Pete liked. He would hang out over their house a lot. One day, I was home alone because I was on punishment for something I had done, or hadn't done – *it's hard to remember because it seemed like nothing I ever did was good enough.* Dave had run away again, and I thought Pete was across the street at the McKnight's house. I went over there to get him, even though I was not supposed to go out of the house. Drew came to the door, and he told me that Pete was inside so I went in.

Long story short, Pete was out with Anna somewhere, and I was violently raped that day by Pete's so-called friend who didn't believe me when I tried to tell him that I was still a virgin. I couldn't tell anybody because I was not supposed to be out of the house. Plus, Drew told me that if I told anybody, he would make something bad happen to me when no one else was around. I never told anyone until years later. ***…None other has ever known…***

...Is This For Real?...

By the time the next school year began, things were really crazy at home. Dad and Ms. Lucy were arguing all the time, and he was staying out for days at a time. Pete, Dave and I all ended up going to the same school that year. That was one of the few pleasures I had in life. I really loved school, and participated in a special program to earn a college scholarship. I completed the program and was given a guaranteed pre-paid full four-year scholarship to attend New York State Teachers College when I was ready to go to college.

In the meantime, Pete's behavior was getting worse and he had started hanging out with some very bad boys. Dave was running away more and more often. The next two parts of this story seem unreal, and if I had not been an eyewitness, I would find it hard to believe it myself. Firstly, one day when Dave and I came in from school, Pete told us to go with him downstairs into the basement because he had something to show us. What he showed us was several large Mason jars filled with money; one with bills including twenty and one-hundred dollar bills, and one with coins. He told us that he left school a couple weeks prior during school hours, and had gone with two other guys and *robbed a bank* near the school. They had stocking caps over their faces, and then returned back to school. *Whaaaaaaaat?*

He told us the police were looking for grown men, not realizing they were just teenagers. Plus, we were never to tell anyone where the money was. He was working on getting us back home to find Mom. We didn't know whether to really believe him or not; but sure enough, there were some zippered bank bags there also. We three made a pact of secrecy until we could get an adult to buy the train tickets for us to go home. Two days later, a huge bomb dropped!! While we were in school in the afternoon, some of the kids in my classroom started running to the window.

Someone said, "Isn't that your brother that the police are locking up, along with two other guys?" I looked out the window and saw Pete look up at me and shake his head, "No". Even now, as I am writing this, I can still hear the buzz of the other kids chattering away. I can remember my breath feeling like it was leaving my body, to see my brother being arrested by what looked like an army of police cars, and uniformed men with rifles.

    The report I heard was that one of the guys, Andrew, was playing around the evening before and snatched a woman's purse. He was caught by some guys when he tried to run. Andrew had a long history of problems with the law, and made an agreement with the police to turn the other two guys in who had robbed the bank with him, if they would promise him a reduced sentence. They agreed, and the rest is history.

    My brother was sent to a reform school with a three year sentence, and I don't know whatever happened to the money in the basement. I was only permitted to visit him one time shortly after his arrest, before I was moved again. Within a few days, everything had changed for the worse again. ***...I come to the garden alone....***

...Catastrophe...

The day after Pete was arrested, Dave told me he was leaving again and would not come back until he had found his way home to Mom. He promised that he would get a message to me somehow that he was okay; and that he would come back for me. He showed me an old rusty gun that he had found, and said he was taking it with him. He then told me that he had found an abandoned monastery not far from where we lived, and that he stayed there some times when he was away from home. Somehow he had also discovered how to use the door key from our house's front door to open the door to one of the storage units of an area supermarket named Loblaw's. He would have plenty food to take with him. Then he left and I continued going to school during the day because I didn't know what else to do. By this time, Dad was so disgusted with everything that he didn't even report Dave as missing.

After three days when I hadn't heard from my brother, I felt like something was wrong, so I began to ask my Dad to report him missing. Dad kept trying to reassure me that he would be back again as usual. After about five days, when I still hadn't heard from him, I definitely knew that something was wrong. Dad did call the police and reported him as missing. After a couple days, they still had not found him. That's when I remembered Dave telling me about the abandoned monastery, and I told Dad and the police what he had told me. The police knew where the place was, and they went there and searched until they found him. He had been attacked by a pack of wild dogs, while trying to protect some wild rabbits he had "adopted". He was too hurt to come home or get to help. Thank God for intervening again in our lives because it was His grace that had caused my brother to tell me about the monastery that day before he left. Dave was hospitalized with some broken bones and bruises for a couple weeks, and then was brought home while waiting to go to a hearing on various charges.

(I don't know if Honey Gramms or Sugar Pops or anyone knows about all this craziness, and if anyone can help us now. I wondered how much worse things could get. All of this was more than my young mind could handle.)

  A few days later, Dad and a couple of his friends were in the living room watching a game and drinking and laughing, when Ms. Lucy walked out of their bedroom completely naked through the hall where everyone could see her and across to the bathroom. Dave happened to be home, and because our rooms were side-by-side and connected by an open air vent, he and I were giggling and laughing about what she had done. Dad stormed out with his friends. Dave and I were still snickering, and it made Ms. Lucy angry. She came in my room and beat me with an electric extension cord until I had bloody cuts all over my arms and chest. After she went back to her room, Dave whispered through the vent that he was going to kill her with the old gun he found. I begged him not to, and assured him that I was all right. After that night he and I began to talk seriously about how we could kill her and bury her in the secret place under the front porch if she beat me like that again.

  The next day, we looked through Dad's papers to find Honey Gramms' phone number but she wasn't home when we called. We tried a different phone number, and got Nana's next door neighbor, Miss Ghee. When I heard her voice, I started crying hysterically in the phone telling her I wanted to come home to my Mom. *(Seven years is too long to be taken away from your Mom, and little brothers.)* Miss Ghee came back to the phone with Nana, and we told her what was going on. Pete was in jail, Dave had been running away trying to find his way home, Dad and Ms. Lucy were fighting all the time and how she kept beating me up whenever she was angry with Dad; especially if no one else was home. Nana told us not to worry, that she would get in touch with Honey Gramms and they would make arrangements to come to get us. We told her not to tell that we had called, but to say that she had called us, because we were not supposed to use the phone if no adult was home.

A few days passed without us hearing anything, but we were still waiting and hoping. In the meantime, I spent a lot of time hanging out with our upstairs neighbor, Miss Mags and her daughter. Her daughter's father was one of the famous old-time professional wrestlers. He was almost seven feet tall, and you may remember his name - "Bo-Bo Brazil". He would take Miss Mags and Suzy and me out to dinner and to the movies, and over to see Niagara Falls from time to time. One night as we were coming back home from the falls, I saw Dave standing out in the driveway, and Ms. Lucy was standing up on the front patio of our second floor apartment. I knew that something was wrong.

As I was getting out of the car, Dave started walking towards me calling my name, but before he could get to me, Ms. Lucy yelled out, "I was wondering how late you all were going to stay out. Nana is dead." For the second time in a few short weeks, I felt like my breath was leaving my body, and I was saying to myself, "This is a terrible dream. I have to wake up now." I remember dropping to my knees and screaming until I passed out. When I came to, the wrestler and Dave were bringing me into our apartment. I later cried until my voice was gone and the only thing left was a raspy sound. In that instant, I felt like all of the hope and love I had really trusted in to help me was dead and gone, and that I was never going to get back home.

I cried until I barfed again and again and then finally Ms. Lucy told me, "enough is enough"; and that if I didn't shut up, she would shut me up. I couldn't stop crying so she "shut me up" by brutally beating me with an electric extension cord again until I had open wounds on my chest, legs and arms. She told Dave to go to his own room because he was standing outside the closed door when she came out from beating me. When he went to his room, I forced myself to be quiet so that she would not beat me again. I did not want him to try to kill her since all I could think of was, if he killed her, he would go to jail. Then I would really be left alone. How would I find my way back home to Mom?

...How To Go On?...

I finally went to sleep, and the next day when I woke up, Dave was gone again. By this time, I had come to the end of my rope. I began to think of ways that I could take my own life and go to heaven to be with my Nana. The hand of my loving God moved for me again giving me courage to at least go to school. During school that day, I talked to a classmate named Sandra Woods who had become my one and only real friend. I shared with her everything that had happened to me and showed her my cuts. She called her father, who turned out to be a Pastor; and he and her grandmother came to the school and picked us up.

They took me to their home, and God worked it out where I actually lived with them for a few weeks. I was very happy; Sandra and I were like sisters. She shared her clothes with me and we went to school together every day. It was at their home where I learned about God as a more personal being, in a way that I could understand a little better. I experienced a peace and love among their family and their church members that was like something out of a movie to me. I really enjoyed going to Bible Study and church with them. Somehow, my Dad didn't come for me right away. He probably had not been home to know that I was gone.

One day a few weeks later, my teacher asked me to carry something to the school principal's office. However, when I got there, my Dad was there waiting for me. As soon as I saw him, I turned and tried to run; but he called out my name and caught me. He began to cry, and asked if I would give him another chance to get things straightened out; or that I could go back to live with Sandra's family if I wanted to. I decided to go home with him because I felt so bad seeing him cry. He and I went out to dinner, and strangely enough, I can still remember as clear as day even what I ate that night. I had an 'all-you-can-eat' shrimp dinner, with corn on the cob, at one of our favorite restaurants. I am always amazed at how the memories of certain details stick out, especially in times of unusually high emotions.

While we were eating, Dad told me that the cause of Nana's death was a heart attack; and that he had wanted to take all of us home for the funeral, but couldn't. He decided not to send me by myself. He couldn't leave Dave alone, and he couldn't take him out of state while waiting for the hearing. He also told me that he and Ms. Lucy were completely done for real this time, and that she had left again. He sat and cried through the whole dinner because he said he had talked to Miss Ghee, Nana's neighbor. She told him all of the things that Dave and I had told them, some of which he had not known. *How could he have not known???????*

I never saw our apartment again (*here we go as usual*), and that night he took me to stay with another "friend" of his, Ms. Jackie, who was a very nice person. I liked her a lot, and she really tried to help me us. Dad went and picked Dave up the next day, and brought him there to Ms. Jackie's tiny apartment. Dave and I wondered if she was the source of Dad and Ms. Lucy's recent arguments because she had a toddler son who looked just like my brother Pete, with the same exact face and head. Neither of them ever said anything about Dad being the father, and Dave and I never asked. We just enjoyed the breath of fresh air for the moment. Dad brought all of our clothes there, and we never went back to the apartment.

To my amazement, here I was preparing to graduate again, because the school year there was broken down differently from my hometown. I had been skipped again that year, and would have a chance to graduate from this middle school into their high school. They were having a junior prom. The problem with that was I didn't know any guys to go to the prom with. I was too young for the guys in my class to even think about asking me because I had been skipped a couple times. I didn't want my brother or my Dad to take me, and the only other person who I would have considered, Mr. Cunningham's son, was away at college. I decided that I would go by myself; but I told Dad and Ms. Jackie that I was going with friends. Ms. Jackie was kind enough to dress me up in her clothes for the prom. She altered one of her dresses for me, and let me borrow one of her fur stoles and a pair of her beautiful dressy heels. Dad had to go to work, and there was no money for me to have a limousine service. I told them I would take the bus. I left out of the house as if I was going to the Prom, but chickened out when I reached the school. I ended up riding up and down on different buses until I thought it was time to go home. I didn't really want to be seen with a grown lady's gown and heels on. They seemed to always believe that I went to the prom, but just didn't have money to buy pictures.

While I was riding on the various buses that evening, I had seen a lot of people going into a large church not far from Ms. Jackie's place. I was able to find my way back there again the following Sunday. I went to the altar and really prayed for my family like Sandra's Dad had shown me to do. I remember feeling such joy and dancing at the altar just like everyone else was doing. I felt clean when I left the church, even though I still did not have a full understanding of all the scriptures or what salvation really did for a person. I just figured it would make me ready to go with Nana when it came time for me to die. In hindsight, I know it was those times in my life where God's love and grace laid a spiritual foundation upon which my faith in Him was truly birthed and rooted strongly.

The following month, just a couple weeks before graduation, Dave's hearing took place and he was sentenced to six months in reform school. I believe it was the same one where Pete was. The next thing I knew, totally unexpected by me, Dad decided that he and I needed to come back home to stay with Honey Gramms. She was now living in Nana's house, and we needed to leave *right away*. Again, I was not favored to stay still long enough to graduate with my class. *Does anyone care how I feel about all of this? ...While the dew is still on the roses...*

...Home Again...

So, for the last time, we left Rose Tree, NY, never to return there to live again. The biggest regrets that I had about leaving there was that I would probably never see Sandra Woods and her family again; and that I was leaving my two brothers there in a reform school. I was praying really hard that I would see them again at home one day. I tried but was never able to find Sandra again. I came back to my hometown as broken and emotionally messed up as any young girl could be and still be in her right mind. **...*And He walks with me, and He talks with me and He tells me that I am His own.*** *(Maybe now, I will get a chance to find my Mom, Texas and Felicia.)*

It was within the first week that I knew it was going to be a nightmare living with Honey Gramms. In the first place, she informed me that it was because of the phone call which Dave and I made to Nana which caused her to get all worked up and have the heart attack. If we had not told her all that was going on, she would not have been trying to get to Rose Tree to come get us. I was informed that she died while packing her suitcase to come for us. Talk about a load of heavy guilt, and the hard part for me was that I didn't know whether to accept that as true or not. *Maybe if we hadn't called.....*

The only thing worse than living with Honey Gramms with other people in the house, was living with her with no one else in the house. There was no one else to take her attention away from me. Again, God intervened and somehow Honey Gramms decided to let me spend a few weeks that summer with my Mom's paternal aunt. It continually surprised me that Honey Gramms knew all of these people who knew, or who were related to my Mom, but yet supposedly did not know how to find her.

Aunt Sissy was a very nice woman, with one daughter and two sons. Her daughter, Rachel, was a teacher and a soft spoken, very genteel woman; but those two boys were just as wild as my own two brothers. The best surprise of all was that Aunt Sissy was a Christian and we attended church every Sunday. Rachel also took me shopping with her, and to the circus and museum.

It was a very good time until the youngest son stole some money, and of course, who else would they blame? The saddest part was that I actually was not the one who took that money, but things turned so ugly, that it spoiled the rest of the summer for me. Honey Gramms absolutely refused to believe that I could possibly be telling the truth, "considering who my mother was." It was a long hot summer, but Thank God, it did eventually come to an end.

...HIGH SCHOOL...

I had come back home with an advanced enough academic record to qualify me to go to a very prestigious, predominantly Caucasian, all female school. The problem was that I was about two years younger than the other ninth grade students; not to mention that my emotional stability was shattered. I passed the entrance exams with flying colors; but my application was rejected because of my age and the counselor's concern for my developmental maturity, or lack thereof. Honey Gramms challenged them in court, and I was admitted to the school under a cloud of hostility from the administration. Many of the students were from financially well to do families, and were mentally brilliant to say the least. Plus the fact that they had boobs out to here, wore makeup and teased up hair, smoked cigarettes, cursed like sailors and most of them had a boyfriend from the all male high school down the road.... *and then there was me...*

I was still wearing the dreaded Buster Brown orthopedic support shoes, with one brown (ugly as sin) pair and one pair of the white and black pony style. My prayer was, *"God help me to get out of these shoes before I actually have to step foot in that school which looks like a mansion and scares me to death."* That prayer must have only gone to the ceiling. I had just turned thirteen and was back to being only permitted to wear the super sized bangs and a ponytail, or a split down the middle with a braid on each side. At least by now, thanks to Ms. Jackie, I had learned to French braid my own hair and so I was released from the dreaded plaits. I was still so skinny that if you looked at me sideways, you might overlook me. I had absolutely no boobs, even though Honey Gramms insisted that I wear a training bra anyway. What I wanted to know was, *"could the training bra help to train my breasts to grow?"* If not, what good was it? I was the only girl that I knew who still didn't even have "the curse" yet. In spite of these challenges to my self esteem, I still had to go to a new school with girls who looked like women to me, and who scared me to death! I was already a month late getting started in the school year because of the drawn out court hearing, and so I started at a disadvantage, which had to be made up. Then I felt like an absolute toad next to the other girls. There was only one other young Black girl in the whole ninth grade. Honey Gramms absolutely adored her. Why??????? She looked just like Urkle from the TV show, with thick glasses and all. No one else at the school even talked to her, and *then there was me*.......... We became "friends", sharing homework and school assignments, and nothing else; especially since she didn't seem to know about anything else.

As for me, I was just trying to learn how to be "normal" in the culture of this school; forget about being "popular." A couple of the Caucasian students took a liking (mercy) to me, and began to help me with my outward appearance. They taught me how to apply makeup using their shades, which may explain why even today I still prefer lighter shades of eye shadow and lipsticks rather than bright reds, burgundies, and dark browns. The girls taught me how to roll my skirts up at the waist to get a "reasonable length" above the knees, and would even lend me their jewelry and shoes during the day. With some practice, I became quite adept at putting everything back to "normal" by the time I reached home, and I actually began to kind of fit in with the other girls.

I was doing well with the schoolwork, but the one class which was a real challenge for me was gym. In Rose Tree, I held my own on the track team; here the focus was primarily gymnastics which I knew nothing about. I knew I was in big trouble the first day they told me to get on the "horse" and at first I couldn't even get on the thing. When I finally did get on it, I was on the stupid thing backward. *What a dipstick!!* The second most embarrassing challenge was trying to climb the rope – am I really expected to get off the floor and up in the air with nothing but that rope to climb up on? How high?? Where is the ladder?? Or at least, a little lift might help?

In spite of my many challenges, I was adjusting slowly but surely. I was doing fine until the day I became a little overly confident and actually let my Caucasian girlfriends "tease" my hair into a bouffant like theirs – yes, my thick Black, all the way down my back, long hair. First of all, when they finished, I had the highest and fullest bouffant hairdo ever in history aside from the Bride of Frankenstein, for those of you who have ever seen the movie. I was the buzz for the whole school that day, with everybody complimenting me about how beautiful my hair was. ……..*whatever!!* Then at about 3:15 that afternoon, my normal time to start "redressing" to go home, I had the shock of my life. We couldn't get my "teased" up hair un-teased or untangled, not matter how hard we tried. I put my Buster Brown shoes back on, pulled my skirt down, and washed the make-up off my face. I just knew that I was going to be a dead duck when Honey Gramms saw my hair which was a great source of pride and joy to her. Sure enough, when she saw my hair, it was a good five minutes before she stopped looking like she had apoplexy or some other paralyzing illness. After regrouping, she washed my hair and painstakingly combed it out inch by painful inch, with my head receiving multiple hickeys from the back of the hairbrush; as a reminder to never tease my hair again. I lost about two pounds of hair, and gained about twenty hickeys. The hickeys worked! I have never teased it again.

Then, something amazing happened as I was going to the store for Honey Gramms near where we lived. I ran into my mother's sister, Aunt Mae. The weirdest thing was that I had only seen her a couple times when I was much younger, but my memory kicked in and I remembered her. When I told her who I was, she hugged me and cried. She told me she thought she knew where my Mom was, and that Texas and Felicia were with her. I told her that I couldn't stay that day because I didn't want to get in trouble with Honey Gramms, but that I would come back the next day earlier in the day. My plan was to play hooky from school for just the one day, thinking my Mom was going to come that day, and then everything would be all right.

...I Want My Mom...

The next day, I left home the normal time as if I was going to school, but I went to Aunt Mae's house instead. She had a hangover from the night before and told me she needed to sleep for a while first. Then she left and said she would be back soon, leaving me there watching television. Well, I waited and waited and she never came back that night at all. Once it turned dark, I became afraid and decided to go to the house of one of Pete's male friends. He had a younger sister my age, and I thought I could stay over with her. His sister gave me something to eat, and hid me out in the shed kitchen on the floor so that her Mom would not know that I was in the house. While asleep there on the floor, I was again violently raped, this time by the older brother. Because I had no place else to go, and I was still afraid to leave until daylight, I just lay there and cried myself to sleep. Why do men think they can just do that to somebody? *I really hope Aunt Mae tells my Mom to come for me.*

This time I had decided that I was not going to give up until I found my Mom. I went back to Aunt Mae's house again and just sat there waiting. Thankfully, I had left the door unlocked the evening before. I waited all that day and in fact, I slept over there that night while still waiting for my aunt to come back. On the third day, early in the morning, there was a knock at the door. It was my aunt's boyfriend, Mr. Pager. Ironically, he was also a long time friend of Honey Gramms'. When he saw me, he was shocked, but I told him I was waiting for Aunt Mae to come back; that she had gone to get my Mom. He told me he would be back shortly and that he was pretty sure he knew where they were.

I had a strange feeling not to trust him, but didn't really have anywhere else to go, so I just stayed there and waited. A short while later, Mr. Pager showed up at the door again, only this time he came with Honey Gramms and some police officers who took me into custody, putting me in handcuffs. Honey Gramms told them I was a delinquent and a runaway, even though I had only been gone for two days. They believed her, and took me to the new police station in the community. They treated me like I was a hooker or something, instead of a young teenager trying to find my Mom. I was made to stand for hours with a yellow page phone book on each individually upturned hand, and each time I let my outstretched arm drop a little, one of the female officers cracked me with a yardstick; telling me the whole time how appreciative I should be to have a grandmother like Honey Gramms. All I could think to myself was, *"but she is not my Mom."*

I was made to go hungry and "punished" for a whole day and into the night for "acting like a delinquent"; and worrying my poor grandmother. Suddenly, in the middle of the night, I was given a lunch pack in a cardboard box, and placed in the back of a paddy wagon and driven I knew not where. It was two days later when I learned I had been sent to a Youth Detention Center, at Honey Gramms' request, since I was acting like my "no good mother." This, in spite of all the good things she and her side of the family had done for me and my ungrateful brothers. (*Does that include stealing us from our Mom while she was in the hospital, and keeping us for almost 8 years, without our Mom knowing if we were alive or dead? So, for this, I should be grateful..?.)* **...And the voice I hear, falling on my ear...**

...A Different Education...

Again, within a few short hours, my life was changed forever, never to be the same again. I was taken into the back of a building, stripped naked, with all my crevices searched, some "skunk" smelling shampoo put in my hair and then showered and brushed until my skin burned like fire. Then, I was put into a cell with the window in the door too high for me to see through; with only a metal cot to sleep on. Somehow, by God's grace, I dozed off, only to be awakened by the sound of a horrible tornado or hurricane outside. I could tell from the sound that there was a violent wind and shaking noise. I thought this was another hurricane like Hurricane Hazel which we had lived through some years earlier. It had torn down trees and killed a lot of people. To make it worse, these people must have forgotten that they put me down here in this basement. It was totally dark, and I started screaming for help but no one came. I screamed until my throat was raw, and I had wet myself but still no one came.

As far as I was concerned, surely everyone outside this brick basement must have been killed, "Oh my God, that means my Mom, Pete, Dave, Texas, Deacon, Felicia, Dad, Honey Gramms, Sugar Pops and everybody I know is gone, and I have no way out of this place." I cried myself to sleep, and I kept waking up screaming again, with no one responding. I was thinking that it's been at least a couple days now and my little lunch pack would soon be gone. Then I would starve to death. The wind must have torn the building down and killed everybody in it; and it has caved in on top of this basement cell. That's why no one knows that I am still here alive. I banged on the door until my hands were bloody and sore, and then I just lay down and cried myself to sleep while waiting to die.

The unexpected sound of a key in the door woke me up and a very tall woman opened the door. She took one look at me and yelled for help. She and another female matron took me to the nurse's dispensary because I had thrown up on myself, wet my pants multiple times, and looked like what "Big Mama" described as a "crazed deer in headlights." I didn't know what that meant, but I figured that I must have looked really bad; based on her immediate reaction when she saw me. I had been so agitated, that I had never even seen the small commode in the corner of the room. After I was given some water to drink, I finally was able to talk and I start crying hysterically (my normal way of crying) telling them that the hurricane had probably killed my whole family.

Finally after listening to me rant and rave for a few minutes, Big Mama realized what I was saying and she just grabbed me and started hugging me; telling me everything was all right, and that there had been no storm. She took me to the window and showed me that the sun was out and everything was normal. For a little bit, they all thought I had experienced some type of breakdown until another matron went back to the "isolation cell" I had slept in. She realized the horrible "storm" noise I had been hearing was the huge, old central air conditioning unit that was right next door to the cell. Also, I wasn't there for days; just a few hours. At that moment, I had learned my lesson about being disobedient and was ready to go home and do everything that I was told to do for the rest of my life even if it meant forgetting about finding my Mom. *But, only for that moment.*

Honey Gramms had other ideas, she demanded that I be held for at least a few days, and insisted that I be tested psychologically, physically, and every other way, both inside and outside; including a pelvic exam to see if I was being sexually active. All of the tests took two weeks to complete. No one believed me when I told them I wasn't voluntarily sexually active, but had been raped twice, once a few years earlier by Drew McKnight and again a couple nights earlier by my brother's friend. The fact that I had never told anyone further fueled Honey Gramms' opinion that I was a child spawned from hell through my mother's family line. She had warned me about it enough times to last me a lifetime.

To make matters worse, by the time I was evaluated by the psychologist almost 2 weeks after my arrival, I had met some girls in that place that told me some things that I had never seen or heard in my life. I had come in this place as green, innocent and naïve as a lime. Except for the grace and mercy of God, I would have been prime meat for some of the hardened criminals living inside the bodies of young females that was on the induction unit where I was housed, and who attended the same school classes I did. You see, out on the street, when I wasn't in the high school trying to play the part of a big girl; I was still playing jacks, jumping double-dutch and in my bedroom at home playing with my dolls. So, here I was in this place with girls who had seen and done things, and knew some things about the street, and then ……..*there was me.*

Big Mama, who was the head matron of our unit, recognized my greenness and put me in a room with a Puerto Rican girl named Myrtle, who was given the job of looking out for me. Her nickname was "Murder" because she had killed her stepfather for beating her mother. Myrtle was like a mad bull with a tight wire temper. She cussed and smoked and told me all kinds of things she had done while out in the street. She also told me she was a "dyke", and had to explain to me what that meant. Then she told me that she never tried to persuade a girl who wasn't really interested in that lifestyle. Thank God!! I know God answered Big Mama's prayers because by the time I finished crying and snotting and telling Myrtle my whole life story, she became my protector for the entire time that I ended up staying in that facility, almost six months. I had no visitors other than Honey Gramms when she came for the family counseling meetings, and I was so angry with her that I did not even want to see her, much less talk to her **…The Son of God discloses...**

...Standing My Ground....

By the time my psychological evaluation was scheduled, Myrtle had already taught me how to smoke cigarettes by inhaling without choking almost to death and wetting my pants like a baby, (like I did on the first attempt). I had also learned how to cuss, although I couldn't use the words correctly and all the girls would laugh. Myrtle told me to demand to be returned to my mother. I went in for the evaluation and when it was over, I stated, "I will not live with my grandmother no "#@$%^"" more, I want to go to live with my Mom." The diagnosis came back "Extremely intelligent, angry, volatile and oppositional. Provide counseling and reevaluate in two weeks." This went on three or four times over the next few months.

When it came time for me to go to my court hearing, a well known harsh judge was on the bench. He was so cruel; he had sent his own son to prison, where the son was killed. He told me he was ready to release me into the custody of Honey Gramms, but I refused, and demanded to be returned to my Mom. He angrily exploded and sentenced me to several more weeks of more testing and counseling. Finally after four months, he told me that if I came before him one more time refusing to comply with his decision, that I would be sent to Slayton Farms until age eighteen. I was ecstatic – I would rather go to a farm with cows and chickens to live than to go back home with Honey Gramms. When I got back to my room and told Myrtle, she started laughing and explained to me that the place was not a real farm at all, but a reform school. I told Big Mama, and she said she was praying for God's intervention in my situation because she knew I would be "dead meat" in a place like the "Farm". By the time Myrtle finished telling me about the murderers, etc., etc. at the "Farm", I was praying pretty hard for my own self.

At the Detention Center, aside from occasional cat fights among the females, it turned out not to be too bad a place – they had an awesome school. That's where I learned how to straighten and curl my hair using hot curlers, how to put on make-up "Black" style, how to play pinochle, and even how to write love letters to boys. We passed notes back and forth through a little hole in an adjoining wall between the girls' unit and the boys' unit. *Where there is a will, there is a way!* It was also there that my curiosity about boys began to develop. I feel like it was there that I began my "Rites of Passage", not through my own personal experiences, but through hearing the experiences of other girls and boys. After a few weeks, I received word that the High School had been informed of my situation, and they had dropped me from their rolls because they did not accept students with criminal backgrounds. *Good for them, they finally had a way out.*

Finally, my last scheduled court date was here; I was told to take all of my belongings with me. I said all of my tearful good-byes. I was still determined that I would rather go to the "Farm" if I could not go home to my Mom. Enter 'Grace' and 'Mercy' again…when I was called into the courtroom, the judge on the bench was not the same one!! Old "Meany" was away on vacation!! This one was kind and soft-spoken. After reading my paperwork, he called me to stand in front of the bench. He said he was shocked that I was there in the first place because I was an honor student both here and in NY, with no record of delinquency or behavior problems. He recommended that I accept the opportunity to return to Honey Gramms', rather than to go to the "Farm". The previous judge had stipulated these as my only two choices, since the location of my Mom was unknown. I stood my ground and assured him that I did not want to be disrespectful, but was not willing to go home to anyone other than my Mom.

The judge said that unfortunately, he would have to honor the previous judge's recommendation, unless some new information had become available. Then (just like in the movies), the courtroom door opened, and my Dad came through the door, running and asking if he could be heard. He related that he had not known where I was until that morning; that he had been out of town thinking that I was with his mother all this time. Then he said something that totally shocked me; both he and Honey Gramms knew the location of my mother, and had known it for some time. My Mom's apartment was only a few blocks from where we lived, and was literally only one city block from where she lived when we were taken!! Daddy asked the judge to allow me to go to my Mom. The judge met with Dad in his office for a few moments and decided to release me to them; with the understanding that I was to be taken to my Mom – *almost nine years later, with Pete and Dave still in the reform school in New York.* Dad drove us to Honey Gramms' house, told me to pack my things and he would be back to pick me up. I went in the room to pack and Honey Gramms locked me in, saying she wouldn't let me go to that, "@#%^& mother of yours."

I sat there for a while thinking, and finally came up with a plan. I told her, "You'll have to let me out sooner or later because I am pregnant." It was a lie, but it worked *...**And He walks with me**...*

...Family Reunion....

Within five minutes the door was unlocked and Dad was called to, "come get this strumpet out of my house right now". I was dropped off at my Mom's doorstep with all of my clothes, and a wave "Goodbye". At least Dad cried a little as he was pulling off. Honey Gramms never even looked back. My Mom was not home at the time. Texas and Felicia didn't know who I was, and wouldn't open the door. I sat on the steps for a couple hours until the upstairs neighbor, Mr. Buster, came home and asked who I was. When I told him, he left and came back in a few minutes with my Mom. I had not known what to expect exactly, but I thought it would be a happy reunion....sad to say, it was far from that.

Mom was cussing up a storm about them bringing me without any notice. There was not even a hug. I suddenly felt totally alone because I didn't know these strangers and they did not know me. Texas was two years younger than me, and Felicia was seven years younger – they had no real memory of Pete, Dave and I. It didn't take long for me to realize that our "family bonds" had been badly broken. Too much time and pain had passed. Deacon was still living with Mom's friend. *Where do I belong???* Even today, although I love my Mom because she is my Mom, the love that I think I should feel for a Mom is not really there. My love for my Dad was also like that for a very long time; especially while growing up because he just wasn't around enough. Eventually, I came to realize that part of the residue of my "holocaust" experience is that my ability to bond with family members is not what it should be. Though I consciously choose to love my parents and siblings, it is not the same as it would have been had we grown up as a bonded family unit. Later, this would also affect my ability to bond with my own husband and children.

After the initial shock, Mom tried hard to make me feel comfortable. She told me that it was okay to call her "Mom" if I wanted to, or that I could call her by her first name. I was shocked and had never heard of anything so disrespectful in my life. I told her that I would rather call her "Mom". As we talked, I would say, "Yes Ma'am", because that was what I had been taught by Honey Gramms. Mom got angry and said, "This ain't no plantation and you ain't no "@#$%^" slave, so stop with the "Yes Ma'am" stuff." That was another step of my re-education.

Dave came home a couple months after me, and was brought to Mom's house. I was brokenhearted to realize that even my brother whom I had been so close to, had become an angry and bitter stranger. He hung out in the streets until late at night, and would come home drunk. He hardly talked to anyone, even me. A few months later, Pete was also brought home to Mom's house. He was so alienated and violent that I was afraid of him. He was physically violent toward all of us except Dave, and would frequently punch us around. He and Dave would argue a lot, but usually would just end up drinking beer together and laughing it off. Within a few months, both Pete and Dave became active gang members.

Once in the heat of an argument, Pete told Dave and me that he hated us because we had abandoned him; that we had left him in Rose Tree and come home without him. *Did we have a choice? Does this craziness ever end?* ***...And He walks with me...***

...A Second Beginning...

This certainly was not the fairytale reunion that we had all dreamed of and hoped and prayed for; but at least we were all back together with Mom. We had some real challenges getting to know one another, and trying to get along with each other, but we all worked real hard at it. As I look back on those days, I can only imagine how hard it must have been for my Mom. When she last saw her three oldest children as she left to go to the hospital all those years ago, we were all young happy, healthy and energetic children. By the time we got back home, we were angry and brooding teenagers, with a real chip on our shoulders.

I learned how to smoke cigarettes and to swear proficiently by then; and didn't mind using my new skills at the drop of a hat. I gave Mom the courtesy of asking her for permission to smoke. Although she told me she would rather that I didn't, she didn't want me sneaking around behind her back doing things either. One of the ways that she handled all of the craziness was to hang out at the bar around the corner which our third floor neighbor owned. She spent a lot of time there with her friends, and we always knew where to find her. We kids pretty much took care of ourselves, cooking and cleaning. Mom did make sure that we were enrolled in school, and that we had the clothes and school supplies which were needed. There were some real problems for each of us for school. For Pete and Dave, they had to go through "enemy turf" to get to their high school, through foreign neighborhoods. Since they were active gang members in our neighborhood, they were in physical danger to get to school and back.

In spite of the truant officer coming to our house again and again, and even with Mom taking them there on the bus herself a few times, they would not attend regularly. Eventually, Mom gave up even trying to make them go, and they just became boys on the corner with so many of the other guys in our area. Texas really tried by going to school regularly. He was so far behind academically; and his behavior was so out of control that they put him in a special education class. Felicia, like me, really liked school and did well until she also lost interest.

As for me, I was sent to the 9th grade of the junior high school for our district, which unfortunately was also across "foreign" gang turf. This, not to mention the fact that the class work was work I had done two years before. I was totally in culture shock, in spite of my "training" at the detention center. I was nowhere near prepared for the girls who confronted me outside of the school doors daily asking me, "Where you from?" (What neighborhood gang?) After my naïve, "I'm from nowhere" caused me to be beaten up multiple times, I learned to start swinging my fists at the same time that I gave my response. Dave had also gotten tired of me coming home with my face messed up and clothes torn; so he taught me how to fight to defend myself. Gradually I fought and won often enough to earn a little respect from the tormentors. I also began to carry a straight razor like Myrtle at the Detention Center had instructed me to do. *Thank God I never had to use it. My threats were enough.*

I spent that entire year of school intermittently fighting my way into and back out of the school; or sneaking in and out before or after everyone else. I actually managed to make the honor roll that year while just showing up for attendance at first period class before skipping out. I did stick around long enough on test days just to take the tests. I played hooky from school and skipped classes so much that one day, after getting washed and dressed, when I asked my Mom for lunch money, she laughed hysterically. It was Saturday!! Finally, the school year ended and somehow, Felicia and I were promoted and Texas was moved up to the next class. Even though my class had a junior prom and graduation, I still did not attend, this time because we couldn't afford it. All of us eventually dropped out of high school. Felicia and I later went back and earned our high school equivalency diplomas. We both went on to graduate from college.

...FRIENDS???...

Then came my first summer vacation back with my Mom. No more picnics or traveling out to the park. Pete and Dave introduced me to "Duke", a friend of theirs who became my first "official" boyfriend. He was a little strange, all he wanted to do was hang out at our house and drink beer with my brothers. Once in a while he would take me to a movie. I thought he was kind of nerdy myself, but at least he was a boyfriend, and after I told him about my horrible history with two guys taking advantage of me, he was kind enough to never try anything with me other than an occasional kiss on the cheek. Thank God for Duke. It was through Duke that I met a very large family who lived in his neighborhood named the Murdocks. The oldest girl, Priscilla and I became good friends. She then introduced me to her friend Miriam, whose grandfather owned a weekend bar and outdoor dance floor in a little town near Atlantic City, New Jersey. Miriam had a boyfriend with a car, and through the three of them, I spent one of the wildest summers in my life.

On the weekends we would actually sneak out after our parents were asleep, drive the two hours down to the club, dance half the night, and be back home by dawn. Of course, I was the chicken who was afraid to drink alcohol, and I spent most of my time on the dance floor. All of this was brought to a screeching halt one August night when Miriam's boyfriend left us down there because he was angry with her. Her grandfather had already left for the night, leaving another guy in charge. There were the three of us – Miriam, Priscilla and me stranded without a way to get home. A few of the young guys who hung out there agreed to bring us home, even though they had all been drinking. We laughed and joked for the two hours home; and stopped and showed them the statues in the large park near our home. We tried to get them to sleep over in their car to rest for a while before leaving to drive home. They refused, opting to go right back, still drinking beer.

By the time we finally reached Priscilla's house, it was later than usual and starting to get light out. We started climbing through our normal back window. All of a sudden, the lights came on and Priscilla's Mom, Mrs. Murdock was all over us with a belt. She beat all of us like we were her own; and threatened to kill us and send us home to Jesus if we ever did that again. I was not hard to convince, so that was my last weekend out with them. There were only a couple weeks for school to start anyway.

The following week, when Miriam's grandfather came home from the club, he told her the horrible news that several of the guys who were our friends from the dance floor had died in a head-on car collision with a train not far from their home the week before. *It was the guys who had driven us home – they never made it back home!* We must have cried for weeks, wondering if it was our fault that those guys had been still out drinking and driving. *Only God knows...* After this, I stopped hanging out with Priscilla and Miriam, and stayed closer to home. I acquired a couple of girlfriends in the neighborhood who like me did not participate or belong to any gang. We began taking walks out all over the city. We would walk the long hike to center city and back, which was like a two hour walk one way. Otherwise, we would walk ourselves over to a large park, only about one hour walking distance away. Usually we had no money and would often end up shoplifting for clothing or food.

One of those girls lived on the first floor of an apartment house near me, and her second floor neighbor would always have a lot of friends and family over. Her name was Ms. Sue, and she lived there with her husband and four young children. She wouldn't let us call her Ms. Sue, just Sue; and we began hanging out up there much of the time. She would have music playing or card games going on, and would cook food for us. She always just enjoyed having a house full of people around. The adults would be drinking alcohol, and occasionally she would give us girls a beer to share among us, but made us promise not to drink anything stronger. Sue was actually the one who talked me into allowing her to pierce my ears. After I told her my life story, she told me to never hang out in the street alone; that if I cut class or left school early, that I could come to her house. She encouraged us to stay in school or to come to her house to be safe. When I told my Mom about Sue, Mom didn't even mind me hanging out over there because at least she knew where I was. What Mom didn't know was how many days, we had hung out in the park or riding the subways while ducking from the truant officers before Sue gave us permission to come there!

    The high school that I was assigned to attend the following year was the same one where my brothers had refused to go to. When I got there, I found out why. It was another constant gang battle getting in and out. I repeated the same pattern of behavior which I had done at the junior high school, yet somehow managing to keep up my grades. I managed to get through that school year.

...Rescue And A "Real" Boyfriend...

The following summer, I reached out to Honey Gramms by going to her house to see her. At first she wouldn't even talk to me, but eventually she did let me come to visit her once in a while. It was on one of those times that I was coming from a visit with her that I met my first "real" boyfriend. Honey Gramms' home was in the turf (area) of a very large street gang. They were known to have ongoing violent wars with the gang whose turf I lived in. I was aware of that and was mindful to never stay in her area until dark. One day I overstayed my time while visiting with my girlfriend across the street from Honey Gramms. By the time I left to go home, dusk had already set in. I began to do a combination of walking fast and running, and took a short cut through a small street near her home. Just as I turned the corner and started walking across an alleyway (breezeway) near the corner, I heard someone say "Pssst" but I kept walking. Then I heard the sound again, "Pssst". Just as I was about to run, a guy stepped partially out of the alleyway in front of me, and told me to stop and not to run. I took one look at him, and nearly fainted. He looked like a movie star. He was one of the best looking guys I remembered seeing in all of my days, and I could tell that he was at least about twenty years old.

I stopped and stood there looking at him from his head to his feet, he had a small gold hoop earring hanging from his left ear, which fascinated me because I had never seen a guy with an earring before. He also had on a huge wide brim hat, and bell-bottom pants, with dress shoes, not just sneakers! Then after a minute or so, I gathered my thoughts, and realized that he could be dangerous and I decided to be brusque with him. Before I could say anything, he reached out and grabbed me to him in a hug, and stepped both of us away from the alleyway. Just as I was about to scream and start fighting, he whispered in my ear to be quiet and to look behind me. I looked over my shoulder and there were about thirty or more younger guys coming up towards us; some from the alleyway and some from around the corner!! They began doing a little chant and making noises like a train; some saying "Choo-choo-choo-choo" and others saying "Whoo-Whoo". One really tall guy walked towards me and said, "Train Time". I was so startled that I stepped closer to the guy in front of me, who was still hugging me and whispering in my ear to "be still".

The tall guy, who I later came to know as "Grass", stepped up to the guy holding me and said, "I stake my claim." The guy who was holding me said, "Back off, this is my dame". Grass threw his head back, laughed and said, "Yeah right. That "b@#%^"" don't know you and you don't even know her name." The one holding me said, "Man, are you challenging me? Everybody knows I am Diablo, and her name is Pookie." All of the other guys started making comments like "Grass, you better know what you're doing man." and "Don't be stupid man, she ain't worth it". 'Diablo' pushed me towards some steps that we were standing near, and told me to sit down and don't move. He didn't have to tell me more than one time.

I don't think I had even breathed for about five minutes or more. He took his hat off, and said to Grass again, "Are you challenging me?" Grass stood there, breathing hard for a few minutes and they just stared at each other eye to eye. The other guys started backing up, and I know it was mercy that kept me from dying of asphyxiation, since I don't believe I was breathing at all by then. Finally, Grass laughed and said, "Come on, Diablo man, I'm just a junior. You know it ain't my style to challenge a senior. I'm just messing with you, man." Diablo smiled, put his hat back on, put his hand out to me and said, "Let's go." Somewhere between the "Let's" and the "Go", I was on my feet and standing almost on top of his feet, ready to move when he moved.

That was my initiation experience with the gang life of a very warlike gang. My brothers had never told me anything about their gang, but I became quite knowledgeable about the gang of which Diablo was the "Senior War Lord." Diablo's real name turned out to be Keith, he was about six years older than me and he became my first real and intimate boyfriend. He treated me with kindness, gentleness and affection in spite of his "other life". We often went out to the movies, to eat, to the park or to the zoo. He actually kept me pretty separate from his gang activity, except for the things that he would tell me about. He took me home to meet his mother, and she told me that I was the first girl that he had ever brought home; and that I was the only one that he had ever talked to her about. Because of the differing gang turfs involved, he had to "sneak" to come see me at my house, and so he only saw my Mom and family once.

After I had been hanging out with Keith for a while, he told me about the first night when he met me. He said that he had been seeing me coming and going to Honey Gramms' house for a while. He noticed I was always clean and quiet and usually by myself, and he liked that about me. He had seen me on that particular night, and had been shadowing me to watch that I got across the street which separated our turfs. Then, he noticed the junior gang members gathering and saw them go in the alley near where I was walking. He realized they were planning to "pull train", which was their name for gang rape of the first girl they saw who was walking alone and unprotected. These guys had even been known to violate girls by thrusting glass soda bottles and things like broom handles into their vaginas. *How absolutely sick was that!!!*

Because of God's mercy, grace and favor watching over me, Keith intercepted their plan that night and rescued me, even though he really knew nothing about me. I naively came to believe that Keith was a "semi-innocent" gang member who didn't really participate in the gang wars (violent shoot-outs with rival gangs) and the violent molestation of the girls. I soon learned that his treatment of me was not fully who he was. He had a very dark side as well. Just a couple months after I started going out with him, he was arrested and sent to jail for rape and attempted murder of a young woman who lived only about 2 blocks from where I had met him. I never told my Mom or family what happened to him. *"Grace and Mercy shall follow me all the days of my life."*

By that time, the summer was almost over, and I started hanging out again with my girlfriends until school resumed. In the interim, Sue and her family had moved to another neighborhood about a half-hour walk from my home. I sought out the comfort of their home more and more often. I had come to really dislike school because of the violent environment, so I had no desire to be there; but I couldn't stay home because I was afraid that the truant officer would come and pick me up. Sue's house was the best place to be for my friends and I ... ***And He talks with me...***

...Could This Be True Love?...

Then the unbelievable happened! One school afternoon, I was hanging out with my friends at Sue's house, eating her extra fluffy North Carolina biscuits and learning how to clean "chittlings." (*Ugh!*) We were cracking jokes, braiding each other's hair and listening to Marvin Gaye records. His big hit, "Let's Get It On" had just come out, and I was in the living room kneeling down on the floor in front of the broken stereo speaker trying to hear the words clearly. The doorbell rang and Sue's little daughter opened the door. When I looked up, a guy was standing there looking at me. Okay....so the other guy (what's his name, Diablo, I think) was no longer the best looking guy I had ever seen!! The freakiest part about the whole thing is that this guy was dressed just like Keith the first time I saw him – he had a similar small gold hoop earring in his ear, a wide brim hat, bell bottom pants and high top Stacey Adams dress shoes. Plus, both of them wore their hair processed, with gorgeous waves. They even favored one another in the face.

How bizarre was that? This guy, Michael, was a lot taller and so much more muscular – Wow! He had the biggest hands I had ever seen, and his shoulder muscles were so big that his shirt sleeves look like they were about to pop. In the meantime, I was still kneeling in the same place on the floor in front of the stereo. *Talk about nerdy!!* About that time, Sue finally came out to see who was at the door, and when she saw him she started screaming and ran to hug him. The rest of the family all started screaming and hugging him and shaking his hand, and I was thinking to myself, "What celebrity is this?" Sue introduced him to us as her husband's nephew who was just coming home from jail. Amazingly, he was also the warlord of the large gang that he belonged to, in another whole area of the city. Okay, this was getting freakier by the minute, and kind of like de'javu. Long story short, I was as instantly in love as a young girl could be, and still be on the ground in the real world. Evidently he was at least infatuated with me too because he kept sneaking looks at me. I was totally fascinated and just sat staring at him drinking his King Solomon Grape wine, and peeling the label off the bottle. I was bedazzled with him, like he was a pirate or something. And then, I had to leave to go home because school hours were over. *No! Don't make me go!*

My two girlfriends and I all agreed that we each liked him, and we decided that we would all flirt with him, and then wait to see who he liked, and then the other two would concede defeat. Hah! - talk about teenage puppy love, those were the days!! We continued hanging out at Sue's house more and more often, even after school. On some of the days we managed to get there, Michael was there almost as much as we were. So, we saw a lot of each other. One day I went over to Sue's home by myself, and Michael was there babysitting. As usual, he had a bottle of "King Solomon's Grape Wine", and he was sitting there peeling the label off of it. Then he totally shocked me by asking me if he could talk to me by myself. He then asked me, "Suppose I was to ask you to be my dame, what would you say?" *There's that word "dame" again.* I said, "Suppose I was to say yes?" As the saying goes, "The rest is history". From that day forward, I was totally in love, and knew for sure that he was best thing that had ever happened to me, and the person with whom I wanted to spend the rest of my life.

Well, my Mom didn't have the same sentiments right away. Her immediate reaction was, "Where did you meet that young jitter hopper?" She hated his earring, his bell-bottom pants, his gorgeous wavy processed hair, and his wide brim hat – *what was wrong with her?* Those were some of the best things about him. Anyway, her animosity towards him only lasted for about five minutes. As soon as he brought her the first bouquet of flowers, flashed that smile and called her "Mom", he had won her over. All of my brothers and my sister liked him a lot; and although he was the warlord from a gang known for its extreme violence, he was absolutely kind and gentle with all of us. He had such a "rep" for who he was in the gang world, that he came and went through our "turf" to see me whenever he wanted to. None of the guys from our neighborhood gang would try to confront him. *Wow!*

One of the positive things about this for me was that Pete was no longer able to beat me up at his own whim and fancy any more. The last time that he slapped me was about an hour before Michael was coming to see me one day, and so I still had a red face when he got there. Felicia promptly told Michael what happened at which point, I saw for one of the few times in my life, the pure raw violent potential that Michael had in him. He picked my brother up over his head, slammed him to the floor, and punched him in the forehead with a huge skeleton ring which Michael always wore. It was the mercy of God that my brother was not killed, but he had a huge knot on his forehead for weeks afterwards. As for me, I knew that I had finally found someone who wanted to, and who could protect me. For that, I was ecstatic. Although, I do have to admit that I felt real bad for Pete.

...Soul Mates...

Michael and I became the best of friends and inseparable, pledging our lifelong love for one another. One weird thing was that we could not talk to one another. I was, and always have been a true talker; but for some reason, I could not have long conversations with Michael. He said he was not "really a talker", and just kind of sat and brooded much of the time. I started out trying to be as vocal as my usual talkative self, but found that it caused a sense of tension in the room. It seems absolutely bizarre as I look back on it, but I remember that we used to write love letters to each other, hand them to each other, and then sit side by side on the couch, holding hands as we read them in silence. Even after reading what the other person wrote, we still would not talk about it out loud. We went out together and spent a lot of time together, and still never really learned how to talk to one another, but somehow we both didn't seem to mind.

After about six months, we decided that we wanted to get married! We asked his parents, and although his mother thought we were nuts, his father said he would give his consent. He was willing to drive us down to Elkton, MD so we could get married overnight – there was just one big holdback—I was only 15 years old and Michael was only 17. My Dad laughed like a madman and said, "When hell freezes over!!" Mom said she had nothing to say, and wouldn't sign the consent. *Now what?* Not to be outdone, Michael and I came up with a plan; we'd have a baby and then Dad would have to give us permission. So that's what we set out to do. The first part of the plan worked, and we got pregnant while I was just barely sixteen years old, and Michael was just barely eighteen. Unfortunately, Dad still said, "No." When I was six months pregnant with our first daughter, Tirzah, Michael ended up getting into some legal trouble. He had gone out with some of his fellow gang members to a city owned playground after hours, and started fooling around breaking windows. They were arrested, charged with vandalism of public property, and sentenced to six months in jail. Way to go Michael – now my Dad is really impressed!!

Things were definitely not going the way we had expected. Now instead of having a husband by my side as we had our first baby, I had to deal with all of this by myself. I felt ashamed even walking down the street alone, not to mention that I was fearful for my life and the life of my baby since gang war was at its highest peak in our hometown. The Vietnam War was going strong and the "neighborhood warriors" seemed like they were more blood-thirsty than ever. The year was 1964 and racial tension was running at a fever pitch all over the country. Finally, when I was about seven and a half months pregnant, the tension in the neighborhood boiled over and there was an all out riot less than one block from our apartment, with stores being looted and burned.

The report was that a White policeman had slapped a pregnant Black woman not far from where we lived. Then her boyfriend jumped the officer, resulting in another officer shooting the boyfriend. Within a few hours, the entire shopping district a block from where we lived was overrun with a huge angry mob of Black people out for blood. Before the police officers could stop it, all of the stores within a ten block radius had been vandalized and/or burned, and this went on far into the night. Because of the location of our home, I watched out of our front windows for hours, part of the time in which my Mom had to go and find my brothers and make them come home. Within the next twenty-four hours, the Armed National Guard was dispatched into our community, where they imposed martial law for weeks. Policemen accompanied by soldiers went door to door, searching people's homes for looted items. Any new items in someone's home for which they could not produce a receipt, were confiscated. What a nightmare!! *And where was my protector?*

I only went up to the Detention Center once to see Michael while he was away, because it was just too disturbing to me to deal with all of the search procedures and other stressful requirements. In spite of all of the challenges, in early January of 1965, I gave birth to our beautiful firstborn daughter, with my Mom accompanying me instead of Michael. There are not many times in my life that I have been as angry with someone as I was with Michael during that time in my life. He missed out on one of the most important events in our relationship.

...Dad and Honey Gramms to the Rescue...

One of the most difficult things that I have ever had to do in my life was to tell my Dad and Honey Gramms that I was pregnant. Even though it was really my choice, I still realized that it would hurt the two of them badly. My Mom just kind of took it in stride, and said, "I hope you know what you got yourself into." Dad cried when I told him over the phone. As for Honey Gramms, she just hung up on me and refused to talk to me for a couple months. In spite of all that, they still came through for me when it was time for the baby to born. Honey Gramms gathered a bunch of her "Green Stamps", which she used to trade in for items from a mail catalogue company. With them, she "purchased" a baby bottle set with the sterilizer, a bottle warmer, a nursery lamp and some other items. She refused to come see us, but she still sent them by Dad. It took me a long time to realize and appreciate that Honey Gramms' way of telling us that she loved us was by the things that she did. *Who knew?*

Dad came the same day that Mom brought me home from the hospital with my baby. I couldn't believe my eyes, and couldn't stop crying when he brought in all the things that Honey Gramms had sent. He went back out to the car, and came back in with loads of beautiful baby clothes, blankets, and other items which he and Ms. Lucy had also bought. The clothes were extravagant and elegant to say the least, with yards of lace, ruffles and silk, and even a cashmere blanket. Wow! There were so many beautiful clothes that Tirzah actually outgrew a few items before she ever had a chance to wear them. It was so ironic how Dad said he ran into Ms. Lucy after years of no contact, without him knowing she had moved back to the city. She was the one who took him shopping for Tirzah – afterwards, we lost track of her again.

Even though I appreciated everything that Dad did for Tirzah and me, I have to admit that there was a period a few years later when I really developed an intense hatred towards my Dad. While living with my Mom, and still feeling like I really didn't belong there either; and as I looked back over my life, I felt that it was all his fault that I was away from my Mom all those years. I felt that he was to blame and because of his actions, that my brothers and I had suffered through some horrible things in our lives.

Thankfully, a few years later, I was able to come to grips with the fact that Dad made his choices based on who he was, and what he knew or thought at that time in his life, at a very young age and with three small children to be responsible for. Given a different set of circumstances, and a different fund of information, perhaps he would have made a different choice. He and I talked about it a few years later, and made a full reconciliation. He is still my "hero", although now his back is not quite so tall and straight these days.

...Gang Violence...

During the time when Tirzah was born, things were very different than they are now. When a Black woman had a baby, the older people didn't let you wash your hair or go up and down flights of stairs, much less go outside, until the baby was a month old, unless it was for an emergency. Even the normal postpartum checkup for women was scheduled for when the baby was six weeks old. My Mom was a real stickler for that, and so I was stuck in the house until the thirtieth day after my baby was born. Finally, the day came that I was permitted to take a walk out with my brother Dave and his wife. He had enlisted in the Army a few months earlier to get away from the gang. He was home on his first leave after Basic Training, and before his scheduled assignment to ship out to Vietnam. He and his wife had just gotten married a couple weeks earlier, and he was fully dressed in his Army uniform.

The three of us were taking a walk to see a family friend who lived about eight blocks from where we lived. Suddenly, two young guys ran past us from behind and we didn't think much of it, so we just kept walking, laughing and talking. About two minutes later, a gang of about twelve young guys ran up behind us and surrounded us. They started shoving my brother around saying he was one of the guys they were chasing. Dave called their attention to the fact that he had on a military uniform and the guys who ran past us did not. They talked about it and had just decided to let us go when a few other guys ran up to us. Sorrow of sorrows; one of them recognized Dave as being a member of the gang he was with prior to the Army.

These guys were enemies of that gang, and evidently Dave had beaten this one guy up pretty badly in school once during a gang rumble. *Drat!!* All of those guys bum-rushed Dave, his wife and myself, and the only thing that I could do was drop to the ground and curl up in a ball to try to protect my stomach since I was still not fully recovered from having my baby just one month earlier. Those guys were hitting us with feet, fists, sticks and whatever else they had. Dave's wife fought all she could before they finally knocked her down, and I looked up long enough to see Dave fighting like a madman, but there were just too many of them. Just about the time that I knew that we were going to be killed out there that night, I looked up and saw a police car coming. In my heart I was relieved thinking we were saved. However, there was only one police officer in the car and he did not stop or even slow down.

A few seconds later, as I lay my head back down on the ground and began asking God to give my baby another good Mommy; I heard a loud piercing bang. I opened my eyes to see the guys starting to scatter, and to see Dave holding on to about four of them still fighting while they were trying to get away. I looked around to see an old man standing on a porch near us with a double-barrel shotgun; evidently that was the sound I heard. He looked at Dave and said, "What you young jitterbugs do to one another is one thing. When girls start getting beat up is another thing." *Thank God!* The three of us were bloody and bruised as we stumbled and ran trying to get to a large crowded intersection not far from where we were. We knew that there were always police at that corner. Horror of horrors, as we were trying to get to help, we ran into a whole different group of guys from the same gang that had just beat us up, and they started coming towards us. When I saw them coming towards us, I started screaming hysterically and when they got up close enough to see that we were already hurt, they changed their mind and told us, "Walk on".

We finally reached the intersection with me still screaming and wailing like a madwoman. There were police cars parked there; and one of them drove us to pick up Mom first, and then to the closest hospital emergency room. That was another nightmare; it was crowded and noisy. There were people bleeding and hurt all over the place, and I went totally ballistic and had to be sedated. While we were lying on the stretchers waiting to be seen, a man was brought in by the police with a huge bread knife handle sticking out of the center of his chest. I heard an officer say the rest of the blade was still inside the man's chest; and that was it for me. I was instantly cured of all my ills. I got up, got dressed, washed my face and told my Mom to take me home to my baby. After that, I refused to come out of the house until Michael came home about six weeks later.

Let me take a minute to share with you my perception of my Mom. When I was brought back home to my mother, I was an angry fourteen year old. In spite of that, this woman who had suffered so much in her own young life immediately opened her home to me. Although the apartment where she lived, and the things that she had, was nowhere near the "middle class" environment that we had been raised in, she held nothing back from me of what she had. My Mom is a beautiful woman who has a "coffee with extra cream" complexion, which requires no make-up to look good. While you probably wouldn't call her 'aristocratic and elegant', I loved the way she carried herself because she was "sassy" and "classy". Known to have a quick smile, she is friendly to everyone; and has an infectious laugh that makes everyone around her laugh. She always had a lot of female and male friends visiting, and everyone would seem to be having a good time playing cards, laughing, and talking or "shooting the breeze" as Mom used to say. Even though we would have been classified as "poor", and even qualified for government surplus food, she still was always sharing what she had.

Although that emotional and spiritual "bond" between mother and daughter that should have been there was irrevocably damaged and broken because of the years apart, my Mom stepped up to the plate when I needed her. For that, I will always be thankful. I was not easy to deal with; and when the time came two short years later, that I decided to be my own woman, Mom helped me in every way that she could. I honor her for the woman that she is. She took the lemons that life dealt her, and made lemonade **...And He tells me I am His own...**

...The 'Plan' Continues...

When Tirzah was two and a half months old, Michael was released and came home. Within a month, I was pregnant again. I guess our "plan" finally worked this time, because my Dad said, "Time to make it legal." So in September of 1965, we were married with me about five months pregnant with our second daughter, and two weeks shy of my seventeenth birthday. Michael was about six weeks shy of age nineteen. He had gone missing a couple days before, and when he did show up the night before the wedding, he was totally intoxicated. The wedding was held in Michael's parents' home, and was a double wedding along with his sister and her husband. Our "honeymoon" was back at my Mom's apartment, with me watching him passed out in a drunken stupor. Even so, I was tickled pink to be married to the love of my life, "my protector".

Honey Gramms refused to come to the wedding, and poor Dad cried through most of it. Mom told me, "You've made your bed hard and now you'll have to lay in it", whatever that meant. All I know is that it sent a chill down my spine and through my tired swollen feet. Only a few of my friends were there because my little brother, who I paid to deliver the invitations, had taken a shortcut and thrown them in the trash. He later told me that he assumed I had already told all my friends when and where the wedding was, but I had not. They couldn't find the house, and as I told you before, I have some of the most helpful brothers that a girl could have (*and still survive*). Oh my God!! I woke up the next morning realizing that I was not only Michael's wife, but I was a "Mommy", with my own responsibility for one and a half babies that I was bringing into the world. Wow!!!! A whole new era was beginning in my life………….. but I suddenly realized that *I still wanted my Mom.*

The following week, we moved into the two rooms on the third floor of my in-law's home. I thought to myself, "I'm grown now and can run my own life" - little did I realize that my personal "holocaust" was not over, but was, in fact, getting ready to go to another whole dimension. A couple months after getting married, I decided that I wanted to go back home to my Mom, and actually packed some things for Tirzah and my pregnant self. As I was standing at the bus stop waiting for the bus, I suddenly remembered what Mom said to me on my wedding day about making your bed hard and laying in it. I changed my mind and went back home and promised myself to never leave my husband again.

The following January, little Lisa made her debut into the world in the midst of the worst major snow blizzard for that winter. It was snowing so badly that my father-in-law was afraid to drive me to the hospital. The ambulance we called refused to come get me, and the police had to come with a paddy wagon to drive me to the hospital. Thank God that Michael was home with me this time, after partying half of the night. He passed out in the hospital lobby when we got there. His new daughter was about twelve hours old by the time he first saw her, but at least I didn't have to feel ashamed of having a baby alone this time, because my husband was there with me (well, in body at least) *...And the joy we share.*

On the day that I came home from the hospital with my little bundle of joy in my arms, Michael dropped us off at the house and said he would go to the store for some things we needed. As I came in the door with my mother-in-law, "Me-Mom" helping me; the phone rang. I answered it because I was the closest one to it. A female voice on the other end asked if I was Michael's wife who had just had a baby, and I answered, "Yes." "Congratulations", she said – "I just wanted you to know that I just had one for him too." Talk about "*Baby-Mama-Drama*" - all of my pregnancy hormones kicked in and I went hysterically ballistic and started screaming and crying like a banshee. My little Tirzah was startled and started holding onto my leg for dear life and screaming almost as loudly as me. Baby Lisa was in my arms crying the cry of a newborn. Me-Mom grabbed me and held me close to her, "What is it? Did something happen to Michael? Where is he?"

Eventually I couldn't scream any more, and sat down crying like Niagara Falls. Finally, I could talk coherently enough to tell Me-Mom what the woman said to me on the phone, and looked up to see her looking at me incredulously. She proceeded to set me straight - *"What the (blankety-blank-blank) are you getting upset about? Aren't you the one that he married? Don't you have two beautiful babies, and doesn't he take good care of you all? He loves you and that's all you need to know. '@#$%' that (*&^%."*

By now, I was sitting there with my mouth hanging open, saying "but I love him". I will never forget the look on her face when she looked at me with a smirk on her face and said "No one woman is enough for my son, and love went out with high-button shoes. Girl, get yourself up those steps and put you and your babies to bed." I think it was total shock that made me start laughing hysterically as I did exactly what she said. By the time I got up in the middle of the night to feed my baby, Michael was sitting there looking at me, crying and telling me that he would never stop loving me. He told me that he did have two other children by someone else, but that they were much older than my children, and he had nothing more to do with their mother. He said it - I believed it - and that settled it. *I can't remember what it was that had me so upset earlier*...***as we tarry there, none other has ever known***.

...Our Own 'Home Sweet Home'...

A few months later, we moved into our own third floor apartment just around the corner from my in-laws, and I absolutely loved having my own family and home. I was a total 'clean' freak, and Michael complained that I drove him nuts following him around telling him not to mess up the house, and emptying his ashtray before he could hardly put his cigarette out. I bathed my babies three times each day until Tirzah's skin broke out with a horrible rash. The doctor said I had washed all of the natural oils and flora off her skin, and that I was to only sponge her off during the day, and could only bathe her once every other day for two weeks. *Yuck!*

Those were some of the happiest days in my early marriage, with just an occasional disagreement between us. The issue was usually about him staying out away from home over night from time to time, and even for whole weekends, supposedly partying with some of his friends. One time he even went all the way to St. Louis without telling me, hanging out with his sister's husband. The only way she and I found out is because they ran out of money and had to call for us to telegram them some money. My entire social life consisted of going around the corner with his sister once in a while to the corner bar, while a friend would babysit our kids for a few hours. Funny thing was Michael never seemed to be there at the same time, even though he was always telling me that was where he could usually be found when he wasn't at home. **...*as I come to the garden alone***

Michael's Dad, "Pop-Pop", helped him to get a job as a tractor-trailer driver; he began taking some overnight jobs, and even a few week long jobs away from home. That began to create some real tension in our family, especially since I was still very afraid of the dark and would sit up in a chair all night when he wasn't home. I would continually whine about it, making him angry. Once he told me that if I didn't like how things were, that I should go back home to my Mom. I had already promised myself that I would never do that again. He gave me a small pistol to protect us when he wasn't there…*me…one of the most squeamish people who lives, with a gun. I think not!*

To make things more challenging, when Lisa was about ten months old, the unthinkable happened – you got it, I found out that I was pregnant again for the third time in less than four years! How does that happen when you're taking birth control pills? Michael accused me of missing my nightly pills, but sure enough, a medical report came out in the news that the particular brand of pills I had been taking had a high failure rate. …great, just what I needed! Things became more strained between Michael and me. He began to spend less and less time at home. The arguments increased in number and intensity. I remember becoming more and more angry, bitter and depressed. By the time Doretha was born, I began to look around for a church to attend; hoping that something would make a difference in our lives…***while the dew is still on the roses.***

Michael and I talked about it, and he agreed that we should start looking for a church to attend together. He set the criteria that the denomination should not be "Holiness", "Pentecostal", or "Catholic", but that almost anything else would do. It didn't really matter to me; I just wanted to go to church. Neither one of us realized that the following week was to be a major turning point in our lives, and in the lives of our children. I had been laid off my job a few weeks earlier, where I worked as a power sewing machine operator in a clothing factory. The clothing union arranged for me to go to a job interview at a factory within walking distance from our home, and I set out with all three of my children in a stroller because I had no babysitter for that day…***and the voice I hear falling on my ear.***

...WHO KNEW?...

I was walking along praying that I would get the job and that it was okay for me to have my children with me for the interview. Then I heard someone call my name and to my surprise, I saw one of the younger daughters of the Murdock family and her boyfriend. The family had moved to the street that I was walking through. We all had a happy reunion, with a bunch of shrieking and laughing. I had not seen them since I moved from Mom's house. I told them I was on my way to a job interview about ten minutes from their home. Ms. Murdock volunteered to keep my children until I came back. What a blessing! I went to the interview, was hired on the spot, and was given a start date for the following week. Things were looking better and better.

I walked back to pick up my babies, and when I arrived, Ms. Murdock was in the middle of teaching a Bible Study with her children and some other young people who had come in. I sat down and listened to "Mother Murdock" talk about the love of God as she explained that God was genuinely concerned about each of us individually and collectively. Oddly enough, as I sat there holding my baby, Doretha in my lap, with my other two children sitting close to me, listening to the lesson – I began to experience a sort of inner peace that reminded me of Sandra Woods' church and family. With this, the "light bulb" came on, and the total realization that it was only God who had kept me through all I had been through in my young life. *With hope and joy, that day opened a new chapter in my life!!* **.... the Son of God discloses.**

..Sharing My Good News...

I left Mother Murdock's home that evening nearly skipping along, with my children in the stroller. I could hardly wait to get home to tell Michael all the exciting things that had happened to me that day, including the reunion with the Murdocks and the new job.

I rushed into the house apologizing for not being there with dinner ready when he came in from work, and started cooking right away. I started talking a mile a minute trying to tell him all my good news, and was half way through my story before I realized that he was just sitting there staring at me with an angry look on his face. Suddenly he yelled at me, "What religion are these people to be having Bible study in their home all day long? Didn't I tell you not to get involved with no 'Holiness' people."

I started crying, trying to tell him that I didn't know what religion they were, because they hadn't talked about that. Then, to my utter amazement, he began to swear and call me 'stupid' and other horrible names, finally storming upstairs and slamming the bedroom door. *Whyyyyy? How can this be?* This is one of the happiest days of my life. How could he not understand and be as happy as I was? I finished dinner, sobbing my heart out; then I fed the babies and put them to bed.

Then I took my bath, while quietly whispering my prayers so Michael wouldn't hear me. I prayed, telling God how happy I was to know that at least *He* really loved me. There in the quietness of my bathroom, I seemed to hear a still small voice speak to my heart, **"You are loved"**. Suddenly I sensed the same peace and joy from earlier that day. Somehow, in my heart of hearts, I knew that "all was going to be well and that I would never really be alone again." How absolutely awesome was that?

….*And He tells me that I am His own.*

BOOK TWO

"And HE Tells Me That I Am HIS Own"

-The Victory Song Continues-

by

September Summer

...Sharing My Good News...

As I sat there in Mother Murdock's living room listening to her teaching about the love of God from the Bible, I began to feel an inner peace which felt familiar to me from an earlier time in my life. It reminded me of when I was a young girl living in Rose Tree, NY. I stayed briefly with my friend Sandra Woods and her family, and attended church with them. It was while there that I experienced an inner sense of true peace and joy that was totally wonderful. It had come at a crucial time in my life when my personal and family life was in total upheaval, and I had lost all sense of hope. *....I come to the garden alone.*

My mind began to drift back to how I felt as I left home earlier that morning, although it now seemed like days ago. Things had become difficult and strained in the relationship between my husband Michael and me. He was spending less and less time at home, as arguments between us increased in number and intensity. I remember having become more and more angry, bitter and depressed as time went by. The year was 1967 and by the time our youngest daughter, Doretha was born, I had begun to look around for a church to attend, hoping that something would make a difference in our lives.

At the tender age of 19, already married with three small children, I had again come to a point in my life where I was beginning to feel overwhelmed and without hope. I had a husband who was only two years older than me, who seemed more interested in hanging out with friends than spending time with his wife and beautiful daughters. He had begun to take more frequent 'over the road' truck driving assignments, leaving me alone with the kids for longer periods of time. I was working full-time as a power sewing machine operator in a factory, and also had the sole responsibility of taking the children to the babysitter in the mornings, and picking them up in the evenings after work.

Whatever happened to the "dream life" that I thought would happen when I married the man whom I loved with all of my heart? My life at home was unhappy, frustrating, exhausting and increasingly tear-filled. .....*while the dew is still on the roses.*

About a week prior to my visit to the Murdocks, I shared with Michael that I would like to start going to church. He agreed that we should start looking for a church to attend as a family with one stipulation which I didn't understand and thought strange. He said we would begin to visit neighborhood churches to find one to our mutual liking, however the denomination should not be "Holiness", "Pentecostal", or "Catholic". He felt that almost anything else would do and it didn't really matter to me, I just wanted to go to church. *...and the voice I hear falling on my ear.*

Neither one of us realized that the very next week was to be a major turning point in our lives. I was laid off my job a few days earlier; and the clothing union arranged for me to go to a job interview at a factory within walking distance from our home. I set out with my three children, Tirzah (3 years old), Lisa (2 years old) and Doretha (3 months old), in a stroller because I had no babysitter for that day. I was walking along praying that I would get the job, and hoping that it was okay for me to have my children with me for the interview. Then I heard someone call my name and to my surprise, I saw one of the younger daughters of the Murdock family and her boyfriend. Unknown to me, the family had moved to the street that I was walking through. We all had a happy reunion, with a bunch of shrieking and laughing. I had not seen them since I moved from Mom's house. I told them I was on my way to a job interview about ten minutes from their home. Mrs. Murdock volunteered to keep my children while I went for the interview. What a blessing! I went to the interview, was hired on the spot, and was given a start date for the following week. Things were looking better and better.

I walked back to pick up my babies, and when I arrived, Mrs. Murdock was in the middle of teaching a Bible Study with her children and some other young people who had come in. I sat down and listened to "Mother Murdock" talk about the love of God as she explained that God was genuinely concerned about each of us individually and collectively. Oddly enough, as I sat there holding my baby, Doretha in my lap, with my other two children sitting close to me, listening to the lesson – I began to exhale, unwind and bask in the inner peace that reminded me of Sandra Woods' church and family. With this, the "light bulb" came on, with an unexpected realization that it was only God who had kept me through all I had been through in my young life. *With hope and joy, that day opened a new chapter in my life!!* **…. the Son of God discloses.**

The sound of people around me laughing and talking brought my drifting mind back to the present, and I was startled to realize it was already dinner time. As everyone began hugging one another and saying their goodbyes, I really liked how they all called one another 'Brother' and 'Sister'. They all called Mrs. Murdock 'Mother Murdock', and it was like one big happy family. Wow! That was soooo cool. I left Mother Murdock's home that evening half walking and half skipping, with my children in the stroller. I could hardly wait to get home to tell Michael all the exciting things that had happened to me that day, including the reunion with the Murdocks and the new job. I rushed into the house apologizing for not being there with dinner ready when he came in from work, and started cooking right away.

I started talking a mile a minute trying to tell him all my good news, and was half-way through my story when I realized that he was just sitting there staring at me with an angry look on his face. Suddenly he yelled at me, "What religion are these people to be having Bible study in their home all day long? They sound like some kind of religious nuts. Didn't I tell you not to get involved with any 'Holiness' people." I started crying, trying to tell him that I didn't know what religion they were, because they hadn't talked about that. Then, to my utter amazement, he began to cuss and call me 'stupid' and other horrible names, finally storming upstairs and slamming the bedroom door.

How can this be? This is one of the happiest days of my life. How could he not understand and be as happy as I was? I finished dinner, sobbing my heart out; then fed the babies and put them to bed. I then took a bath, while whispering my prayers telling God how happy I was to know that at least He really loved me. There in the quietness of my bathroom, I seemed to hear a still small voice speak to my heart, "I do love you". I sensed the same peace and joy from earlier that day and all of a sudden I could hear my Nana's little voice singing her favorite hymn, "Rock of Ages cleft for me; let me hide myself in Thee. Let the water and the blood from Thy wounded side which flowed." For the second time in one day, the 'light bulb' came on, and in my heart of hearts, I knew that "everything was going to be all right." ....***And He walks with me..***

...Surprise!...

When I awakened the next morning, Michael was gone to work already. For the next few days, he hardly spoke to me except for an occasional grunt. I was still saying my prayers in secret, and had even managed a couple short visits to Mother Murdock's home for her to pray with me. I made sure that everything was done at my home, and that dinner was ready as usual. I really wanted for my marriage to be stronger and happy, not miserable because I wanted to go to Bible Study. Then something amazing happened in the middle of the night three nights later. Michael woke me out of my sleep yelling and thrashing about in the bed. I shook him, at which point he woke up profusely sweating. Long story short, he had some type of horrible nightmare, which must have been super-duper scary. The first thing that he said once he was fully awake was, "I need to go with you to see Mrs. Murdock so she can pray for me." *Whaaaaaaaaaat???* I was in such shock that I was afraid to go back to sleep, thinking he was going to change his mind before the morning came.

Well, Michael did not change his mind! He actually took the day off from work the next day - which was a miracle in itself - and we went together to see Mother Murdock for prayer. She prayed with the two of us, telling us about the blessing of having a loving spouse and children. She also talked to him alone for a long time. For the first time in a good while, he had a real smile on his face by the time we left her home. For the next year or so, our marriage blossomed and we had one loving and happy home. We spent all of our non-working hours together, either doing things at home or taking the children out to the park, movies, zoo, or visiting relatives. Although none of the members from either side of our families visited us, we made a decision to reach out to them more often. Michael stopped taking over the road trips for a while with the truck, and made a real effort to spend more time with the children and me.

I have to laugh as I think of the time that Michael gave me some money and sent me out for a few hours with a couple girlfriends, while he watched our three young daughters. First of all, I was totally blown away because two of the children were still in diapers (cloth) at the time; which was a real struggle to get him to change when I was in the house, much less out. *"No, you go ahead. We'll be fine. I know how to change diapers."* Out of the door I went and after a couple hours of shopping and eating out, I came home. I can honestly say that I had a scared feeling in the pit of my stomach to see what my house would look like, but I was certainly in no way prepared for what I found when I opened the front door.

What a sight to behold!!! The house looked like a snow blizzard had hit, with white flour from the front door to the back door, all over carpet and upholstered furniture. My poor babies looked like little snow babies with flour all in their eyes and long thick hair, as they chased each other throwing flour up in the air and at one another. The two with diapers on were walking gap-legged from the weight of the wet diapers hanging down to their knees, and one had a very "unpleasant" smell. When they looked up and saw me coming through the door, before I could un-stick myself from the spot where I was standing, they all three ran and jumped on me laughing and screaming with the glee that only young children could have in this situation.

Finally, I was able to get into the door and after catching my breath, I called for Michael, with no response. I walked through the downstairs and he was nowhere to be found. I finally found him upstairs in the girls' room sleeping on the lower bunk bed with a dry cloth diaper in his hand snoring "to beat the band." After keeping myself from hitting him on the top of his head, I finally shook him awake. Long story short, he laid down earlier with the girls, trying to get them to go to sleep. Their endurance proved to be greater than his.

After he fell asleep, they went downstairs and tried to get into the cookie-jar, knocking the flour canister to the floor instead. Once they saw the flour all over the floor, the rest was history. Who needs cookies when you have five whole pounds of beautiful white flour to play with? Screeeeeeeeeeam!!! Needless to say, our carpet and furniture were never the same, and my children were never left alone with their Dad again until they were out of diapers. ***…And He talks with me…***

...Trying to Find Our Way...

Although we still visited the Murdock family regularly, Michael wanted us to find an actual church that we could attend together as a family; one with activities for our children. We visited a number of churches multiple times, but never found one where he felt totally comfortable. It was also during this time when I realized that another form of contraception had failed me and I was expectant with our fourth child. Amazingly, Michael and I both were very accepting of this turn of events, or at least it appeared that way to me. From the first trimester of this pregnancy, I had complications with severe lower back pain. The doctor finally told me that I had to discontinue the type of work that I was doing. The force of the vibration when I pressed my foot on the pedal of the power sewing machine was more than my body could tolerate, with so many young children. I was placed on 'precautions' with no heavy lifting or activity. Michael resumed 'over-the-road' driving to replace the loss of my income. Our 'togetherness' began to gradually wane again. ***...and He tells me I am His own...***

I asked Michael to teach me how to drive so that I could use the car when he was away in the truck. He complained that after driving for work, the last thing that he wanted to do was deal with a "cry baby" pregnant woman trying to learn how to drive. I promised on the lives of all that was precious to me that I would cooperate. After about 3 weeks of intermittent begging and nagging, he finally set a date to take me out for the first lesson. It was definitely not my fault that within five short minutes of the driving lesson; as he was yelling at me to turn right, I forgot my right from my left and turned left. I tried to tell him (without crying) that this was the kind of thing that could happen to anyone, especially if the person was really nervous like I was.

However, as I opened my mouth to say it, without any control from me, the tears started running down my face. Michael lost it. "Pull over", he screamed, "This is the end of this #$@^ lesson." I started begging and sobbing, "Nooooooooo, it's not fair." That joker took me back home, and he went to bed; with me boo-hooing like the world was coming to an end. I guess he felt badly because a couple days later, he took the kids and me over to his Mom's to visit. He promptly lay on the sofa and went to sleep, and I told Me-Mom about my "driving lesson". She took me out for about two hours in Michael's car, and "patiently" showed me what to do. I've been driving ever since. *...and the joy we share...*

I had a couple brief problems when I snuck the car out in the dark a couple weeks later, while Michael was asleep - the man at the gas station had to tell me how to turn the lights on, where the gas tank was, and that there was more than one kind of gas. Oh, the other "little" thing was when I was parking in front of the house; I "accidentally" knocked one little brick out of the front wall of the house while backing up. I hadn't learned how to feel when the tire was up on the curb, our street was so tiny, and the curb wasn't that far from the house. *As far as I am concerned, this proves that the failed driving lesson was not my fault. You could hardly notice the missing brick anyway.*

...Tell Me It's Not So...

Michael began to work more and more hours away from home, and not long afterwards, he came home and announced that he decided he was too young to go to church right now. He said he wanted to be able to party with his friends again. He and his brother-in-law left the house together, and it was three days later when my husband came home again. Over the next few months, Michael was gone most of the time. I was home alone with the total care of the children. I began to suffer with depression, and cried almost continually. On top of that, I was in the house for days at a time because of the uncomfortable lower back pain.

It became increasingly difficult for me to even get out of the bed in the mornings, so I would take peanut butter and jelly upstairs with me at night so Tirzah, the four year old, could make sandwiches for all the kids until I could get up. One morning, as I lay in the bed in a stupor with pain, I heard a loud knocking on the front door. Even as I crawled out of the bed on my knees to the window, I had a "knee-jerk" feeling in my gut because my little Doretha was not in her crib in my room. The knocking was becoming more insistent, and finally I made it to the window; managing to open it enough to look out while still halfway on my knees.   ...*as we tarry there...*

To my utter surprise, there were my three babies out on the steps, standing in pouring down rain with two police officers. *Whaaaaaaaa???* Simultaneously as it began to register in my mind that I felt a cold breeze coming through my bedroom door, one of the officers told me the front door was open and asked if it was okay for them to come in. *I must still be dreaming.* I dragged myself downstairs. After about 5 minutes of listening to the three munchkins speed talking - well, actually two, with the other talking 'gibberish' – I figured out that Tirzah and Lisa had helped Doretha climb out of her crib. Then, the three of them put their raincoats on (with no shoes) and went out of the house. Now they were all three standing there holding tightly to fountain sodas. *Lawd, help me!!* Where had they gone? *"To see Mr. Tommy."* He had a restaurant around the corner, across a very wide 2 lane street and a busy intersection. *Why??????????* Because *"Mr. Tommy told us to come see him again"* (the day before when we were all there together buying bread).

The three of them had their pajamas on, except for Doretha's bottoms which were missing (later found balled up in the corner of the crib, along with her overnight diaper). She had nothing on her bottom, and of course they had no shoes on because *"we didn't want to get ducky (slippers) wet in the rain."* As I sat there listening incredulously, the enormity of what just happened began to sink in. I began to cry hysterically, just to think that my children could have all been killed at one time. The police officers spotted them trying to get across the street to the restaurant....***none other has ever known.***

Finally, after my loud sobbing subsided, the police officers advised me to get a lock installed higher up on the door. I was informed that normally they would have taken such young kids out in the street alone down to the police station, to be picked up by Child Welfare. However, God had intervened through Mr. Tommy who saw the police officers stop traffic as the kids crossed the street. He told them that I was a good mother and the children were very well taken care of. *Thank God for His mercy and grace.*

...Lord Help...

That event really frightened me and I began to wonder if I really was competent to properly care for so many young children by myself. I felt like I was at the end of my rope, and there wasn't even a "knot" in it to hang on to. Then, a few days later something happened which again was the tender hand of my loving Heavenly Father. A girlfriend of mine came to the house and invited me to attend her church with her for a special program. I agreed, and that was my first introduction to a place that I would come to call my own "home church" ... *I come to the garden alone...*

The Pastor and everyone were very loving and friendly, treating us like we were long time members. The children and I began to attend regularly, and the Pastor and his wife became our surrogate family. My biggest regret was that we did not find this church when Michael was still interested in going, instead of at a time when he was no longer interested. The other ironic thing was the girl who invited me stopped coming shortly after we did. The church also had a Bible School, and I was ecstatic to be able to start doing some type of structured learning again. I dropped out of high school a couple years earlier at the age of sixteen to get married, but my desire to read and learn remained strong. At last, I had something that I could pursue for my own personal satisfaction and growth; and which still allowed me time to take care of my family responsibilities. *...while the dew is still on the roses..*

Speaking of family responsibilities, you know the saying that a mother who really loves her children will "always think of their preservation over her own". Well, for some people, it works just a little differently. My tests came a couple of times during this timeframe. One evening the kids and I were leaving from a program which had been held at the church, and we were all laughing and talking up a storm. We got in the car as usual, and after everyone was settled, I turned the key in the ignition.

Suddenly, there was a loud noise like some kind of explosion or something, and without another thought in my mind about anything (or anybody) else, I jumped out of the car like "Jumping Jack Flash." I broke out in a run down the street like an Olympic champion runner. By the time I remembered that I had left all my babies in the car, I was a good quarter of a city block down the street. Then the "real mother" in me kicked in and I did do the right thing. "Yes" – I took my life in my own hands and went back to get my children. When I finally inched my way back up the street, expecting at any moment to see an army tank or something, I found all of the kids still sitting in their places in the car. They were all laughing hysterically, including Pastor who was telling me that it was just a truck backfiring. Shucks man! That was not funny!! Wow…I didn't even know that I could still run that fast.

As a result of that incident, I began to have safety drills with my kids; and we developed our primary rule for emergencies. My children all lived by this rule until they grew up and moved out – *"If you see Mommy run, don't ask any questions, just follow her. She may not remember to shout or give any warning, and we will not talk about what is going on until we have run far enough away to feel that we have reached safety."* This rule was to be followed at all times, and in every location, even when Mommy is hysterical! **...*and the voice I hear...***

...Night Terrors...

In spite of everything that I tried to do to make Michael interested in myself or the children, he continued to become more distant. He was away from home for days at a time. When he was home, he was so tired that he would go to sleep as soon as he sat still. Being connected to my church family became like a 'lifeline' to the children and me. The women also began to help me with the care of my children. When I was about seven months along in the pregnancy, things began to seem like they were settling down. The children and I were in a comfortable daily pattern of living, but the bottom was about to 'really' fall out. I began having a disturbing dream over and over, night after night. I dreamed that I was being attacked on my back by a huge monkey, which was biting me again and again on my upper back. The dream disturbed me so much that after about a week of having it, I shared it with my Pastor's wife.   *...falling on my ear...*

She asked if I knew what the term "monkey on your back" meant, but I had no idea. She explained to me it was a street slang for someone with a drug addiction. As a nurse, she took the time to explain to me about illicit drug use. *What did I know? The hardest 'drugs' I ever took were prenatal vitamins. (Oh, and a little Vodka from time to time a few years before.)* The whole concept of drug addiction was Greek to me. She told me certain signs to look for to see if my husband was possibly using street drugs. The only thing that I could tell her was that he slept a lot when he was home. Two days later I was gathering dirty clothes to take to the dry cleaners. I picked up Michael's jacket to put it with the rest of the clothes, and I felt something heavy hit my hand.

I looked in the pocket and there was a Sucrets throat lozenge can which was old and partially rusty; it sounded like there was something metal rattling inside. There was a heavy rubber band wrapped around the can which I removed to open it. Inside I found a bent teaspoon, a syringe, a rubber finger cot, and an elastic tourniquet band like nurses use to draw blood. To this day I don't know how, but I knew from the cold chill that went down my spine that this had something to do with what my Pastor's wife was telling me about two days earlier. *...the Son of God discloses...*

I called her on the phone and described what I found. She came to my house and confirmed it was intravenous drug paraphernalia which I.V. drug (i.e. heroin) users would use. I heard her, but didn't believe her, because I absolutely would never believe that about my Michael. She left and I put the can on top of the china closet in the dining room. I put the jacket in the dry cleaners with the rest of the clothes. *Guess who came home straight from work for the first time in weeks*? Michael came rushing into the house, grunting as he ran past me up the stairs to the bedroom. He yelled downstairs asking me if I had seen the jacket in question. I told him I had put it in the dry cleaners, at which point I wouldn't even begin to tell you some of the words he called me. He flew into such a rage that the kids started screaming and crying, so I handed him the can from the china closet. He snatched the can from my hand and ran into the bathroom, slamming the door. *...and He walks with me...*

Over an hour later, after hearing no sounds from him since the door slammed, I called my Pastor's wife and asked her what I should do. Following her instructions, I opened the bathroom door and laying there on the floor with the tourniquet still around his arm…and the syringe on the floor next to him…was my husband. *...and He talks with me...*

I could tell he was alive because of how hard he was breathing. I closed the door and ran back to the phone almost unable to speak. It seemed like I could hear someone outside of myself saying, "Oh my God. Oh my God. Oh my God". At some point, my Pastor's wife hung up because some time afterwards, she and the Pastor rang the doorbell. My little Tirzah let them in because I couldn't move from the couch where I was sitting. I must have cried myself to sleep because it was dark outside. None of the lights in my house had been turned on yet. The kids were all huddled up around me on the sofa crying. Pastor turned the lights on.

Pastor went upstairs to check on Michael and found him still on the floor, snoring loudly. Pastor and his wife fed my children and put them to bed after washing them up in the kitchen. They then sat up all night with me as we waited for Michael to wake up. He finally did around daybreak. ***...and He tells me that I am His own...***

...Sorrow upon Sorrows...

That day was the beginning of many sorrows for my family, the likes of which I had not yet seen. I thought surely I had been through some of the worst things that could happen to any one person in their lifetime. When Michael awakened early in the morning, Pastor talked with him at length. Michael promised that he would never do it again, but of course that promise didn't last more than a couple days. He stayed in the house for the first couple days, but returned to his pattern of staying out again....***and the joy we share...***

One evening shortly afterwards, I was leaving our church with a group of friends, walking to the bus stop to go home. Michael hadn't been home for several days and had taken the car with him. As we stood at the bus stop, "happenstance" had my husband to stop at a red light just in front of me – and there was another woman in the passenger seat of our car. He did not see me, and as I was walking over to the car, he leaned over, pulled her closer to him and kissed her. By that time, I was up close enough to tap on the window, which I did. I looked briefly at my husband's shocked face, and then I just turned and walked back towards the church. I was only able to hold the scream that was coming up from the core of my being like bitter gall, just long enough for me to get inside the building. Then I began to scream hysterically. *I wondered how much one person's mind could take before they would go stark raving mad!!...**as we tarry there...***

Pastor and his wife intervened again, taking me home and staying with me for hours. Thank God the children had been left with a babysitter and were already in the bed. Michael stayed away for 3 days before coming home, crying and apologetic again. At this point, Pastor asked Brother Love from our church to reach out to show support to my husband. The two of them talked over the phone quite a bit and developed a rapport. Michael even invited the brother over to talk a couple times. I thought, "Maybe this is going to help." ...*none other has ever known.*

The following week, Michael left home on his motorcycle supposedly going to meet Brother Love at the church. Instead Michael and a buddy of his went the opposite direction and had a horrible collision with a tractor trailer. The friend had massive head trauma, and Michael's foot was almost amputated at the ankle. Amazingly, Michael's mother was in a supermarket at the end of the block, at the exact time of the accident. She was one of the first people to arrive at the scene, and was with Michael while waiting for the ambulance. A few days later, I overheard a discussion some of his family was having in the hallway of the hospital, that the "accident" was something that these guys had done purposely, attempting to get money from the trucking company. *[I need to say, this was never confirmed]*. However, the plan had gone horribly wrong because the motorcycle and riders were not just "hit" and knocked away, but became entangled under the tractor trailer and was dragged a few hundred feet before the driver even knew they were hit. It was not until this point that I finally begin to get a real glimpse of the depths of the drug addiction with which my husband was struggling. ...*I come to the garden alone...*

...Mommy Again...

This pregnancy with my fourth child, Esther, was difficult from the beginning; and at the end of the pregnancy, I was a whole week past due with no signs of true labor. The doctors thought I had miscalculated, but I knew for sure that something was wrong because of the extreme low pelvic pain I was experiencing. I kept going back and forth to the hospital, and they kept sending me back home. Finally, true labor began but Michael was nowhere to be found. Once again, my Pastor and his wife sat up with me as I paced the floor at home for almost two whole days with back labor pain. ...*while the dew is still on the roses*...

Unexpectedly, Michael came home and insisted that I go back to the hospital. After an examination, I was told that I was not actually ready, and that I should return home again. At this point Michael went ballistic. By the time he finished cussing and raging, refusing to take me back home, my water broke while I was still in the exam room. A couple hours later, Esther made her entrance. Sure enough, during the delivery, the doctors found her to be partially dehydrated, with the skin on her little arms and legs having a greenish hue. The report was that she was truly past due, and would surely have died had she not been delivered within those few hours. Thank God that by grace Michael came home at the crucial time. The next day he was gone again until the day I was to come home from the hospital. ...*And the voice I hear*...

Over the following year, Michael was again away for increasing lengths of time; so much so that when I became pregnant with our fifth daughter, Rose, he insisted that he could not be the father. Never mind that I could only use an ineffective barrier type birth control because my blood pressure had not stabilized following the birth of Esther. Michael adamantly refused to do his share by using additional protection; but of course, it was all my fault. His attitude of blaming me was also the same attitude that I received from my family, his family and some people at the church. I never thought that I could be "ashamed" to be having a child for my husband, but it was so. ...*falling on my ear...*

I thought that no pregnancy could be more challenging for me than with Esther, but "Boy, was I wrong?" The fifth pregnancy seemed like it drained me to the "core of my soul", physically and emotionally. I had no self esteem. I hated myself for being pregnant again and hated Michael more, for leaving me to handle it alone. I was exhausted and depressed, and as mean as a snake. If anyone looked at me for more than a few seconds, I would scream at them, "What are you looking at?" I felt like an amped hotwire ready to explode with minimal provocation. ...*The Son of God discloses...*

How could my life have come to this? I was only twenty years old, with four (4) children and another on the way. My husband was a drug addict and MIA most of the time. I couldn't work outside of the home because it would not be worth it to pay a babysitter; not that we didn't need the money.

...Where is the real Michael?...

Michael was still somehow managing to hold on to his job driving a tractor trailer over the road, in spite of his increasing heroin abuse. Then when I was about halfway through the pregnancy, the "other shoe" dropped and Michael was fired from his job for stealing from the company....***and He walks with me...***

That's when things unraveled even more quickly. First of all, he began to steal things out of our home to sell. My sewing machine that I used to make our dress clothes disappeared out of the dining room. Other items like fans and our stereo system walked during the night. I received a phone call on more than one occasion from the police to see if some appliance they found him trying to peddle was ours or not. I found myself and Me-Mom several times down at the central police department in the middle of the night, trying to convince some judge to have mercy on Michael and let him come home to me and my four kids. I guess the judge felt sorry for us because they continued to release him over and over on his own recognizance, with nothing more than a warning....***and He talks with me...***

My Pastor and the people from our church became a source of food and other necessities for my kids and me more often. Michael forbade me to apply for financial assistance from the welfare department of our state, claiming he would work it out. Things were spiraling more and more into what felt to me to be like an endless black hole. My only connection to any sense of sanity was my involvement with and support from our church. I continued taking courses in the ministry training program taught by the Pastor and his wife. I was totally amazed to be able to graduate and be licensed at the first level of ministry, even while all of the craziness was still going on at home. ***...and He tells me I am His own...***

It was so comical the day that we had the licensing ceremony from our Bible School, because there were about six women in our class who were pregnant. We all looked like full "fat ticks" lined up sitting next to each other on the front row. The keynote speaker was a guest minister who made the point to mention about 20 times that we certainly were a "prolific" congregation, (Tee Hee). I wanted to ask him how many of our kids did he want to take home with him. My Pastor just kept a huge smile on his face, and had his chest stuck out like he was the father of the universe or something. *....and the joy we share...*

Michael remained absent from home most of the time. One day in my late pregnancy, he came home and announced that he was moving back to Me-Mom's house without me or the children. I lay almost catatonic with depression, in a fetal position for a couple days. I vaguely remember Tirzah, who was five years old by then, bringing bread, peanut butter and jelly into my bedroom. Every once in a while I would kind of wake up, and all the children were laying in bed with me with the television on. I refused to even answer the phone. I finally woke up enough to decide that "enough was enough." I waited until I put the kids down for a nap, turned the gas stove on, blew all the pilots out, prayed that God would forgive me, and climbed into the bed with the kids. Sure, I had more than enough, but certainly was not willing to leave my little ones here to suffer at the hands of other people. *As we tarry there...*

We all slept from mid-afternoon until it was dark outside. When I woke up in the dark, my first thought was "Uh Oh, I don't think this is heaven." Then by the time we all became fully awake, and I realized that we were still alive, I felt disgusted that I couldn't even do "this" right. *Disgusting weakling!!* However, when I came downstairs, I realized it wasn't my failure at all - all of the gas in the house had shut off for an "unknown" reason. Imagine that! I had to call the gas company to come out to turn the service back on, and they had no idea of why it was off in the first place.

It was bitter cold outside, and if we were going to stick around, we definitely needed some heat. As I lay in my bed that night thinking about it, I knew that the merciful hand of God had intervened for me one more time. That would have been a horrible thing for my family to bear, for my children and me to all be found dead....***none other has ever known...***

...Rather Die With You...

A few days later I went to Me-Mom's house to ask Michael to come back home. He and a couple friends were in the dining room busily involved with inhaling something that kind of looked like little pieces of black tar, along with smoking marijuana. He didn't realize immediately that I had come in and was standing in the doorway watching them. When he looked up to see me standing there, he told me that I should not be there, that I should be home with the kids. I told him that I wanted to be with him, and was even willing to do what he and his friends were doing if that was would it would take. I had never taken any drugs in my life, other than over-the-counter medications; but felt like I would rather do drugs with Michael, than to have to live without him. ***...I come to the garden alone...***

I told him so, while crying hysterically. He told me that I didn't really want to do drugs because that stuff would take me straight to hell. I pleaded with him, "I would rather go to hell with you than live without you." I will never forget the look that came over his face. Then Michael did something for which I have been eternally grateful, even though on that day I was too distraught to appreciate it. He picked me up with my big pregnant belly, carried me to the front door, and set me outside on the front steps. Then, without another word from him, he turned around and went back in the house, locking me outside. I pounded on the door, crying and pleading with him to let me in; and was totally heartbroken when he walked away from the door and said, "Go home." After carrying on like a madwoman for about 15 minutes or so on the steps, I got in my car and cried and snotted all the way home. I felt like my life just wasn't worth living. When I did reach home, I called my Pastor's wife, and as usual, they came and sat with my children and me for hours. ***...while the dew is still on the roses...***

Soon after that, my fifth daughter, Michelle, was born. It was Pastor and his wife who took me to the hospital. When I called Me-Mom's house to let them know I had the baby, she said that Michael hadn't been around for a couple weeks, but she would let him know. Life can be ever so strange, because of all my children, Michelle came here looking exactly like Me-Mom. When Michael and his Mom came to see us at the hospital a couple days after the delivery, they both took one look at the baby and became very apologetic about accusing me of having been unfaithful. I tell you; only God knows just how to take care of those who trust in Him. Here's the ironic part, by the time Michelle was two weeks old, she no longer looked like Me-Mom. She looked like my Mom, and still favors her more. *Go figure!* *... and the voice I hear...*

I thank God for the ability to laugh because I believe humor is a real gift that God has always given me as the way to stay sane. I needed to get something from the pharmacy around the corner from our home a few days after coming home from the hospital with Michelle. I was rushing before the babies woke up. I got dressed in a maternity dress and slip – after all, I was only going around the corner! I took the big stretched out elastic panel in the front of the slip and straight pinned it together. I walked quickly to the store, bought what I needed and was leaving. As I stepped out of the door, I heard a little "pip" sound. The next thing I knew, my slip was on the ground around my ankles, just as some guys from the block were coming near!!

I didn't have enough time to bend over to pick up my slip without them noticing it. So, I just stepped over the slip, took one of the guys by the arm and started talking to him so that he would look at my face, and kept stepping. I never looked back, and by the time I reached home, I was nauseous from trying not to laugh hysterically out in the street. *What a putz*!! The very next day, I packed the balance of those maternity clothes to take to the Goodwill center.

...Got to Get Myself Together...

Finances were tight for us, but we managed to squeeze through financially with help from the church and a little help from family members. After two months, I was on my feet and ready to go back to work at the garment factory. ***...falling on my ear...***

How was I going to afford to pay a babysitter for taking care of an infant, two small children home all day, and my older 2 when they came in from school – all of this on a factory worker's salary? The mercy of God again intervened. One day as I was standing in the front door of our home pondering on this, I saw a young woman walking across the street pushing two small children in a stroller. I called to her and asked if she knew of anyone in the area who kept small children in their home. She came over and told me that she had been watching me for some time now, and that her heart went out to my children and me. She was a single divorced Mom, and she had enough income coming in that she was able to stay at home to take care of her children, Wonder of wonders! She offered to take care of all my children for only $50 (yes, fifty dollars) per week....***the Son of God discloses...***

Long story short, she and I became the best of friends and my children absolutely loved her. Her name 'Yasmine' was a little hard for them to remember, so they nicknamed her, "Miss Playground". She became their second Mom and my lifesaver again and again, after I returned to work. There were many days when I would come home hardly able to put one foot in front of the other, to find that my children had already been fed and bathed, with homework already done. As the saying goes, "God is good all the time, all the time God is good." ***...And He walks with me...***

In addition to Yasmine being my friend and babysitter, others of her family also began to look out for us. Her Dad fixed my car at little to no cost on more than one occasion; and her sisters and brothers adopted my children and I right into their family for holidays and outings. I began to feel more at peace, and even began to sleep at night without having every light on in the house…with candles and matches all over the place in case the lights ever went out. ***…and He talks with me…***

Our family began to settle into a comfortable pattern, still attending church regularly and even getting to go out for recreation once in a while. We usually went to a "drive-in movie" because that was inexpensive and convenient with little ones. Things were quiet for a change, although the kids and I all missed Michael terribly. We never heard from him in those days, but we all prayed together for him before I put the kids to bed. One evening while Pastor was away on vacation, a guest minister spoke at our church. At the end of the sermon, when it was time for the altar call, he called me to the front of the church to say a special prayer for my children and me. If you are more than 10 years old by now, I'm sure you have come to realize that some things in life are just not explainable in normal terms. ***And He tells me that I am His own…***

That minister told me that he felt like I had survived many challenges in my life, and by the grace of God had always managed to land on my feet. "However", he said "when I look at you, I see a huge fist winding up like a Joe Palooka punch. There is a major crisis coming to your family, and you had better get as close as you can to the altar in prayer and stay there." ***…and the joy we share, as we tarry there…***

As he was talking to me, all of a sudden, I had an overwhelming sense of dread, and began to cry. I drove the kids home that evening after service was over. After bathing them and putting them to bed, I took a drive out by myself. I drove to an area not far from home, got out of the car and stood there looking up at the big bright moon and what looked like thousands of stars. As I stood there looking up at the sky, I began to wonder what could possibly happen to me that could be worse than any of the things that I had already come through in my life. The two "worse" things I could think of would be losing one of my children, or losing my own mind.

At that point, I begin to pray and all I could say from the depths of my heart was, "God, even if I go crazy and don't remember to hold on to You, I ask You to hold on to me, and never let me go." I had no way of knowing what was coming my way within a few days. However, in hindsight, as I look back years later, I can honestly say that God heard and has answered my simple prayer over and over….***none other has ever known…***

...On the News...

During that time, my sister Felicia had started coming to visit, and she would stay over with us from time to time to help me with the kids and house. She had a little daughter of her own by then, Delores whose age was between Esther and Michelle. One night while Felicia was staying over, all of us were soundly sleeping when I was startled out of my sleep by the sound of someone banging loudly on the front door. I looked at the clock and it was about 2:00 a.m. I staggered over and lifted the window to see who could be banging like a madman at this time of night. As I looked out the window, it suddenly seemed like I must be still asleep. Outside in our small street, there appeared to be a sea of uniformed policemen with helmets on, bullet proof vests, and rifles or handguns pointing upwards towards the window that I had just pulled up. ...*I come to the garden alone...*

Whaaaaaaaaaaa?? After almost falling out of the window, and hearing Felicia behind me asking what was going on, I realized that I was not asleep. Then I realized that one of the officers was still banging on the door yelling out Michael's name. I finally was able to breathe in enough air to be able to say, "Michael doesn't live here anymore." He asked who I was, and I told him that I was Michael's wife. Then he demanded that I open the door immediately or he would have it kicked in. I whispered to Felicia to go back into the room with the children, to make sure they were covered, and to close the door. *"Father, this is it, please keep me in my right mind".* Then I went down and opened the door. A swarm of police officers rushed past me, before I could step aside. The one who had been knocking seemed to be in charge and demanded of me where Michael was. I reiterated that he didn't live there anymore, and that he had moved back to his mother's house several months earlier....*while the dew is still on the roses...*

Just then I saw several men start up the steps towards the bedrooms. I quietly called out to them, asking them not to wake my children. They continued up the steps, so I asked that I at least be able to have my girl children and sister put covers over themselves. In spite of my tearful pleas, the "boss" stormed up the steps past the rest of us, while the other officers blocked my way. The officer opened the kids' bedroom door with a loud bang, and a search was made of their closet and under the beds. Astoundingly, the only one of my children who woke up was my little Tirzah. The "boss" asked her where her Daddy was, and she said in all the innocence of childhood, with a little smile on her face, "Oh, Daddy lives with his own Mommy now." I believe it was her half-sleep childlike response that made them leave the room...**and the voice I hear...**

However, they continued to search every nook and cranny of our home, from the roof to the basement. After they were satisfied that Michael really was not there, the officer in charge informed me of the following details concerning why they were looking for him: *Michael and two other guys had committed armed robbery of a grocery store not far from our home!! The owners were both in their seventies, and someone whom the guys probably expected would be easy victims. What the guys had no way of knowing was that both the husband and wife were long time members of a hunting club, were expert shooters, and had a gun in the store. Michael and his best friend, Mark went into the store while another friend stayed in the car, to be the look out.*

In spite of Michael's foot being in a cast from the motorcycle accident, and him walking with one crutch, he carried a shotgun into the store and held the couple at gunpoint. Mark asked the couple for their money. Instead of waiting for the woman to give him the money from the register, Mark began physically jerking the husband around. The woman pleaded with Mark to leave the man alone, explaining that her husband had recently survived a heart attack and was not well. Mark became more aggressive with the husband, while Michael looked on holding the shotgun. Suddenly, the woman reached under the counter and pulled out a pistol and shot Mark, killing him immediately. *[She later testified that she hadn't planned to shoot, but feared for her husband's life if she didn't]*. She then turned and shot Michael in the chest, not knowing the shotgun was broken. Somehow he managed to drop to the floor and crawl out while she was still shooting at him. The driver drove off, leaving Michael; who still managed to get away as the woman turned back to attend to her husband....***falling on my ear…***

The officer said they knew for certain the Michael was badly wounded because of the trail of blood he had left behind. They believed he couldn't have gotten far, and were not even sure that he wasn't already somewhere dead. If he were still alive, the officers believed he would have to try to come home sooner or later. Regardless, an "All Points Arrest Warrant" had been sent out for him, and he was considered "Armed and extremely dangerous."

As I stood there looking at the officer's mouth and hearing the words coming out of his mouth, my mind began to withdraw from what was being said. I thought of Michael somewhere bleeding to death and of Mark's wife and five young children roughly the same ages as mine. I said out loud, *"Okay God, I really would like to wake up from this nightmare now."* ***…the Son of God discloses…***

The policeman's attitude softened a little, as he said to me, *"We will be surrounding your house and the adjacent streets until your husband is caught. He will not get away. If he calls you, it is crucial that you tell him to turn himself in because right now, we consider him an armed and dangerous fugitive. If we find him and he resists arrest, we will not hesitate to shoot to kill. For your sake and the children, tell him to turn himself in."* He went outside, and after I locked the front door, I immediately called my Pastor and his wife. His wife informed me that she had been trying to call me for over two hours, but the line was busy (we were not on the phone during the time). She had seen the late night news and the story about Michael and the robbery were on the news. Oh My God!! This is actually happening!! *...and He walks with me...*

I turned on the news and sure enough, it was on the radio and on the television, alerting people in our neighborhood to be on the lookout for Michael who was armed and dangerous. There for the whole world to see was my husband's picture, holding the shotgun. I guess it must have come from the security camera at the store. I tried to call Me-Mom but didn't get an answer. *"Father, I stretch my hand to Thee...no other help I know."*

My Pastor and his wife offered to come, but I felt ashamed to have them come to my home with the "police army" outside. There were men on the roof across the street, men hiding in alleys, men in the back yard, and men every place else that I could see out of the bedroom window.

...What Do I Do Now?...

Somehow I fell asleep for a few hours in the bed with Felicia and all of our kids together. Following were the long days and nights of waiting to hear something about the condition of my husband. I phoned his mother, Me-Mom's house hundreds of times, with no answer. This went on for about two weeks, with policemen following me to work, and following my children to school. ***...and talks with me...***

After the first couple weeks, the crew outside began to be smaller gradually until only a few men were left in parked cars. Finally, about three weeks later, Michael's brother-in-law, Butch, came to see me. He told me to come with him to Me-Mom's house without the children. I was so afraid that I was going to be told that Michael was dead, I could hardly breathe. When I got there, Me-Mom was not home. Butch told me that he was going to make a call and let me talk on the phone to Michael. I was so terrified, not knowing what to expect, I just started bawling when he told me that Michael was still alive. When I asked where Michael was, I was informed that since I was such a "church girl" that I couldn't be trusted to not 'tell the truth' if the police came back and asked me if I knew where he was. ***...and tells me I am His own...***

Ironically, as Butch dialed the phone, for some reason the call did not go through, so he had to get the operator's assistance. This caused him to say the number out loud and I made a point of memorizing it. Finally, I heard Michael's voice, and it's amazing that either of us knew what the other one said, because we were both blubbering like infants. He shared with me the part of the story which the police officer did not know. Michael had called a friend the night of the incident from a phone booth a couple blocks from where the incident had taken place. This friend picked him up, and drove him in the trunk of their car out of town before the police had time to send out the alarm. He had been driven to a relative's home. The relative had been taking care of him for the last few weeks. The bullets were still in his body, and plans had been made to take him further away to another relative's home in another state up north. He asked that I pack the kids up and come to go with him. I was numb and could still hardly believe all of this craziness was real. *"God, are you still holding on to me?"* Why does it seem like I am a total magnet for the most bizarre things that can happen to someone? **...*and the joy we share, as we tarry there...***

    I asked him how would the kids go to school, and how would we get money to take care of them? He didn't know, but asked me to trust him that he could work it all out. I told him to let me think about it for a couple days, and I would let him know. Butch drove me back home. As soon as I was in the house, I called the phone number I had memorized. I couldn't believe it when Michael answered the phone. He was angry about me calling him back. I told him that I just wanted to talk to him alone, without Butch standing there glaring at me. He told me to call him the next day, and then he hung up. The next day when I called back, the relative he had been staying with told me that Michael had been driven to the place further away the night before. I was informed that I was not to be trusted and that I had to wait to hear back from my husband when he was in a safer place. What kind of craziness is that!!!!!!!!!!!!!!!!!...***none other has ever known...***

...I Have To Keep Moving...

I cried hysterically for almost two days. Then, I decided to pull myself together and do what I needed to do to take care of my five daughters and me. I returned to work in the factory, and eventually all of the police officers left from the vicinity of my home. The kids and I prayed for Michael every night, but I tried to make things as normal as possible for them. To help them kind of enjoy life again, I would take them on long drives on the weekends, or to whatever free activities that I could find. I also kept them involved with our church family. This went on for well over a year, until something totally unbelievable happened to me again *[that seemed to be the story of my life!]*

I was moved by the clothing union which I belonged to, to another factory for work. I was pleasantly surprised to find that two of Michael's sisters were also working at the new place. One of the sisters told me she lived within walking distance to the job, and so she began to bring lunch for the three of us often. We would all sit together for lunch and laugh and talk, or go to the nearby shopping district. This went on for about six months, with neither of them ever mentioning anything to me about Michael. I just assumed that they didn't want to make me feel bad, so I never asked them about him.

Hah! One day about six months later, I received a phone call at work from the police asking if I was Michael's wife. When I confirmed that I was, they informed me that Michael had been arrested at a loud party the night before, because the neighbors had called the police complaining of the noise and the "drug smell". The police had gone to the house and arrested the whole group. While processing Michael, an officer in the station recognized his face from the "Wanted" files.

I was absolutely floored that the police from another state would have my phone number at work! I asked the police officer how they found me where I lived, when Michael was living in another whole state. Well - hold on to your pantyhose! As it turned out, Michael had actually been back in the city for about nine months!! He had been living with the sister who lived in walking distance to the job. *Whaaaaaaaa!!* That was not possible!! How could this be!! I went home that day in utter amazement. By day's end, I had received several messages from Michael, which I thought was quite ironic. All of a sudden he remembered us, when we had not heard from him for over a year. This, although he was not far from where I worked. Long story short, he asked me to plead to the judge on his behalf, asking for mercy because he had a wife and five kids. *"God, I'm really starting to hate this guy."*

At the trial, the D.A. asked that Michael be sentenced to 15 years for the crime, saying he was a true menace to society. In spite of my feelings of anger towards Michael, I couldn't imagine him in prison for 15 years. So, I did what he asked. The judge again extended mercy to him, telling him it was for the sake of his family. He was sentenced to only 3½ to 15 years, with time credited to him for the one year that he had actually been in hiding. *Michael should get on his face in thankful prayer day and night.*

In fact, Michael actually only spent about 2 years in prison. I determined to never take my children inside the prison walls even to visit their father. However, after receiving several requests from him via Me-Mom, I yielded and took the younger kids while the older ones were in school. At our second visit there, I learned from the guards they thought I was Michael's girlfriend since his "wife" had already been there several times. I even heard them snickering and talking about who should actually have rights for "conjugal visits." That was my last visit to the prison with my children. Several weeks later, I hesitantly made another visit to the prison, and decided that it was not something that I would do again. It was more than I could handle, and I had no desire to be a part of it.
...*I come to the garden alone...*

...In Need Of A Miracle...

Shortly afterwards, I was laid off from my job. I had no income since the last factory I worked in had failed to pay into unemployment for me. While I was waiting for an appeal with the State Unemployment office, I didn't want to ask the church for any more financial help. My children and I had already received from them so much generous assistance. The mother of a friend of mine, recommended me to the nursing home where she worked. I was hired part-time as a Nurse's Aide on the overnight shift. Even so, my salary was not adequate to take care of five children, so Yasmine suggested that I apply for financial assistance from the State Welfare department. I applied for help one week before Christmas. The caseworker who took the application cried with me as I shared my situation with her. She promised that she would make sure that we would receive help in time for Christmas.

The next few days came and went with no check coming. Finally, Christmas Eve was here and still no check had arrived. As I drove to work that night on gas fumes I prayed for enough gas to get there and back. I worked that night with a heavy heart, thinking that for the first time in their young lives, I did not even have decent food to give my kids for Christmas, much less toys or a tree. When I reached home Christmas morning around 7:30 a.m., I couldn't believe that Felicia and the kids were still asleep. My kids were normally up at the break of dawn. As I sat down in the living room with tears running down my face, I heard what sounded like a truck pull up outside and stop in front of my house. I went to the window in time to see a UPS delivery truck, with the driver coming up my front steps. I opened the door before he had time to knock, and he handed me an envelope which I had to sign for. *What can this be?* I had never received anything by special delivery in my entire life!!...*while the dew is still on the roses...*

When I opened the large brown envelope, inside I found a business envelope, with a check in it for more than $900 from the State Welfare department!!!!!!!!!!!! Oh my God!!! The caseworker had somehow kept her word. I wanted to scream and cry, but didn't want to wake the kids up. I was shocked that they were still asleep. Then my mind kicked into high gear – where could I cash a check for that amount of money at 8 o' clock on Christmas morning? *"God help me."* The thought about the small pharmacy one block from our home came to my mind, and I practically ran to get there. On the door was a big "Closed for the holiday" sign. As I stood there with my mind skipping to and fro, all of a sudden I thought I saw a flash of light inside the store. As I stepped up to the window and pressed my face to the glass, I saw the owner behind the counter getting something off a shelf!!! I tapped on the window, and since he knew me he smiled and waved, pointing to the sign on the door. I frantically signaled to him to come to the door, which he did, telling me the store was closed. He had only come there to pick up a package he had inadvertently left there the night before. (*Thank you, God*)

I showed him the check and told him that I had no money for food that day, and no toys for my children for Christmas. He opened the door and let me in, explaining that he had no real money in the store with him that day; but wished that he could help me. Then I had the idea to buy a few of the dolls and toys in his store, and just let him hold the check until two days later when he would be open for business. He then said he would give me the couple hundred dollars of his own money which he had in his pockets to buy food, and that we would settle everything later. I gathered a couple toys for each of my kids, and even something for my sister Felicia and her daughter, crying so hard, I could hardly see. He gave me a box of gift wrap, at no charge, and I ran all the way home, hoping the kids were still asleep – and they were!! I knew this was definitely God at work; it was now almost 9:00 a.m.!!

I quietly woke Felicia and asked her to wrap the things while I went around to the market, which I was hoping was open.

Surprise! The market was open for just the morning that day. I bought everything we wanted for dinner, and some other things that we needed. As I was going home, I realized that there was no Christmas tree, but I was so happy about everything else, that I tossed the thought out of my mind. I reached home and the kids were stiiiiiill asleep – this was really freaky by now.

About two minutes after I got back in the house, and as Felicia and I were putting the toys under the living room window, there was a knock at the door. When I opened the door, I almost fell out of it. There was my younger brother, Dallas standing there with a Christmas tree!! *Oh my God* –this was all totally surreal. He had been out with friends all night, and on his way home, he walked past a street lot where Christmas trees had been sold. The sellers had abandoned the unsold trees. My brother said he wondered if I had a tree. Since I had no phone at that time for him to call to ask, he had walked over an hour and a half carrying a tree bringing it to my kids, along with a tree stand. I was beyond words by this time, and crying like a river. Dallas didn't even stay for breakfast. Somehow, Felicia and I put the tree up and as we were banging the nails into the stand, the kids began to get up one by one! It was almost 10:00 a.m.!! Needless to say, that was one of the very best Christmases that I had ever experienced. (*Talk about a modern day miracle*) ***...and the voice I hear, falling on my ear...***

... Moving...

A couple weeks later I received a letter in the mail informing me of a job training program sponsored by the Welfare department. I signed up for the program, and through them earned my GED (High School Equivalency Degree). This was a real motivator to me to pursue a profession that would give me enough money to take care of my children on my own. Meanwhile, I was still working part-time at the nursing home. I enrolled into a two year course to become a Legal Secretary. After only 3 months, I realized that I preferred working with the patients at night over taking shorthand and typing. I asked to change my career choice to become a Certified Nurse's Assistant. My late decision caused me to have to wait until the following school year to get into a program.

It was during this time that I started asking people to keep an eye out for a bigger house for me, since we were still living in a two bedroom house which was totally too small. We didn't even have enough room (or money) to have dressers for clothes. Yasmine gave me the idea to collect hard blue plastic milk crates from grocery store trash bins. We stacked the crates to build a "wall" of storage units in the kids' room for clothes, toys, etc. Imagine my total shock, a few years later, when I saw the same size plastic "cubes" being sold in stores in all different colors. (Ha-Ha) *Wow! We had designer crates before they even came on the market!!*

Pastor suggested that I begin to "visualize" the size house I wanted, including the number of bedrooms, yard, basement, etc. I began to do just that, and less than two months later Honey Gramm's friend, Pop-Pop, called to tell me he had a fully furnished four bedroom house which he was looking to rent!! I went to see the house which was beautiful; including a huge wrap-around open porch, a side yard with a large weeping willow tree, and a finished basement with a washer and dryer. Two of the bedrooms had 2 complete sets of bunk beds each, and the master bedroom was also fully furnished. *Can you imagine that?* There were actually enough dressers for everyone to have several drawers of their own. I definitely wanted this house, but was more than sure I couldn't afford it. I was just managing with the $250 per month that I was paying for the miniature house, much less however much more this huge house would cost. *Are you sitting down?* Pop-Pop told me that I could pay him the same amount of money that I was paying for the small house, and there was no deposit required. (*God at work again!*)

Needless to say, we moved shortly afterwards, and Pop-Pop even paid for the moving van. It was totally wonderful to have enough room for my children. Things were really starting to look up. In the midst of all this, my car died, and my Dad came to my rescue again. He gave me his old car because he had just bought a new one. He even paid to have the paperwork transferred, since I didn't even have money to do that. I told you before – *my Dad, my hero.* I was still working part-time at the nursing home at night, so my sister and another young lady moved in with us to be with the kids, and to help with their care. I began to exhale slowly, and things were stable again for a while.

...Adrift...

Then, totally unexpected by the church, our Pastor returned from a ministry trip to Florida with a major announcement. He announced that he decided to sell the church building, and relocate. He told us he had investigated and learned that with the money we were spending each month for just a building; that we could move the church to Florida and buy a larger building, with plenty of land attached. The invitation to go with Pastor and his family was offered to anyone from the church who would like to take the opportunity. Wow! After the initial shock to my brain, I began to think that maybe this was just what we needed for a brand new start in life. At first I agreed that my children and I would go. Then I thought about my parents and even Michael. Although he had certainly not considered me or the kids in the choices he made, my past experience of being taken from a parent gave me an uneasy feeling. I couldn't bring myself to do that to my children. With many tears and sad goodbyes, several families left, but the rest of us were left to fend for ourselves….***the Son of God discloses…***

What would my children and I do now? Pastor, his wife and the church had been like our immediate "family" and support in so many ways for the last few years. *What now?* Who would pray with me now in the middle of the night, and who would I call when I was feeling overwhelmed? I had no answers for any of these questions, and this threw me into a depression for a while, but I continued to work and busy myself with my children. I prayed, but it didn't feel the same. Reading the bible didn't have the interest for me that it had when I could talk about it with Pastor and my close friends. I tried visiting a few churches for a bit, but felt that we would go in as strangers and would come back home still strangers. After a while, I would send the kids to a neighborhood church on their own for Sunday School; and I would just listen to church music and ministers on the radio on Sunday mornings.

I began to sink deeper into the depression. Finally, I came home one day after a really difficult time at work, and made a decision again that I was tired of living. I was just a little more than a teenager myself, but had five children to care for; and a husband who was in jail not even thinking about us. That evening, after putting the kids to bed, I thought maybe I would feel better if I could find a church to go to. I drove back over to where our old church building was, and there was another congregation there having service. I went in, but for some reason, being there just made me feel more sad and hopeless. I left there, and as I drove home through the park, I decided to end it all by driving my car off the bridge into the water. I figured that if I did that, I couldn't back out because I couldn't swim. *But, hold it*! I couldn't possibly do that without seeing my kids and sister at least one last time to say "Goodbye". I went home, took a bath (couldn't do this without being clean and having on fresh underwear like Honey Gramms had taught me); kissed everybody good night and went out to get in the car. What do you think happened?? **The stupid car would not start.**

Now what? I was all cleaned up and ready to do this, and had already said my "goodbyes". I was such a failure, that I couldn't even bump myself off right. After considering a couple other options and deciding that nothing else was feasible for right now, I decided to take a long walk to clear my head. About four blocks from home, I saw a corner bar; and had the really bright idea that I would get intoxicated. Maybe then I could figure something out. Mind you, it had been years since I had any alcohol to drink; and had never been a "real" drinker in the first place.

I went inside and strolled up to the counter, realizing I didn't know what to ask for. Then I remembered many moons before when I tried a little "Vodka and orange juice." I also remembered that in the movies when someone was upset, they always asked for a "double". I ordered a "double Vodka and orange juice". After standing there just looking at me for about three minutes, the bartender poured the drink and sat it in front of me. I paid him and tried to smile like a "worldly wise woman".

At this point, some crazy looking guy decided to come over and wink at me, asking if he could sit next to me. I got indignant, *"You can if you want to take your life in your hands. My husband will be here in a few minutes, and he's really jealous."* He opted to keep moving, but I felt like he was still watching me. Back to the movies, I remembered that the person always threw their head way back and drank the whole thing. Well, if they could do it, so could I. I took a deep breath, threw my head back and took as much as I could get in my mouth, with the intention of drinking it all straight down. But something strange happened – as that liquor hit my throat and travelled downward, it turned to liquid fire. To make matters worse, some of the "flame" that was still in the back of my throat decided to come back up through my nose. *Ugh!*

I did not have the time (or clear vision) to find a flame thrower. Then I realized that my hands and feet were going numb, and I was slowly sliding off of the stool. If you have ever seen that old Amos & Andy movie, you will understand my instant prayer – *"God, please don't let my feet fail me now."* I pasted what I hoped was a nice smile on my face, in between trying to discretely gasp for air. All while mentally trying not to go "number one" on myself, I forced myself to stand up to what I believed to be a straight position. I did a little wave, with the fire still running up and down from the back of my nose all the way down to my belly. I then turned as elegantly as I could towards the door.*"…and He walks with me, and He talks with me…*

Wait! Who moved the door all the way over there? I reached for my purse, and tried to remember the times Honey Gramms made me stand up straight and walk with those books on my head. I walked out the door and held it together long enough to get out the door and ten feet or so to get around the corner. I was afraid someone would follow me out. By now, I realized that I had, for once in my life, reached my goal one hundred percent. I was intoxicated all right, totally plastered! *Now what!* I don't have my car, and am about four loooong blocks from home. Anyway, I can't go in the house like this because I can hear Honey Gramms' dire warning playing in my head – "If a man gets drunk and passes out in the gutter; after getting up and bathing in the morning, he will still be Mr. ... But if a woman gets drunk and is even still able to walk, she will always be 'that drunken floozy'."

By now, it is about midnight and freezing cold so there is no one out on the street. Suddenly, it dawns on me that I am still "technically" afraid of the dark, and now I am afraid to even try to walk the blocks to get home. After sobbing my heart out, with frozen tears on my face, and standing on a dark corner, I remembered my friend's mother who helped me get the job. She was one of the older ladies from the church who used to pray with me, and help me with my children from time to time. I decided to take a bus to her house. By the grace of God, I made it safely there without passing out completely, although I kept dozing in and out.

Her son opened the door to let me in and I just fell to my knees and crawled over to the couch. "Mother" came down the steps. She sat down and held my hand until I cried myself to sleep, incoherently trying to tell her what happened. The next morning, I was absolutely floored when "Mother" told me that my sister had called her the night before as I was leaving the house. Felicia told Mother that she felt afraid for me when I left the house, because I had a strange look on my face; and that I said, "Goodbye" instead of "Good Night" to everyone. Mother said she had been praying for me from the time I left home, until I arrived safely at her home. *Once again, God's grace and mercy had kept me.* I decided that would be the last time that I would try to take my own life. If God loved me enough to look out for me like that – I must at least have some little value....***and He tells me I am His own...***

...Time To Get A Life...

After the fiasco with the girlfriend the last time I visited with Michael, I decided not to subject myself or my kids to the trauma of going behind those prison walls again. Michael and I had no communication for months. I wrote to him, but he did not write back, or even try to call us. After a while, he wrote me a scathing letter about me not wearing my wedding rings when I had last come to see him. He had a lot of nerve! I lied and told him that I just forgot to put them on – I didn't want to tell him that I had to pawn them to help pay the rent; and then had no money to redeem them.

I was spending all of my time either working or with my kids. When Michelle was almost two years old, some of my friends decided that I needed to "get a life." Although I wasn't really interested at first, I finally agreed to let my babysitter's boyfriend set me up for a blind date. That was how I met "Ricardo". My initial impression was that he was "totally weird". He was the first West Indian I ever met in person, and he had the most beautiful lilting accent. But he wore the strangest clothes I had ever seen on a man. In all of my life, I had never seen a man wear a pink shirt with pink ruffles on the front, not to mention his tendency to mix plaids and stripes. All of the kids fell instantly in love with him, probably because he brought them gifts and money from day one. He spent hours laughing and playing games with them. Then, to top it off, he loved taking them out on Saturdays to the wrestling matches or Roller Derby (competition skating) events at an arena near where we lived.

As for me, there was something endearing about him, in spite of the strangeness. For one thing, from the very start, he showed the protectiveness towards my children and me that I had wanted from Michael for a very long time. The first time that I invited him to dinner, he gave me a piece of advice that really touched my heart. He came to dinner carrying a bag of groceries, and instructed me to, "never let a man put his feet under your table to eat from you and your children, unless he has brought some food for the house with him." I have repeated that recommendation down through the years to many young women, especially single mothers.

Initially, in spite of the estranged relationship between my husband and myself, I still didn't feel free to get really involved with Ricardo. Sure enough, within a couple months of meeting Ricardo, something happened that confused my emotions even more. One day as I was in the kitchen cooking, I suddenly heard a bunch of loud noise and squeals from the living room. Then, I thought I heard the kids saying, "Daddy's on the television!" *Whaaaaat!* I ran into the living room in time to see Michael being interviewed by a reporter. There was a special news program on with a few prisoners at the facility where Michael was incarcerated. The topic was a new "early prison release program", being offered to men with families. Of course, there was my husband on the screen as big as day crying and talking about how much he loved his wife and children (*Did he mean the same ones that he hasn't even called or written to in months?*) I stood there in complete disbelief, thinking '*Here we go with another fairy tale drama again.*' Out of the hundreds of men in the huge prison where Michael was incarcerated, how is it possible for him to be one of the first men they would interview on national television?

Does everyone's life seem like something out of a horror book, over and over? Can anything about my life ever be normal? How could *one* person have a history of a childhood kidnapping, a bank robbing young brother, an armed burglarizing husband, etc., etc. , all in less than 25 years? As I sat down in the middle of the floor staring into space, I had a horrible feeling in my gut that somehow, my world was getting ready to be turned upside down again.

...*Reconciliation?*...

Even Ray Charles could see what would happen next – but not me!! I began to get a myriad of calls from reporters, and even from Michael himself. The reporters wanted to know how much difference it would make in my life and the lives of my kids for their "loving" father to come home to help take care of us, and to help raise our children. Then Michael suddenly remembered our phone number and called daily. The promises began, "*If you apply for me to get out to come home and help you and the kids, I promise I will be the husband and father that you all deserve.*" After my initial skepticism, I began to think that possibly this could work. After all, we had a nice big house now, in a pretty nice family oriented neighborhood; and maybe – just maybe – Michael did really still love me. After just a few days of thinking about it, I agreed to petition the courts to release my husband to come home early. I also helped the older kids to write a note of petition, in their own handwriting. Who could resist the handwriting of such obviously young children? Within less than 30 days, the request was granted....*and the joy we share as we tarry there...*

We were all ecstatic. Felicia and I planned a little party with the kids to celebrate. I told Ricardo that my husband was coming home, and the kids started crying as he left. They wanted to know why Ricardo couldn't still come to see us and Daddy. (*Oh, the bliss of innocence*).Once the release was confirmed, I knew that I had a much bigger hurdle to climb concerning Michael coming home. I had to tell Dad and Honey Gramms. I felt so apprehensive that I waited until just two days before Michael's release date to invite them to dinner and to share what I hoped would be good news. Dad expressed concern that I might be setting myself up for a disappointment, but Honey Gramms' response was shocking, even for her. "*You have 30 days from the day that he comes through this door, to pack your things and move out of this house.*" I stood plastered to the same spot for about ten good minutes after they left, still thinking that I could not possibly have heard her right. Why would she want to move my children and me out of the best home we had lived in to now?...*none other has ever known*...

I thought to myself that she would surely calm down after a couple days, and understand that I was trying to reunite my family. Two days later, Me-Mom rode with me up to the prison to pick Michael up. I signed about twenty-five papers, stating that as his wife, I assumed accountability; and that I was to report any misbehavior on Michael's part to his parole officer. We all came back home and had a wonderful dinner after the kids came in from school, and Felicia came in from work. After dinner, as I prepared to drive Me-Mom home, Michael suggested that he could take her home while I got the kids into bed. This would also give him the chance to get some of his clothes to bring home. When he left out of the door that night, *I had absolutely no inkling that was the last time that Michael would ever set foot back in that house again.* When he didn't come back that night by midnight, I called Me-Mom's house to see what happened. She told me that he was exhausted, and would be home the next morning.

Three whole days later, I received a phone call from Michael telling me that he was sorry; but that he still was not ready to settle down to be a husband or father. Me-Mom drove her car and followed him as he brought my car back. That same day, I received a letter in the mail from Honey Gramms, stating that we were to vacate the house within 30 days; or she would have Pop-Pop go to court to have us evicted. Now, I understood what that horrible sinking feeling had been in my belly just a few short weeks before, when I saw Michael on television. Not only was I now husband-less, but we were about to also lose this beautiful home that we had prayed for. I thought about calling Honey Gramms to tell her that Michael would not be coming back, but I made a decision then and there; to never subject myself to her control again. I wanted to call Dad, but didn't want him to inadvertently tell Honey Gramms what Michael had done.

...We Will Make It...

The next day, I called City Hall, and asked what I could do. They referred me to the Public Housing authority in our city. I explained the situation, and was told to complete an application. I was told there was a waiting list for the better neighborhoods, so that the only unit that I could get in time with the number of bedrooms needed for my family, would probably be in a high-rise project building. I cried and pleaded for a place that would be "female" safe, since I had five young daughters. The intake worker cried with me and said she would see what could be done. I thanked them for whatever help I would be given.

I went home and began to pack, praying that God would somehow intervene with a miracle, as He had done over and over again. I humbled my heart and called Ricardo, and explained the situation. He took a cab (probably paying half a week's salary) to get to our house, on the other side of town from where he lived. He came in and worked his usual charm on my kids. By bedtime, they were full of snacks and smiles again. As the next couple of weeks rolled by, I was feeling more apprehensive by the day, but continued to pray for a miracle as I packed. About three weeks through the thirty day period, I received a phone call from the intake worker at the Housing Authority. Here was the answer to our prayers – although the entire waiting list had hundreds of people, there had only been one other family as large as mine on the list in front of me. That family had decided to move out of town, which brought us up to number one on the list for a four bedroom unit. Wow*!!...I come to the garden alone...*

How ironic that the size of my family which had initially appeared to be a "stumbling block", had turned out to be a "stepping stone". *Who knew!* Within 3 days of that call, and with a lot of help from friends and Ricardo, we moved into a newly refurbished duplex apartment with 2 floors of our own, and not in a high rise building! It was not the beautiful porch front house we had to move from, but it was definitely better than where we had been in the little two bedroom house. Pop-Pop privately told me that we could take all of the furniture with us. *What a wonderful thing, not to go back to the milk crates for dressers.* (Tee Hee)

The children all adjusted quickly into new schools, and I continued working part-time at night. It was during this time that Ricardo and I became almost inseparable. Michael remained out of touch again for months. Shortly thereafter, I received my letter of acceptance into the state financed vocational training program to become certified as a Nursing Assistant. In the same envelope, I was offered the option to upgrade to the course for Licensed Graduate Practical Nursing at the same school. That was a "no brainer", so I enrolled into the one year LGPN (Licensed Graduate Practical Nurse) program to begin in the fall.

...Down South...

While waiting for my school program to begin, Michael's Aunt Sue invited the kids and me to travel with her and a few of her family members to North Carolina. This was Michael's grandparents' home. I had never been further South than the state of Delaware, and was totally ready to see "down South". Felicia and I packed up our kids and joined the caravan of five cars heading to N.C. We adults were just as excited as the kids were. I don't know who "oooh'd" and "ahhh'd" more – the kids or us, at things that we drove past on the highway. Everything was totally new to us, being the city-bred children that we all were.

We made it to N.C., with just one little "lost" episode in Washington, D.C. Just as I stepped out of the car in N.C., all of a sudden I heard a loud buzzing sound near me. I looked up in the sky just in time to see a group of flying insects zooming towards me. As they got close enough for me to see what they were – I broke out in a hysterical run, screaming "Dr. Needles - ruuuun ." About 10 seconds later I realized no one else was running but me; and all the adults were bent over laughing at me running from "Skeeter Hawks" (dragonflies). Since none of the creatures had attacked me with their "deadly" pointers, I came back feeling rather stupid. I explained that as children we were told that those things were poisonous. I was promptly informed that the "Dr. Needles" were actually good to have around because they ate mosquitoes. First lesson for the city "klutz".

After meeting the "in town" family, my crew and I were led to "over the creek", where G-Mom and G-Pop lived, with Michael's Aunt. Although it was a little distance out of town, thank God it was a nice modern brick house with an indoor bathroom; not like many of the wooden shacks we had passed, with outhouses. When we arrived it was evening, but still hot as blazes. We were all beat, so we showered and turned in early. The next morning, the kids were up bright and early, out in the yard playing with 2 chickens which they named "Ducky" and "Lucky". Things went pretty smoothly the first day, aside from the killer heat. The kids loved being out in the open; and I loved the freezing cold water that came up from the water pump in the yard with a little effort. ***…while the dew is still on the roses…***

Around 10 a.m., Felicia and the kids and I rode into town to the supermarket to pick up a few things like peanut butter, jelly, hot dogs, and other snacks. After riding around a little, we went back in time for supper, which we had been told would be at 12:00. We all washed up and went to the table to sit down to eat. The food looked totally delectable – golden fried chicken, plenty of vegetables and huge biscuits. I could also smell fried fish.

Just as we said "grace" and I started to fix one plate – Felicia's daughter came in and said "Where is Ducky and Lucky?" We thought she was in the bathroom but it seems she was outside being a little 3 year old detective. G-Mom said, "Who?"- while at the same time pulling the cover off of the fried fish. Esther said, "Ducky and Lucky, the friends we were playing with outside." G-Pop said, "Gal, is you talking about them chickens in that bowl on the table?" My hand stopped mid-air with that big beautiful golden fried chicken leg. We all turned and looked at the table at the same time.

Even as I began to feel a twist in my stomach, all of a sudden Doretha started screaming, "Mommy, the fish-eees' eyes is looking at me." By then, all of us began to understand what G-Pop had said about the "…chicken on the table…" I was saying, "*Oh my God*", just before total pandemonium broke out. All I could hear were kids screaming and crying, "Murderer, you killed Ducky and Lucky"; "I want to go home"; "Turn your head, don't throw up on the table", and "Ugh, the eyes is looking at me". Then, all the kids broke out in a run outside to the yard. I was kind of feeling like barfing on the table my own self by then. G-Pop is standing up and yelling at the top of his lungs, "What the $#%@ is wrong with you young-un's?" "I been up 'fo day this morning catching them fish."

G-Mom was sitting there staring at me with her mouth hanging open like she couldn't believe her eyes or ears. I gathered my thoughts enough to start apologizing for everybody, when I suddenly realized that Felicia had not moved for the entire outburst. I had to look closely just to see if she was still breathing. Finally, after G-Mom had cleared the table, we got everybody back into the kitchen, and very apologetically made peanut butter and jelly sandwiches (for me too). All of the kids ate in between sniffling and tears, with their eyes stretched wide and looking like they were about to take off running at any moment. That night was a real challenge getting them settled down, bathed and in bed. I was so totally upset for my kids, that if I thought we could find our way back north by ourselves, we might have left that night.

The next day started out kind of gloomy with the kids moping around, but thank God for the resiliency of children. By lunchtime, they were back to running and playing, but definitely no longer interested in the few chickens still roaming freely around the place. I felt badly, but all of us "northerners" were in total agreement; our cuisine for the rest of the week consisted primarily of cereal, and peanut butter and jelly sandwiches. I never ate so much peanut butter in one week in my life. I think I was back at home before the roof of my mouth was fully unstuck. All in all, everyone agreed it was a wonderful trip while we were away, and even more wonderful to get back home. ***...and the voice I hear, falling on my ear...***

...Something New...

One thing I did learn from that adventure was how relatively easy it was to pack the family up and get out of the city to see other places. Throughout my children's young years after that, we spent many, many hours at the large park in the city we lived in, or at the zoo, or taking a long ride in one direction or the other just to sightsee. Money was limited, so we would pack lunch, which was usually the good old faithful "p b & j", some fruit and a big thermos of Kool-Aid. Then, at least twice per summer, I managed to take us to some place really special like Dutch Country, Blue Mountain Campground, Crystal Cave, or to the shore where we would stay at least 2-3 days. Our menu was still pretty much the same, but at least we would see there was more to life than the corner where we lived.

Finally, the summer was over and it was time for school for the kids and for me. Ricardo and I talked about it, and he initially was supportive. He had his own place, but since he worked the graveyard shift; he agreed to sleep over at my apartment during the day to have someone in the house while I was in school. It sounded like a good plan, but after about a month, Ricardo complained about not getting enough rest. I decided to ask my Mom's mother, Mom-Mom, to stay with the kids and me during the week, and go home on the weekend. Again, it sounded like a good plan, but something began to happen with my relationship with Ricardo. I was going to school full-time all day, working part-time overnight, studying as much as possible and getting only 2-3 hours of sleep most days. I had no real time for a relationship, and even though I would get a babysitter and squeeze in a "date" once in a while, Ricardo became increasingly distrustful of me. He began to accuse me of seeing someone else when I was supposed to be in school.

The situation came to a head one evening, after I was three months into the class; in spite of me trying to reassure him. I walked to a small store near home after all of the kids were in bed. Mom-Mom had gone home for the weekend. Ricardo had been in the house when I left out; but when I came out of the store, he was standing behind a nearby telephone pole trying to keep me from seeing him. I chose to act like I didn't see him. After I returned home, he came back into the apartment, went into his overnight bag and pulled out a handgun. I looked at him without saying anything, as he took the bullets out, and started cleaning the gun. He said something to the effect that he wanted to make sure his gun was clean in case he had to use it. At this point, I began to feel a real rage rising on the inside of me, which was more than the fear which I was also feeling.

I asked him what was he thinking of to bring a gun into my home, when I had small children. I began to talk to him as calmly as I could, although I wanted to jump on him and scratch his eyes out. He sat quietly while still cleaning his gun. Finally he reloaded it and put it back into his bag. At that point, I sat aside what little "religion" I was feeling, since I hadn't been to church in a good while by then. I brought up some cuss words out of my belly that I long since thought I had forgotten. As I stood up to open the door for him to leave, God intervened on my behalf again, because he put my key on the table and left without even saying another word.

Before he was out of the front door good, I went into the bathroom, looked into the mirror and said to myself, *"Girl, you must be crazy, sniffing glue, eating dog food or truly psychotic. I can't believe you got in that crazy behind man's face like that."* For the first time in many months, I got on my knees that night and thanked God for keeping my children and me safe, again. Ricardo tried to phone me several times, but I refused his calls, and after a few days, he stopped calling. The kids and I continued on with life as usual, with Mom-Mom still helping out. I was ecstatic to be back in school, and loved the program, and then…***the Son of God discloses…***

...*Uh Oh!*...

About three weeks after the incident with Ricardo, I woke up with a fresh chest cold, which I couldn't seem to shake even after trying all kinds of things for about two weeks. It was time for midterm exams for the trimester; so I went on to school, intending to come home after the tests. As I sat in class, my chest began to feel tighter and tighter, until suddenly it felt like a vice compressed my lungs and I could not catch my breath. I don't know how I had the strength, but I just got up and walked out of the classroom, got into my car and drove myself over to the hospital emergency room. As many older people say, "God takes care of babies and crazy people". For surely, He took care of me and everyone I drove past that day.

I was purple by the time I reached the hospital, and was rushed immediately inside. I was placed for hours on oxygen and given several bottles of intravenous fluids. Finally, I began to feel like the elephant had lifted up off my chest. It was only at that point that my thinking was clear enough to remember that none of my family knew where I was; and that my kids and Mom-Mom were waiting for me to come home. I didn't want to startle Mom-Mom or the kids. The only person that I could think of to call quickly was "that" Ricardo. I called him, and after being assured that he would take care of things, I drifted off to sleep. When I awoke several hours later, the doctor told me I had suffered a severe asthma attack. He wanted to know how long I had asthma. *What!!*

I told him that he was mistaken because I never had asthma. He assured me I had an asthma attack, in addition to being dehydrated and exhausted. I was sent home to be on bed rest with a referral to see my own physician for follow-up; along with some medication to help me breathe. *This is unreal*!! I went to see my own doctor the next day. Some further blood and urine tests were done, and I was given an appointment to come back in a couple days. Thank God, it was mid-trimester break time. I went home and slept for the next three days. When I went back for my follow-up visit, that man told me something that made me feel like "someone had just walked on my grave", as Mom-Mom was fond of saying.

"CONGRATULATIONS, YOU ARE ABOUT THREE MONTHS PREGNANT", was what I thought came out of his mouth. But, inside I knew that couldn't be possible because I could only have children for my husband. *"I know you're good Doc, but you messed up this time. You need another rabbit."* He sat and let me rant and rave like a hysterical maniac for about five good minutes, before finally offering me his condolences and best wishes. He then had the nurse escort me outside with one referral slip for Ob-Gyn clinic, and a separate one for "Family Planning Clinic" for possible abortion services. The choice would be up to me as to which referral I would use. I sat in my car in hushed silence for a couple hours, trying to figure out if Doc would take back what he said, if I called him on the phone. After all, I had been faithfully using birth control and I had not slept with Michael. Somehow, my mind could not comprehend that I could actually get pregnant for someone other than my husband, even though he wasn't around.

I don't remember much about that afternoon, other than staying out in the street as long as I could. Ricardo stayed with the kids that day for me since Mom-Mom went home for a few days. Finally, after I felt faint from hunger and thirst, I went home. Call it "intuition" or whatever you want to, but when I opened the door and Ricardo took one look at me, he started laughing. I walked past him and into my room, sat on the bed and cried until I had dry heaves. I thanked Ricardo for watching the kids, and asked him to go home. He walked past me without a word, wrote something on the wall near where I sat, turned around and walked out the door saying, "Call me when you need me." I looked to see what he wrote on the wall, and was floored to see *"Boy, August 15"*. If I tell you that I wished I had the pistol he had been cleaning previously, you had better believe it.

"Anyway," I said to myself, "it doesn't matter, because I am not having no more babies." I knew that I didn't believe in abortion, *but that was before I found out I was pregnant for the 6th time.* Now, this was war!! I made a call to the Family Planning Clinic the first thing the next morning, and was scheduled for just two days later. I made arrangements for a babysitter other than Mom-Mom or Ricardo, and set everything in order.

Early on the morning of my appointment to take care of my "situation", I had another major asthma attack. By the time I dropped to my knees trying to catch my breath, I had promised God, Adam, Eve and every other living creature that if I could just get some air; I would not do what I had contemplated doing. My second daughter, Lisa, woke up early and came down to get a glass of water. She found me in the floor gasping for air, and called my neighbor, who called Ricardo. That was the second of many asthma attacks that almost took me out; throughout the entire pregnancy. I was rushed to the hospital multiple times, unable to breathe and delirious from lack of oxygen. I wondered if this was a punishment from God for being pregnant outside of marriage. **…and He walks with, and He talks with me…**

...Only One Option...

Ironically, when I called Michael and told him that I needed to talk to him, he came without his usual complaining. That was again one of the hardest things I ever had to do in life; to tell my husband that I was pregnant with another man's child. I felt lower than a worm; and he had the nerve to be indignant. He started pleading with me to have an abortion. He tried to negotiate with me saying that he would come home and do what was right, if I really loved him enough to do what he asked. I pleaded with him to forgive me, and to love me enough to accept me along with my baby.

He refused, while holding his ground. I told him that I had already made the decision to have the baby, which was a part of me, no matter who the father was. He left, saying he would call me later; but as usual, he didn't. This time, something changed in my heart towards Michael, and I began to feel even a more intense bitterness towards him. After all, it was never my choice or desire to be with someone other than him in the first place. It certainly was not my choice to be pregnant again. It had all stemmed from his choice to not come home to his wife and kids. I had been left with making the choice to have someone else help me with my children. After all, I was still a very young woman in my mid-twenties. In spite of my resolve concerning having the baby, I went into another real depression. I couldn't return to school because half of the time, I could hardly lift my head from the bed. To Ricardo's credit (and despite his dangerous jealousy), while I was so ill for most of the pregnancy; he took excellent care of my children, our home, and me (including bathing me when I was too weak to lift my head from the bed).

He cooked, cleaned, did homework and even "braided" the girls' hair – well, let me just say that they loved him enough to forgive him for what he did to their hair. They had the nerve to go to school wearing their hair proudly like it was a badge of honor or something. *Screeeeeeeeam!*

One day, a long time girlfriend of mine called. After we talked for a while, she told me to get dressed because she was going to take me out of the house for a while. She took me over to an area shopping mall to buy some things for the baby. While we are the mall, I passed an exhibition table from our local community college. Because I was bored out of my mind, I picked up one of each of the brochures, and a few days later filled them all out and had Tirzah to mail them for me. I really did not expect a response, but was just fooling around.

To my complete amazement, within a week I received a letter of acceptance into the Registered Nursing Program at the area community college, along with a committal letter from the federal student loan agency to cover the complete cost of the tuition. *Whaaaaaa? Is this really, really real*? Yes! Not only was it for real, but I would have just enough time to have the baby and recuperate for 6 weeks before classes would start. O-H M-Y G-O-D!!! I am really going to go to college for Registered Nursing, instead of going back into the LGPN program. At that time, because I was not able to work, I was receiving financial assistance from the State Welfare Program again. To add to the wonderment of it all, when I called my caseworker and told him about the approved application and student loans, he informed me that I still had some available time and funds from the job training grant I used at the previous school. This money could be used to help cover the costs of my books, baby-sitter, uniforms and transportation. O-H M-Y G-O-D!!!...***and He tells me I am His own...***

...A Son??...

Finally, after what seemed like an eternity, I had the baby. Wonder of wonder...miracle of miracles...ninth wonder of the world...amazingly...everybody hold your breath...in between the anesthesia, I thought I heard the doctor say, *"Mother, you have a strong healthy baby boy."* Oh my goodness! Is that really what he said? I could hear myself saying, "I'm sorry Doc, there must be some mistake, I can't have boys." Then I heard someone in the room laughing and saying, "That's no mistake, that's a real boy". I looked up just in time to see Ricardo, Jr. (R.J.) giving someone a "yellow" shower. *Wow! I have a son – who could imagine?* By the way, remember the "handwriting on the wall" by Ricardo early on in my pregnancy? My son was born only 1 day later than his Dad predicted. *"Go figure!!"*

It was quite an adventure learning how to take care of a male child, after having 5 daughters. Not only were his physical characteristics different from the girls (muscle strength, etc.), but his personality was different (much more independent at a younger age). One other thing that was totally bizarre was that after the baby was born, my asthma attacks began to gradually wane. The obstetrician later told me that I must have been one of the women whose body has problems with carrying a male child because of the testosterone, especially after having several girls. *Boys are such show-offs!*! The testosterone can act like a severe allergen in these cases where the mother's body has only experienced high levels of female hormones. The last attack I had was about four months after delivery, and it was only a minor one. *Thank God*! Unfortunately, Ricardo, Jr. didn't get off that easily. He had his first full blown asthma attack at seven days old and was troubled with it throughout his early childhood. Thankfully, he never had to spend a single night in a hospital for it – the attacks always responded to emergency room care quickly. (Later, per the doctor's predictions, R.J. pretty much outgrew the asthma attacks when his body went through the changes of puberty.)

Just as R.J. reached his first 6 weeks, my classes were set to begin. Although Ricardo was still staying with us at the time, he was still working at night, and couldn't be trusted to awaken during the day to a soft new baby's cry. Therefore, I made arrangements for his care with the same girlfriend who had taken me to the mall when I picked up the college applications. She had a home-based daycare. After crying all the way to school the first day that I dropped R.J. off, I entered my little "corner of heaven on earth" – well, until the real work started any way. I have no words to describe how fully blown away my heart and mind was the first day that I sat in the classroom as a college nursing program student.

I listened to the welcome speech, along with the dire warning that for the next two years, our lives would not be our own. I knew that I didn't care what it would take to complete it. I needed this to be able to take care of my children and to be able to provide them with a decent life. I would rather hurt someone than have anything stop me from making this good paying career mine. I was totally appalled when I saw three people get up and walk out when the professor said that no one could successfully work a full-time job and complete this nursing program. I remember thinking to myself, *"Does that include the job of full-time Mommy to five young children, and a new baby?"* As I sat there thinking about what responsibilities I had at home – I began to be fearful of whether I could do this or not.

Then, I remembered what my whole purpose was at this point in my life for *needing* to get a better education. It wasn't just for a good report card anymore. It was to be able to buy food and clothes for my children and not have to "sell" my soul to an abusive man to do that. I HAD TO MAKE IT!! This was affirmed in my heart even more resolutely after talking to two other young female students. They each shared with me how totally unlikely it was for me to come off the street directly into the Nursing Program, because of the huge waiting list. They both had been taking "General Studies" courses for two years, waiting to be transferred into the nursing curriculum!! They wanted to know how did I get in immediately, and who did I know? I just smiled and said, "I know people in high places"....*and the joy we share, falling on my ear...*

...Right Place, Right Time...

There is a common saying, "God may not come when you want Him, but He is always on time." Just a couple weeks after I started attending the nursing program, I was out one day with Ricardo taking care of some business to apply for a new thing the government was giving out called "Food Stamps". While at the office, I ran into some friends from my old church, Thomas, and his wife. He had previously been the lead musician before the church moved out of town. I was instantly embarrassed when they saw me with my baby, because I had to introduce Ricardo as his Dad. The brother and his wife both had met Michael on several occasions, and knew he was my husband. They were so gracious as to not ask me about Michael, but extended an invitation to Ricardo and me to come with the children, to fellowship with them at their current church. They told me that their Pastor was similar in many ways to our previous Pastor, especially in how loving and caring he was about people.

Ricardo and I were back to arguing a lot again and things were not going well. I had come to realize quite some time before, that Ricardo had what I felt was an unhealthy obsession with me, and a "dangerously" crazy jealousy. I had observed him following me at times when I left the house. He would often falsely accuse me of being with other men, even though all I did was go to work and school. It seemed that no amount of reassurance on my part satisfied him; and it was becoming more unbearable for me each day. In addition to his false accusations towards me, I began to hear bits and pieces about him being quite the "ladies' man" in the neighborhood.

By the time we ran into Thomas and his wife at the Public Assistance office, I was ready for some serious changes in my life. Ricardo and I talked and agreed to visit the church the following week, along with the children. The rest is history. I was immediately comfortable with the people, and knew that we had found another "church family". Many were young people like me, with young children close to my kids' ages. I felt "at home" quickly, and there were also a couple older ladies there who were like mother hens to all of us. I think I joined the second week, and the children and I became involved in Sunday School and other activities.

The people there filled the huge vacuum which was left because of the disconnect within my biological family's relationships. The women helped to take care of one another's children, and the men looked out for everyone, including the single women with children. Wow! I had some "real" brothers and sisters now. When they learned that I was in school full-time, the women did everything in their power to help lighten my load, including making casseroles for us, and many other labors of love.

The craziest thing is that just as happy and comfortable as my children and I were, that's how miserable Ricardo became. He would put on one face in the public with smiles and happiness; but then get home and accuse me of everybody from the Pastor to the janitor. He also resented the fact that the children had other places to go and friends to visit. Eventually, I decided that Ricardo and I should just be good friends, and "joint" parents to R.J., and leave it at that….***none other has ever known…***

...Busy, Busy, Busy...

Meanwhile, back at the college, I was dealing with total culture shock, while trying to reawaken my intelligence neurons. They had gone to sleep somewhere between baby 3 and baby 4 – and by baby 5, those little suckers didn't want to fire at all. I kept reassuring myself that the twenties was definitely too young to be going senile. I had to get used to being back in school full-time with a 16 credit load, while still working part-time at night at the nursing home.

Eventually, the Pastor offered me a part-time job as church secretary during the day around my school hours. At least, this would help with finance by allowing me to get 3 hours of sleep at night instead of sleepwalking through the dark halls of the nursing home, and still trying to function during the day in class. In the crevices of time in between, I had to still do what was needed for my children and then find 3-4 hours to study most days. I did so much reading that in the first semester I had to be treated at an area Eye Hospital for "sprained optical muscles" behind each eye. I eventually overcame this, not with less reading, but with eye "push-ups" - little exercises to strengthen the muscles. Imagine that – me, the one who absolutely hated exercise, having to "exercise" my eyeballs. *What kind of stuff is that???*

Then, at one point I went completely insane and succumbed to my 4th daughter's tearful requests to become a teacher's assistant in her kindergarten class. It was on a volunteer basis 2 days per week for 4 hours. *Girl, whaaaaaaaaaaaaat ails you*?? It's amazing how the "psychosis" of youthfulness gives us a sense of immortality in the teens and twenties. By the mercy of God on behalf of the children, the kindergarten "thing" resolved itself for me the day I almost had to tie my hands to my belt to keep from "spanking" (murderizing) a totally out of control child. That was the first year that the school system decided to use "Behavior Modification" for the children – to completely ignore all negative behavior, and only praise all positive behavior. "Don't see Johnny punching, kicking and scratching other children like a maniac – but praise Sue for sitting quietly, "I like the way Sue is sitting nicely in her chair". *Did you notice that half of Sue's dress is on the floor because Johnny ripped it off as he ran by her?"*

The "end" came for me on the day when I realized that it was not a good idea for me to work with young children who lived by a different set of rules than in my home. My kids knew to only test me to a certain limit. They knew that if I started looking at them with that "mad cow" look in my eyes, then it was time to cool out. These other children didn't know that, and it wouldn't be fair to them to have to learn it while I held my breath. So, I quit one particularly challenging day, and walked out in the middle of the class time. I felt like looking back and saying to the teacher, *"I like the way I didn't kill somebody's child."*

To make matters worse on the same day, I got home and had a call to come back to the school immediately. My second child, Lisa, saw fit to use the karate techniques which Ricardo had taught her recently, to drop kick a boy in her class. He had been trying to bully her. The problem was that Lisa did so well, she broke the boy's arm. Okay - her behavior definitely did not fit into the Behavior Mod program for that day. But, what happened next really wasn't fair either. Guess who was suspended from school for the rest of the day – no, not the bully; but the little lady whose mother sent her to school every day in such pretty little dresses.

I had to take her back to school the next day with her strutting like a peacock; as the other kids cheered her on for taking care of the bully. Meanwhile, I felt so embarrassed for having this miniature female "Bruce Lee" turned loose on the world by Ricardo. As I neared the principal's office, I could hear a man's voice talking loudly and insistent. As we got closer, I could hear the man demanding to see the "big boy" who dropkicked his son, breaking his arm. Just then the boy looked up and cringed as he saw Lisa. By now, I began to realize what was going on and began to turn back, but the principal saw us. Long story short – the boy told his Dad a "bigger boy" broke his arm, rather than tell him it was a girl. Dad, who was no small man himself, came to "deal with" the culprit. Then here I show up with a girl in a cute little dress, and smaller than his son. *Oh Boy!!*

As the principal corrected the mis-information, the Dad looked at Lisa as if he wanted to drop kick her himself. Just as my foot was shifting into position to execute the same deadly dropkick which I had also learned from Ricardo, the Dad laughed and walked away. Thank God! I would have hated to have to show my daughter that her mother was as unladylike as she. That's it! No more Bruce Lee movies or karate lessons for the girls. *Save it for the boy child!* ...***I come to the garden alone...***

...Meanwhile, in College...

Concerning Nursing School, my degree belonged almost as much to Mom-Mom and Ricardo as it did to me. Without them and the people from the church, I would never have made it. Those three years were some of the most grueling of my young life. It also didn't help that I have always been one of the most squeamish people in the history of the world. I definitely went completely against my natural disposition, all because Nursing was considered to be among one of the highest paid, and most secure jobs on the market. With six children, and no "real" husband, I needed a "real" job. However, there were definitely a few times when I almost gave up the "ghost."

The first incident took place during an Anatomy and Physiology class. We were supposed to dissect a fetal pig. Excuuuuse me!! I don't even really eat pig; so why would I want to "cut" one up – and a baby one at that. Ugh!! Well, I called everyone I knew who could pray and asked them to pray that I not actually have to "touch" that thing. I went out and bought the dissecting kit and equipment because it was mandatory. Then, I went on a 3 day fast, praying for a miracle. The class was instructed to bring an apron, a face mask and a pair of rubber gloves with us to class. On the morning of the project, I showed up for class in full operating room garb – covered from my head to my feet, including a bonnet and booties. I had on a face mask and goggles so that very little of my face was uncovered. I had on surgical uniform pants over my pants and a full floor length paper gown, plus elbow high heavy rubber gloves. After I got "garbed" in the bathroom, I knew how David felt when he tried to walk in Saul's armor. However, I was not giving up even an inch of my protective "armor".

By the time I shuffled down the hall to the lab, I was bawling like a baby and sweating so hard that my goggles were steaming up. I cried so badly that I wet up the whole top of my "armor". By the time my classmates figured out who was behind the get-up, they got together and petitioned the professor to "puh-leeze" excuse me from actually dissecting the pig. They asked that I be permitted to just identify and label the various types of cells from the body tissue samples under the microscope, while they did the actual dissecting. The professor laughed so hard that she cried, and then she agreed to their requests. If I could have, I might have bent over to salute her, but I couldn't – so I just said "Thank You" a thousand times. *Don't tell me there is no God!!*

The second incident which almost killed my nursing career at the outset occurred during the maternity/Ob-Gyn rotation. The people who did the assignment must not have known who they were messing with when they assigned me to observe a Caesarean section. *What??*- Isn't that where they cut through the woman's belly? Won't there be blood and stuff? *Excuuuuse me*!! I let my finger do the walking and made the "famous-by-now" prayer call to all my prayer warriors. I also did another 3 day fast…my assignment was changed the night before to the regular delivery room!! Shucks! I figured I could do that with my "eyes closed" – I'd personally delivered a child there myself 6 times and survived.

Duh!! The problem was that is exactly the position I was in when I had my own children, with "my eyes closed" from anesthesia. I didn't fully think about the reality of the situation until I was already standing in the delivery room. I was looking all cute in my pretty white uniform, and patting the woman's husband's hand, telling him to be brave. Were my eyes closed when the doctor said "Look, the head is crowning?" Ooooh no, I was wide awake! All of a sudden, the baby's head popped out with a little b-l-o-o-d on it, and then things started moving in slow motion around me. Way off in the distance, I could hear somebody saying "breathe, breathe". I thought they were talking to the Mommy, when I realized they were talking to me as I was on my way gliding down to the floor. *What happened*?? As I wrote my report later, all I could say was, "things definitely look different from the other end of the table."

The third bombshell came when it was time for me to be an observer in an operating room. Again – *someone had forgotten to tell them who I was*!! Would the scheduler never learn? They actually had the nerve to have me assigned to observe a heart transplant. *Whaaaaaaaaaa!!* I was told in great detail by other students how the chest would be "cracked open" with an electric saw straight up between the ribs. *Ohhhh no!!* Are you kidding me? The phone came back out and the plates were put away, this time for just 1 day, because I only had a 1 day advance notice. I cried and tossed and turned throughout the night, before getting "the call" the next morning, which I was hoping for. I was reassigned to the Short Procedure/Outpatient room, where minor surgeries such as splinter removal were performed. *Yes!! Even I can handle that.*

I arrived by 6:00 early the next morning, and changed into scrubs, looking all chipper and professional. It was a good morning laughing as the doctors and nurses told corny jokes and talked about their social lives. As the minor procedures, like suture removals, were done, I secretly looked away, up at the walls, lights, ceiling, etc. I was so smooth that no one noticed that I didn't look directly at what was being done, minor or not. Wow! This was a breeze. Maybe I would even think about doing this every day; since I was trying to figure out what area of nursing I wanted to work in.

About 11:00 A.M., as we were wrapping things up, I was feeling really good. Shucks! I didn't even have to "faint backwards" away from the sterile field, like the instructor told me to do if I started feeling faint. Then the phone rang – everybody looked at each other, and some folks starting swearing. Our room was needed for an emergency "dirty" surgery (not necessary to have everything sterile), to be done on an in-patient. He had major abdominal surgery a few days before, but the wound had become

Infected, and the edges had "dehisced" (separated). The wound needed to be flushed out and re-sutured. As I listened, I start thinking to myself, "Well really, how bad can it be since his original surgery was days ago?" I figured there probably wouldn't even be any "real" blood…right?

Wrong! There was plenty of blood, along with an extremely foul smell, from the huge hole in the man's stomach; through which one of the surgeons put his whole hand almost up to the elbow prodding around. Sure enough, his hand came out with a green looking surgical sponge which had been left in the poor guy. The good thing for me was everyone was so focused on the retrieved sponge, that no one even noticed the student nurse who was also 'green'; with her head down between her knees to keep from passing out at the sight and smell. Okay!! Maybe this was not really the area of nursing where I belonged! I guess that explains why I later signed on to work as a Psychiatric Nurse-Therapist, and stayed in it for almost thirty years; very little blood and yuck. **…*while the dew is still on the roses…***

...Major Situation...

Finally, I made it to the last semester of my Nursing Program, and began to look forward to graduation with anticipation. Then, an unforeseen crisis occurred, which "shook my world". There was a young lady, Rita, whom I had befriended. She would often come to visit with the kids and me; and at times, I would ask her to babysit with them for me. It was at the beginning of my last semester that she came and told me she was almost 7 months pregnant and needed my help and support. I was blown away that she had been able to keep it a secret from everyone up until that time!! Being the young "mother hen" that I was, I chose to help Rita by making sure that she registered into a prenatal clinic. I enlisted Ricardo's help so that between the two of us, she always had someone accompanying her to her clinic visits.

One morning as I was preparing to leave for school, I received a phone call from Rita's Dad, explaining that she had been in labor all night and that they were leaving to go to the hospital. The problem was that her Dad couldn't take time off from his job to stay with her. I agreed to take a day off from school, and to meet her at the hospital. Ricardo came into the apartment as I was preparing to leave, and I asked if he would go with me to see about the young lady. When we arrived at the hospital, she was in full blown labor, but was in the room alone. When I spoke to the nurses, they were less than compassionate, as they reported that Rita had been very uncooperative with them. She had refused to have anyone touch her until she saw me. I gowned up, and we went through the balance of the labor and delivery together. She delivered a big healthy baby boy. I waited until she was brought back to her room after a few hours in recovery; and was sitting there watching her sleeping when Ricardo came into the room.

He had been asleep out in the waiting area, and said he was coming to see that I was okay. He and I sat and laughed and talked in hushed voices so as not to awaken Rita, when suddenly he started crying. My exhausted mind was trying to figure out why he was crying, but I was in no way in my lifetime ever prepared to hear what he said - *"I am the baby's father."* In my mind, I was thinking to myself, "It sounded like he said he is the baby's father." Out of my mouth I said, "What baby?" He started blubbering about, "It happened one night when you had gone out with some of your girlfriends, and I was mad with you and was drunk. She was there babysitting when I came in, and was flirting with me, and it just happened." By this time, Rita had awakened and seeing Ricardo crying, she started sobbing, "I'm sorry, I'm sorry, I'm so sorry." As the clarity of what was being said came through to my understanding, I realized my chest was tightening up and I was not breathing. Somehow, from somewhere way down deep inside of me, I heard myself saying to her, "It's not your fault; he is a grown man old enough to be your father." *Whaaaaaaaaaaa??? How can this be???*

At that inopportune time the nurse brought the baby into the room. I was still frozen to the chair. As I looked into the baby's face, I saw my son's face with just a few differences in the features. Somehow, I stood up and pulled myself together to go to the nursing station to let them know that I would be leaving, and that Rita would be alone with the baby. I got into my car, and as I was driving home with my mind in a fog, I was thinking, "This is a bad dream and is not even funny." When I finally reached home and sat down, I began to fully realize it was not a dream and that I was completely awake. I didn't know what to do!! I called my Pastor, and as I heard his voice, I began screaming hysterically. Pastor just began to pray over the phone, still having no idea of what was going on. Finally, after some time, I calmed down enough to tell him. He and his wife came to my home and sat with me for a while, as he kept reassuring me, *"No matter what, God is going to bring you through this."*

I received a call from Rita the next day telling me that her father was sending her and her son back to live with her Mother. She again apologized profusely. She pleaded with me not to tell anyone else who the father was. I honored her request, and never shared the information with anyone until years later. As far as I was concerned, that was the death of the possibility of ever having an ongoing relationship with Ricardo. It was also the end of my college days for the time being. I couldn't concentrate or make myself go back and deal with the work. Plus, I actually never wanted to talk to another human being, "ever".

Pastor let me stew for a week, and finally said, "Enough is enough, get moving." When I contacted the school a few days later and told them I had been AWOL due to a serious family crisis – I was told that I had forfeited the credit for the work done in that semester, and could not graduate that year. ***...and the voice I hear...***

By the mercy of God, I was not expelled all together. However, the Nursing curriculum was very time specific and structured; and the classes I needed to complete would not be available until the following year. After all I had been through to get to this point; this was definitely a low blow. I had to remind myself often of my whole reason for going to college in the first place – to make a decent life for my children. I was determined not to give up. Thank God, I did return the following year and graduated with Honors. Six weeks after completing the course, I passed the State Board Exams. Who would have ever thought it??? *Me, the high school drop-out – a Registered Nurse!!*

There was one disappointment – when it was time for me to graduate from the Nursing program, I couldn't afford the fees for both the special Nurse's Pinning ceremony, plus the full college graduation. I opted to just attend the pinning ceremony. We marched in our uniforms and Nursing caps. *What a blast*!! Life is so strange, again I did not get to walk in a graduation...***falling on my ear...***

...What You Gonna Do, Michael?...

Through the several years which had passed following Michael's early discharge from prison, he had not involved himself in any way in our lives. I had a couple superficial relationships with guys, but was still really in a "waiting mode", thinking that maybe Michael would decide to come home. After a couple years, there were a few times when he called and we kind of talked about reconciliation. Nothing serious ever came of it. While I was still very much in love with Michael, I did not have the inner strength to take care of all my children basically by myself; and deal with Michael's addictions and multiple women too.

Eventually, I started refusing to listen to his promises at all. He would occasionally call and promise the kids that he was coming to take them out. Nine out of ten times, he didn't show up at all, or he would show up too late to go out, with potato chips or something. After a couple times, this caused me to begin to develop anger and bitterness towards him. It was bad enough that he had so deeply disappointed me, but to repeatedly do that to my kids was unforgiveable to me. The other maddening thing that he would do often when he did finally come to take them out to spend the day with him, was to leave them at Me-Mom's house and show up hours later. The kids never seemed to really mind most of the time, but it would cut me to my heart each time. I made the decision to personally just stay away from Me-Mom's house.

In spite of these challenges, things began to settle into a fairly "healthy" routine for myself and the kids. I had a decent paying job then, and I enrolled the kids into several community activities, including the Brownies and Girl Scouts. Ricardo would still come to see R.J. and the girls, and would often take them out to eat or to the movies or to the wrestling matches. Although I decided to forgive him for what he had done, I knew I could never bring myself to fully trust him again. Just about the time that things seemed to really be smoothing out, I came home one day to find that our apartment had been burglarized!! There are no real words to describe how "violated" I felt when I realized that someone had actually been in our home and touching our things, uninvited. During the same timeframe, one of the ministers in our church was running workshops to teach people how to become first-time homebuyers. Following the break-in, I began to aggressively pursue that possibility, although I had no money saved for a down payment.

Pastor fully surprised me one day when he informed me that he had done some research and found an organization which would give me a $1,000 grant. I could use it as a down payment on a house. As we began researching the information, the issue was raised that I was still married, which could affect the application process. There was some concern that since Michael and I were separated but not divorced, if I were to purchase a home, he may try to assume some of my assets. I went to several counseling sessions with my Pastor, and we contacted Michael on multiple occasions to see if there was any possibility of reconciliation. In spite of agreeing several times to come in for joint counseling, Michael failed to show for any of them. We placed the house application on hold for about six months; with me living in constant fear for myself and the kids in the apartment which was previously burglarized. Finally, I came to the conclusion that Michael was not interested in reconciliation or our safety.

At that point, I made the difficult decision to file for a divorce. I called and left several messages with Me-Mom for Michael to see if there was still anything left to be done for our marriage. He did not respond at all. I filed for, and was granted a divorce without contest. Once the divorce was finalized, I made application for the mortgage. With the help of my church, my children and I bought our first "home"…..*the Son of God discloses…*

...This Is Sooo Hard...

I began working extra hours, up to 50 to 60 hours most weeks taking care of children, bills, student loans, and whatever else was needed. I received no financial help from Michael. Ricardo also cut back on the occasional help that he provided for us. Ricardo had begun to visit less and less often, especially after he asked me to marry him, and I refused. My entire life became work and children, with occasional attendance to church. After several months, I began to experience a serious depression. With the total responsibility of six young children, and very little family support, I was "dying on the vine." Eventually, I began to lose interest in church, and wanted to start having a social life like my coworkers who were my age (late twenties). I began to feel more and more boxed in, with no relief from the care of my kids. I took them a lot of places, from the Poconos to Wildwood to Dutch Country – *but what about me??* "Does anyone realize that I have never had any real freedom in my life?" ***...and He walks with me...***

Then I was only a few weeks from my thirtieth birthday. I decided to do something "just" for me. I secretly bought myself a pair of roller skates, a bicycle, and an electronic toy named "Simon", which had just come out on the market. I hid all of my "presents" in the basement until the big day. I did not want to share them with anyone, especially my kids who seemed to envelop my entire life. However, I learned a true lesson about selfishness – no real good can come of it. Firstly, after the kids went to bed that night, I put my bike in my car trunk and drove to a nearby park. I didn't want the neighbor's kids to see me riding my bike on the block and tell my kids the next day. (What a putz!)

Well, someone should have reminded me that if it was dark at home with the street lights on, that it was doubly dark in the park with minimal lights! Now, being still "slightly" scared of the dark, I couldn't even enjoy riding through the park. After all, "Jack the

Ripper" or his brother might jump out from behind a bush at any given point. Okay, one time around was enough – back into the car the bike went, back through the rear basement door, and back in hiding until months later, when I ended up giving it to the kids. *Phooey*!!

Secondly, after returning home with my "chariot", I figured I would ride my skates. After all, I could do that in the basement where there was light. Funny thing was, I never noticed before how smooth and slippery that cement floor was. I also definitely never realized how the floor was on a serious slant – not until after I had put on my beautiful new shoe skates, and stood up. Without even having to put any effort out, I simply started "rolling" down the decline. Sure enough, the "rolling" almost immediately became "flying"; with nothing to stop me as I was propelled towards the cement wall at the bottom of the decline. All of this as I pulled down every overhead clothesline on my way down the hill – while trying not to scream. The kids might hear me – and they might want to share my skates. Not!! Whump!!!!!!!!!!! Thank God for the washing machine just before the cement wall!! *"Did anybody get the license plate of that Mack truck that I ran into?? Meanwhile, can someone else please help me to get up off my back because I am laughing and crying too hysterically to get up?"*

I laughed until I was gagging, all the while trying to do it quietly, and without needing a Depends diaper. Finally, I managed to stop doing the "turtle" on my back long enough to turn over and crawl on my knees back up the incline to the steps. Once there, I managed to sit down and take those "rockets" off my feet. I kept imagining my kids waking up the next morning looking for Mommy; only to find her knocked unconscious and lying on the basement floor with her "birthday" skates on. *Such a wiener*!! I decided that I should go upstairs now, and wait until the morning to nail all of those clotheslines back up. By the way, my kids never suspected a thing, or wondered where the "wheels" suddenly appeared from when we had to move our upright piano months later. If you ever need to move something big and heavy, skate wheels work wonders (just like rockets).

Third and lastly, a few minutes before midnight while it was still my birthday, I decided to play with my last new toy. I brought out my new electronic "Simon" game, away from all the little prying eyes. Oh my goodness!! Someone should have told me how loudly the thing beeps. Is that a soft knock on my bedroom door after I have only been playing for about 3 minutes? *"Who is it?"* I hear a little voice, *"Mommy, I was sound asleep but I dreamt that I was hearing the beeps like from the new game I saw on television."* "Girl, you must have been dreaming, go back to sleep."

I learned something else that night too – it's impossible to play "Simon" under heavy blankets while trying to muffle the sound. Aside from the fact that "Simon" doesn't listen to "Shhhh"; it's too dark to be able to clearly see the lights on the game. You need to see the lights to play it. By the time I was soaked to the skin with sweat, and my eyes were sufficiently blurred, I finally gave up the fight and went to sleep.   Happy 30th Birthday to Me!! **…and He talks with me…**

...Dioje...

While my children were young, we usually had a dog for a pet and protection. We had three different dogs with the same name, "Dioje" (pronounced Dee-OH-Gee, with the emphasis on the "OH"). I heard someone else call their dog by that name, and I just thought it sounded so "French" and aristocratic. It was okay to have a "French" German Shepherd. It added a little class to our house. I'll just share a little with you about how absolutely "special" Dioje #2 was. He was an absolute maniac!! He would run through the house just as fast when he was fully grown (huge), as he did when he was a little pup. He would chew your shoes, your clothes, the furniture and probably you, if you let him. No matter how much training we did, the only civilized thing about that dog was that he was housebroken (well, most of the time).

One of his favorite pastimes was catching mice – we didn't need a cat. The problem was, Dioje would then bring you the mouse and want you to play with him. Ugh!! He kept us running from him with a mouse hanging out of his mouth often. I came in the house one evening, tired and frustrated after having worked a long 16 hour shift. Dioje had trash from one end of the living room to the other; and was romping through it like he was in a playground. That was it. I was done!! I certainly did not need one more thing to take care of!! I told the kids to take Dioje around the corner to the park near us, and to tie him to a tree for whoever wanted him. All of the kids went up the street looking like they were on a "death march". Meanwhile, Dioje was jumping and prancing and acting like his normal frenzied self.

About 5 minutes later, I heard a sound at the door, which I thought was the kids. As I opened the door, who bounced in but Dioje, almost knocking me down? He had chewed through the rope and beat the kids back home. This cycle was repeated three times that night. I even threatened the kids with their lives if they didn't tie him good enough to hold him to the tree. After the third time, I gave up, and decided to forgive him. However, when I got up the next morning, that dog had turned over almost every waste basket in the house; and had shredded one of my shoes. I guess he was showing us his displeasure. I packed his butt into the car, and off to the local animal shelter we went. On the way there, I got a moving violation ticket for an illegal turn, while trying to move the hound off the steering wheel. It didn't matter, *"I am getting rid of this dog today."*

I had to drag him inside, with him fighting me and squealing like a stuck pig. I guess he recognized this as the place where he normally got a shot. I finally got up to the counter, and explained that we could no longer take care of this "wonderful" dog. The receptionist asked what his name was, and I said with the thickest French accent I could work up, "Dioje".

She looked at me over her glasses and said, "I know how to spell "dog", but what's his name?" After the 30 seconds it took for me to realize what she said; I was so stunned that his name spelled "d-o-g" that I never even answered her. After staring at her, speechless for a full minute, I just turned around and walked out the door, never even looking back.

...I'm So Tired...

I kept barely managing the whole endless treadmill of work-work-work, and the full responsibility of my children (*food, clothing, shopping, cooking, washing, Parent-Teacher meetings, discipline, injuries, and referee, on and on and on*). Then, one Sunday morning, I woke up and knew that I could not take another day of it. I had been having uncontrollable crying spells all throughout the day for several weeks. Either something had to change, or I was going to go crazy on that day.

I called Me-Mom's house and left a message for Michael that I needed to drop the children over there for a visit after church. I went through all of the normal routine, feeling like I was in a fog or something. While we were at church, a girl friend asked me what was wrong. We went outside during the service, and I broke down and wept uncontrollably. I told her that I did not want to walk off and leave my children for someone else to raise; because of my own childhood experiences. However, I was feeling like I was going to lose my mind at any given moment.

She suggested that I take a one week break from the kids; and that I should leave them with Michael and his family. I told her that I didn't want the kids' lives disrupted away from their home. Together we came up with a plan. I would ask Michael to come stay at the house with the kids, and I would stay in my friend's spare bedroom. I left church that day and dropped the children over to Me-Mom's house, with instructions that I was exhausted and that Michael would need to bring them home. For the last few years, he had continued the same pattern of picking them up occasionally, only to leave them at his parents for someone else to end up bringing them home. On this particular Sunday, I went to the market, did laundry and made sure everything was set that they would need for the upcoming school week. I left some money in an envelope and taped it to the television, along with a note to

Michael; explaining that he would need to "inconvenience" himself for a week, and stay at the house with his children. I did not want R.J. to be separated from his sisters while I was away, so I made no arrangements for Ricardo to come take him.

I left no contact information, but wrote that I could be reached at work the next day as usual. I then packed my bag, and "went away", alone from my children for the first time since Tirzah was born. She was in her last year of high school, so figure how many years it had been. My emotions were wound so tight, that I laughed and cried all the way to my girlfriend's house, and for half of the evening.

There was no such thing as a cell phone back then, so I had to keep calling to the house to check if the kids were home yet. After multiple calls, one of the kids answered, saying they were just coming in the door. I told them to make sure that Michael read what was in the envelope before he left them, and I hung up. I did not call back that night because I didn't want to be cajoled into coming back home without a break. I took a nice hot bath, and for the first time in years, had a solid night of sleep – without trying to keep one ear open. When I arrived at work the next day, there were several tearful messages from the girls. I called the house, only to have Tirzah tell me that Michael did not stay with them the night before. He and his girlfriend had left them alone all night. He told them that if he didn't stay, he knew for sure that I would come back that night.

You could have fried an egg on my head, I was so angry. I called Me-Mom's house and told her to tell her son that I was NOT coming back until my week of rest was up. He had better take some responsibility for his children for a change. Michael called me at work and thoroughly cussed me out. I held my ground and told him I was not coming home, and hung up the phone. I refused to take any further calls from any family members for the rest of that day. However, I did tell Tirzah to call the Pastor if there was an emergency. I called Pastor and gave him my work number and my friend's home number.

When I called back to the house later that evening to check on the kids, I was told that Michael had come back. He had some clothes with him to stay for a few days....*and He tells me that I am His own...*

...Run-A-Way...

I slept almost all of that week when I wasn't at work. The crying spells had become minimal. However, I woke up the morning that I was supposed to go home, and couldn't catch my breath. I had a full-blown panic attack. After talking with my friend again, we agreed that I should stay one more week. I called and told Michael that I was going to stay for another week. He totally amazed me by agreeing. He said that he didn't realize how hard it must be, taking care of all these kids by myself all the time. He said that I must feel like I'm in prison or something. Wow!

From the time our children were born, Michael had taken very little physical care of them, even when we lived together. Several years earlier, I had finally taken him to domestic court for child support, because he absolutely refused to help me with any of the financial care of his kids. In spite of his ongoing drug abuse, he managed for quite a while to still work at truck driving. He showed up to court with a high paid lawyer, while I had a court appointed one. I thought the judge was going to fall off his seat when Michael's lawyer ran down a list of expenses to explain why he couldn't pay child support – after all, he had two Dalmatians which ate $100 worth of food each week, his girlfriend with her kids, and their mutual son.

After a few minutes, the judge told Michael and his lawyer to shut up and take their seat. The judge then asked me how much I wanted to receive each week. He agreed, very unhappily, when I asked that Michael only be ordered to pay $50 per week for child support, because I had a decent paying job. The judge told Michael to sell his dogs if necessary; that he was getting off "like a fat rat"; and that his pay would be garnished if he failed to pay consistently. I wasn't trying to take all that he had. I primarily wanted to show Michael a principle that he should be helping with his responsibilities, whether he was at home with us or not. In spite of the court order, over the next few years, I received less than $500 in payments from Michael, but just never bothered to go back to court to have his pay garnished.

While I was on my "rest break", I had Tirzah to come to the job, and gave her money for the house; and spending money for each of the kids. We laughed and cried and had a good visit. As each day passed, I began to feel like I could really breathe and think clearly again. It was near the end of the kids' school year, and by the end of the second week, I made a decision. I called Michael and told him that I could not bring myself to come home yet, and that I was going to find me a room to rent for the summer.

It must have been divine intervention on my behalf, because although Michael balked, he didn't go ballistic. I agreed that I would pay the mortgage each month, and that I would give them money for food and weekly allowances. I put the word out at work that I was looking for a room to rent. The very same day, one of my coworkers, Marilyn, told me that she had a finished basement bedroom available for rent, and we came to an agreement for 3 months. Marilyn had a granddaughter staying with her, who was like the ages of my younger children. We decided that it was okay for me to give my children the location and phone number where I was, and that they could come visit me there.

According to the reports that the kids gave me, things seemed to be okay at home; although the older children seemed to be doing most of the actual parenting of the younger ones. Michael reportedly would disappear from time to time, and Ricardo had to help them out at times. As for me, I saw or talked to the kids only by phone or when they visited me. I spent most of my free time alone that summer, occasionally going out with my sister, Felicia. I went to church occasionally, but slept in most weekends. I couldn't get enough sleep. It seemed like the more I slept, the more I needed to sleep.

... Please Don't Make Me Do It...

As the summer drew close to the end, I began having unexpected crying spells again. On top of that, I began to hear reports from the younger children of increasing conflict and tension between the two older girls, Tirzah and Lisa. When I had been home, I occasionally had to play referee between the two of them. As is often the case with second children, Lisa had a tendency of trying to prove that she was the boss, not only of the younger kids, but also of the older sister. Tirzah, who tended to be softer spoken, eventually began to hold her ground; hence, it would lead to occasional screeching "cat fights".

The more I heard of what was going on at home, the less I wanted to be there. At the end of the summer, I made the decision to "*stay a little longer.*" Needless to say, Michael was not a happy camper this time, for sure. However, I didn't care what he wanted. I was just starting to feel "sane" again, and couldn't imagine going back yet. Bottom line, I ended staying away from home for **one whole year!** It was finally during the one year anniversary week of my leaving, that I had to really come to grips with myself. I came to realize that if I didn't go home then, I would probably never go back again. **God help me…I went home!**

Book Three

"The Joy We Share As We Tarry There"
-The Victory Song is Sung-

by

September Summer

About the cover of Book Three – *All of my life, I have had an aversion to cats, and have been afraid of them. Two years ago, my daughter asked me to take her cat* **"Boots"**, *as she was moving into an apartment which didn't allow animals Hence, I agreed to take Boots for a trial period, and although we have had our bumps and bruises, God has taught me to love her, when I thought never could (like loving myself). In this, there has been another level of healing in my soul.*

..How Did I Get Here?...

The end of the spring found me completely burnt-out, the year that I "ran away" from home. I was depressed and suffering from insomnia night after night. I would find myself at the most unexpected and inopportune times, during any given day, with tears on my face. I would not realize it until someone asked me why I was crying.

It wasn't that I was tired of being a Mom. I loved my children deeply. The problem was, I felt like there wasn't enough of me to go around to properly care for six children. I found myself feeling more and more resentful towards everyone. No one seemed to see and really understand that I was literally "drowning" in all of my responsibilities and concerns.

As far as my kids were concerned, they were no different from other children their ages, a combination of sugar versus spice. My oldest daughter Tirzah made me very proud by graduating from high school the year before. Shucks! Not counting my returning to school for my GED, she had done better than her Mom or Dad. That is definitely not to say that she didn't give me a "run for my money".

...Testing the Limits...

I had already laid down the 'law' when Tirzah was still in kindergarten and grinning at the little boys. The minimum dating age in our home would be 16. However, that didn't mean that I was *really* intending to let them "actually" start dating that young. That was the age I was when I got married! The "law" was my way of trying to "psych" all of my kids out when they were real young. By the time they would reach age 16, I figured they would have changed their minds and be more focused on going to college.

We-e-e-ll, "Ms. Thang" (Tirzah) decided at age 15 that she was going to have a boyfriend; the son of one of our neighbors. Of all the boys in our block, I felt like Danny was probably one of the wildest. Plus, I was hoping that Tirzah would at least have chosen a boy in our church, not a little "hoodlum" (like her Dad). Tirzah and I went through a little power struggle before I finally just pulled out the "parent privilege card", and said "No, you are not permitted to date Danny". Honestly speaking, I was working so many hours; I was surprised to learn later that she had been sneaking to see him, while using his younger sister as an excuse to visit their home. By that time, Tirzah had reached the magic age (16). I put my foot down and told Tirzah that she was absolutely not to be in their house when I wasn't home, and that Danny was not to be in our home either.

Well, being "Eve's daughter" (Ha-Ha), Tirzah did exactly the opposite of what I said. In the spring of 1982, she and I began to prepare her things for her upcoming Senior Prom and graduation. I added even a little more overtime hours to my schedule to pay for expenses. I was already busy as usual, working 50 to 60 hours per week just to pay mortgage, buy food and clothes, and pay bills. I relied heavily on Tirzah and Lisa, my two oldest daughters, to keep the house organized and to monitor the younger kids. One Friday evening, a few months before time for Tirzah to graduate from high school; I agreed to stay over at work to work an extra eight hours. Tirzah asked if she could go to a birthday party in the neighborhood with a girlfriend from school. Because she and Lisa had been working so hard to help me, I consented with the understanding that she was to be home by midnight. She also had to give me the name, address and phone number to the house where the party would be.

My sixteen hour shift finally ended at 11:30, and a male friend picked me up to drive me home. I reached home to find no Tirzah in the house. I called the phone number she had given me earlier, only to find that the number was disconnected. My first instinct told me that she was across the street at Danny's house, so I went there first. I was informed, (of course) that she was not there. I told Danny to tell her she had better be in my house by the time I came back from where she said the party was. Duke walked with me around the corner to the party address Tirzah had given me. By then, it was about 1:00 a.m. As I knocked on the door of the home, a Hispanic woman came to the door holding a baby, saying "No speak-a English". In my mind, I was saying, "Okay, this is getting uglier by the minute." I was fuming as we walked back to the house, not to mention that I was cross-eyed tired to the bone.

When I went into the house, Tirzah was upstairs in her bedroom taking off her coat. As I started asking her questions, she became belligerent and arrogant, which really angered me. I was still trying to get my exhausted arms out of my coat. Suddenly she raised her hands up to a defensive mode like someone boxing. I looked at her in total disbelief. I said, "What was that? Were you trying hit me?" Arrogantly, while swinging her head like she was talking to another kid, she said, "No, I thought you were trying to hit me!" At this point, I said, "Oh, and so if I was going to hit you, were you going to stop me?" By this time, my tiredness was decreasing as my anger was increasing. I took my coat off, folded it neatly and handed it to Duke, while he looked at me incredulously.

I then gave Missy "permission" to fight me back, and then proceeded to give her an old fashioned "beat down" just like I was one of her girlfriends from the streets. I used all the body moves my brothers had taught me years before, and made sure not to hit her in the face to leave any evidence. By then, Lisa climbed out of her bed and got under it. She later told me that my eyes were "bugged out", and that I looked like a madwoman. After a few minutes, I walked away from Tirzah, and went into the bathroom, putting my face into a towel and crying like a baby. I was so angry that I wanted to scream, but didn't want to wake up the whole neighborhood.

As I came out of the bathroom, I saw "Ms. Thang" putting her coat on. I asked her where she thought she was going, and she said, (still swinging her head) "Out!" As I looked at her, I started giggling, and informed her that it was okay, that I was going to my bed now. I told her, "When I wake up in the morning, if you are not in your bed, I am going to put a contract on you! There is no alley in the city small enough to hide you!" She swung that head again, and said, "You're crazy. You can't put no contract out on me for nobody to kill me."

By now I was laughing hysterically, probably from exhaustive delirium. I 'swung' my own head and said, "I'm not going to pay them to kill you. I'm going to pay them to find you, and then I am going to come and kill you myself! Then, I'll go to jail and laugh for the rest of my life." (I was totally exhaustedly psychotic by now) Then I put on the biggest 'head swing' that I could muster up as I turned, walked into my room, and passed out on my bed sobbing loudly like a wounded bear.

...Be Careful What You Ask For...

I believe I fell asleep before my head hit the pillow, and the next thing I knew it was daylight. I got up to go check on the kids. Tirzah was laying on top of her bed with all her clothes on, including her coat, with tear stains dried up on her face. The good thing that came out of that episode is that as each of my daughters started coming into their 'age of rebellion', Tirzah would take them aside and have the "talk". I was informed years later that she would tell them, "Don't push Mommy too far because that woman goes crazy!" (Tee Hee)

The day after the "beat down", I called Michael and told him to come and get Tirzah. He was still living with a woman who had a little boy for him and several of her children. Michael informed me that he didn't have any place to put Tirzah. He told me that he would come and talk to her. I left to go to the market, but had an uneasy feeling. I doubled back just in time to see Tirzah going down the street with a suitcase. At the same time, Michael's car pulled up, and she started running. He had to run to catch her. I told him that if he couldn't take her with him, that he should drop her at the police station, because I'd had enough. He did take her with him, and she stayed for a few weeks. However, she started calling me the very next day after she left to ask if she could come back home. It seemed that there really was no bed for her, and she had even less comforts there than we had at home. Although I cried for almost two weeks, I told her, "You have made your bed hard; you sleep in it for a bit." On top of that, the Prom was a closed deal as far as I was concerned.

Eventually, I did allow Tirzah to come back home, and she gave me no further problems. She graduated without further problems. The regret that she had missed her Prom plagued me for a long time afterwards. That is one thing that I would do differently if I had it to do all over again. After all, a Senior Prom is only a once in a lifetime event, never to come back again.

...At My Limit...

This was just one of the types of stressors that I had been dealing with in raising my children as a single parent. This was not what I signed up for when I said "I do". I was sooooooo tired of being a referee, as well as everything else that a mother and father was needed for. Michael was no help, since he had his other "family. Ricardo was "teaching me a lesson" since I didn't want to be back in a relationship with him. What kind of craziness is that? It's no wonder that my brain and heart were "fried" by the spring of 1983 when I "ran away". That was the year of Lisa's Senior Prom and high school graduation. Of course, I was also very proud of my second daughter's accomplishments.

High school graduation was another "rule" in our home; it was not negotiable. I made sure my kids knew they "owed me" the high school diploma, and anything beyond that, they owed to themselves. Therefore, even though I was not staying at home the last couple months leading up to Lisa's Prom and graduation; I helped to pay for whatever she needed. I also went to the house to see her off for the Prom, and later met them all at the graduation.

Once the graduation was over, I stayed away from home for the three months of the summer of 1983. I was in desperate need of rest to avoid a complete mental, emotional and nervous breakdown. I loved the feeling of being free, and at times would ride out in the evenings with the car windows open, listening to the radio. Sometimes I would just "listen" to the silence. Then I would find something to eat, take a shower and go to sleep, with no sense of weariness or dread. Thank you God! Within a few weeks, I was so noticeably at peace that my patients and co-workers began to speak about how much better it was to work with me.

...Working to Recover...

During that time, Caesar, one of the social workers I worked with invited me out to dinner. Wow! For the first time in my life, someone was attracted to me who had many of the same interests I had – we both loved reading various kinds of books, listening to "quiet" music such as jazz and soft rock, and even taking day trips to museums or the zoo. Unbelievable! I now actually had a male friend who also liked to talk about as many different things as I did, from what was going on down the street to what was going on across the globe. He was in the last stage of completing his Master's thesis, and of course the "editor" in me kicked in. That became a project we could do together. He wrote it and I typed it for him. As a reward, I was treated to some of the best restaurants in the area, and "wined and dined".

All of those things were good, but there was another part of the relationship which I found to be amazing – he continually told me things about me that he felt were positive. During the previous months when I was feeling so overwhelmed; I had done less and less to keep up my appearance other than the very basics. I had previously stopped wearing make-up because I felt it didn't matter, and I did as little as possible to my long, thick hair. While I remained meticulous with my personal hygiene, I did nothing extra. Even my sister, Felicia, questioned me about why I was no longer being the 'well dressed lady' whom she loved to tease about being *"Miss Sidid-di-fied"*. I came to realize that she didn't really mean any harm by her teasing, and she had no way of knowing how sensitive about it. I didn't want people possibly thinking that I was trying to be better than other people. It was another area in which I felt that I never really fit in – my paternal Grandmother and Dad's side of the family had raised me to be "genteel, prim and proper", with the need to always act like a lady and to always walk with your head and shoulders held up high. Yes, I even went through the posture training with the books on the head, plus many books on proper etiquette.

Then I married Michael, who could care less about how "gentlewomanly" I acted. In fact, I was often the butt of jokes from him and his friends and family. I became more relaxed in my speech and mannerisms. As a result, Honey Gramms began to call me 'farmer' with real disdain in her voice and in her facial expression. On the other hand, my husband's family frequently teased me about being so 'prissy'. Long story short, by the time I began to go out with Caesar, I had about as much self esteem as a dust ball had a chance in a windstorm.

Caesar was much older than me, and had been estranged from his wife for ten years. He admitted that he had done the same thing for years that Michael was doing, with the substance abuse, until it had cost him his family. He had been raised in a good Christian home, had his own business at one point, and was well educated and extremely intelligent. By the time he asked me out, he said he had been in recovery for five years, and was on his way back to becoming the man of quality he had been. He used to tell me that he saw me as a "rare jewel", whose real value had not been recognized by myself or others around me. At first I figured he was just "shooting the crap", as a part of his "man game". But, after a while, I began to believe that he genuinely cared. He took me on as a "project", and was gentle, kind and affectionate towards me. This began to rebuild within me a sense of my being "somebody" of worth.

...Is This It?...

During our time together, I began to believe that I wasn't "less" than a real woman. In fact, I had a right to fix myself up, hold my head up and take pride in the person that I was. No matter that I wasn't like anybody else, it was okay to just be me! At times, I can still hear him say, "Girl, pick yourself up, dust yourself off, and get to stepping." Then, there were the times when he would make me stand in the mirror and tell myself how beautiful I was - not perfect – but still beautiful. Of course, after a while, I fell like the Titanic for him, hook, line and sinker. I began to believe that he was going to be the man with whom I would spend the rest of my life. Screeeeeeeeeeeeeeeeeech!

Wouldn't you know that after I invited Caesar to attend church with me a couple times, that he began to really get his heart right with God? He was honest with me and told me that in spite of how he felt about me, he could not see himself raising a second set of young children since his were all adults now. Here comes the hammer! Whyyyyyyyyyy God?? This is not fair!! Sure enough, from that point, things became uncomfortable between us. He completed his thesis and began preparing for a fall graduation from his Master's program. He then began going to church with his wife, and within a few months they decided to reconcile. He gave me the good old cheer-up talk, and of course told me what a "good" woman I was.

Even as the words were still coming out of his mouth, I held up my hand to stop him, but he kept talking. I wanted to slap him and scream in his face, *"SHUT UP ABOUT ME BEING 'GOOD'! Being 'Good' AND a token will get me on the bus, and I had better not try it without the token. Look at ME for who I am! Don't look at me because I am "good"; because I have been told my whole life to "do good" and "be good". What has it ever gotten me? Absolutely nothing!! I thought for sure that of all the people in my life, at least YOU understand that I always do my very best in everything that I do –but it's never quite "good" enough.* It still never makes people love me or stay with me.

When I was a child, Honey Gramms always told me to do a 'good' job. She never ever once told me anything about the job that I already worked so hard to do, except "the next time, do better." In school, when I worked so hard to do "good", what happened? I made 'good' grades, but was ostracized by other students because I was "Miss Goody-2-shoes." When I got married, I worked hard day and night to be a 'good' wife and Mommy, and what did it get me? A husband who didn't love me, and 5 children to raise by myself! When I met Ricardo, I strove to show him that I was a 'good' woman, and what did it get me? A son to raise alone and one of the worst betrayals a man could commit. Exactly, what the heck can ever be, "GOOD ENOUGH"?

All of these thoughts are rushing through my mind hysterically while Caesar is still talking; my mind is like a run-away train!! *"I HATE THAT WORD "GOOD". Why do you have the right to compare me to some standard that you have set in your mind, to judge that my 'good' is not "good enough", after I have opened up my heart to you? Why does everyone else but me get to decide when I am 'good' enough? I'm sick and tired of loving people, and never getting real love in return. How dare you tell me that there is nothing wrong with me, and how I shouldn't take it personal? Excuu-uuuse me? How much more "personal" can my personal broken heart be?*

If Caesar could have heard all of the thoughts flooding my mind, he probably would have run for his own sanity. Talk about a "catch-22" – I am so angry I want to puke, but who can I be upset with? (1) Him? – How can I be angry with someone who had decided to get right with God and go home? (2) His wife? – I guess not, she is a Christian, and they are legally still married. (3) My kids? – It's not their fault their Dad(s) turned out to be less than perfect. (4) God? – I am too much in awe of God for that, and scared He might strike me down with lightning or something horrible. As far as I knew at that time, God was a stern and pitiless taskmaster like Honey Gramms, just waiting for me to mess up, so He could drop the hammer.

Then who? – Why of course it has to be with my own self! It has to be me who is the problem. It's me with the fifty-nine kids, and it's me who always tries to do my very best, only to end up hearing, "You're such a "goo-ood" woman, so don't take it personal." Listen Bud – go tell that crap to someone who really wants to hear it! Goodbye and good riddance! As hard as it is to say, I really do wish you and your wife the best. (*Sniffles*)

...Back At The Ranch...

Meanwhile, as "The Days of My Life" are playing out, the summer is drawing closer to the end. I begin having unexpected crying spells all over again. On top of that, I am getting phone calls from my younger children about increasingly frequent fights and tension between the two older girls, Tirzah and Lisa. Prior to me leaving home, it was not unusual to have to play referee between the two of them. As is often the case with a second child, Lisa had a tendency of trying to prove that she was the boss, not only of the younger kids, but also of her older sister. Tirzah, who tended to be softer spoken, eventually began to hold her ground; hence, it would lead to occasional screeching "cat fights".

The more I heard about what was going on at home, the less I wanted to be there. By the end of that summer, I made the decision to *"stay away a little longer."* Needless to say, Michael was not a happy camper this time, for sure. However, I didn't care what he wanted. I was just starting to feel "sane" again, and could not imagine going back to what felt like a prison, just yet.

...Got to Do What I Got to Do...

Bottom line, by the time it was all done, I ended up staying away from home for **one whole year!** As the one year anniversary of my leaving drew near, I had to really come to grips with myself and realize that if I didn't go home now, I would never go back again. What could I do? I knew the trauma of growing up without your Mom. *I went home!*

It is quite an understatement for me to say that it was one of the most challenging times of my life. I didn't want to be a mother who had failed her children by deserting them; but was truly not sure if I would survive parenting my six children as a single parent. I had no reason to believe that Michael would continue to make his presence available to us once I returned home. I shut myself away in my room for a three day fast and prayed to God for His supernatural strength to help me do what I knew needed to be done. During those three days, I came to an inner resolve that I would do all that I could for the next ten years or so that it would take to finish raising my daughters and my son, the youngest child, to age eighteen.

My sister and I set out with a male friend very late on Friday night, supposedly driving to New York City to celebrate my "last free weekend". Ironically, we ended up getting lost because none of us really knew the way. Our "party" turned into a late night meal at an all night diner, and back to the house. The following Monday found me back at home in my own house when my children came in from school. I think Michael broke a speed record getting his clothes packed as he left! As I sat in the house by myself, waiting for the kids to come home, I began to relive the day that I was brought back to my mother after the nine year separation. I began to feel apprehensive and very uneasy.

Sadly, as my children came in one by one, I felt the same sense of emotional distance and isolation as I felt when I had come home to my Mom. In hindsight, I believe that I sat there and unconsciously built a wall of protection around my emotions to prevent possible rejection. My oldest daughter had moved out into her own apartment during the summer; and my second daughter, Lisa, sulked and pouted because her father was gone. The four younger children seemed happy enough to see me, and I tried to lighten things up by having cake and ice cream. I didn't know what to feel.

...How Can This Be?...

I felt like a stranger in my own home, and found myself slipping into a serious depression. On top of that, the company I worked for began to have financial problems, and I had to change jobs. While it was a very disconcerting time for me, the changes would actually have a major positive result in our lives. That school year was a much lighter load for me financially since I now only had four kids at home in school. Lisa was in her first year of college, and had decided to move in with Michael during her visits home. I began to notice a decided change in the atmosphere in the neighborhood where we lived. Suddenly, there was an increase in drug activity, and an increase in violence and burglaries.

One day near the end of the school year, my third daughter, who was fifteen years old, came home and told me she had been invited to her girlfriend's wedding. I asked her what she was doing associating with a girlfriend old enough to get married. The young lady was one of her classmates who was pregnant, and the father was also fifteen. The two of them were planning to marry and then live with the girl's mother. I began to feel a sense of panic. This situation led to a strange set of circumstances, which changed all our lives in a way we would not have imagined.

Ricardo had moved just a couple blocks from where we were living, and he and I were getting along as good friends. He helped us out with money at times, as well as with spending time with the kids whenever I needed a break and wanted to go out to a movie or something with friends. Michael was back to his drugs again, and we hardly heard from him. One day, a couple weeks prior to Doretha's 'wedding invitation', Ricardo had begun to make little hints about me becoming his wife. At the time, I didn't take him seriously. I thought both of us had a clear understanding that I could never trust him again because of what happened years earlier with the young lady he had the child with.

However, he began to say slightly more pointed things. Finally, one day as I was cooking, he came in and fell on his knees in the kitchen. He told me that another woman had asked him to marry her. I laughed at first, thinking he was being a jokester, as usual. As I turned and looked at him, I was totally floored to see tears in his eyes as he told me that he would not wait for me any longer than today. This would be my last opportunity to accept him or he would marry the other lady, whom he did not love. He said he really loved me, but wanted to be married and have a wife. I was dumbfounded! As I realized that he was serious, I asked him to give me a little more time to seriously think about what he was saying. He refused, saying that if I did not agree that night to marry him, he would marry the other lady the next day at the Justice of the Peace.

At that point, I became angry, and told him to do whatever he felt was best. I was belligerent and asked him who did he think he was to give me an ultimatum, when as far as I was concerned, we were getting along just fine as "best friends"? Shucks! Why did he want to try to put more demands on me? The only thing that we really didn't do with one another was to sleep together; and he was quite aware that we both were seeing other people. He stormed out, and I pouted myself to sleep; not truly believing for one minute that he would really marry someone else.

Boy! Was I more than a little wrong? He married the other lady the next day like he said, and called to tell R.J. he had a new stepmom. What kind of crap was that? If he really loved me, how could he marry some other woman? Where did he find the hussy anyway? How did he know she wasn't some floozy? How did he know that I didn't really love him anyway? (I actually did) Didn't he know he was supposed to stay with me and my kids regardless of whosoever else he was fooling around with?

...Something Has To Give...

I stewed and brooded and stormed around for the next few days, complaining to all of my girlfriends. Then, on top of this insanity, Doretha comes to tell me about some stupid child getting married. That took me over the top, and I decided right then and there that I had my fill of where I was living. I needed a new start; and decided to start looking for a "safe" place for my children and me. After all, if Ricardo was not going to be coming around, some folks in the area may start getting some ideas about breaking in.

I went to my new job in a real funk on that weekend, and whined to anyone who would take the time to listen. One of the few people who took pity on me long enough to not walk away, was one of the nursing supervisors working that Sunday. She was going through her own 'valley' with some family issues. So, we listened to each other.

Just before time for my shift to end, Ms. Gray called to ask if I wanted to hang out with her for a little after work. She invited me to a Jazz concert taking place not far from where I lived. At first I said I couldn't; but called her back to say that I would. I needed to stay out of my depressing neighborhood for a couple more hours. When I called to check on the kids, Ricardo was there, which really sent me over the edge again. Ms. Gray and I went to the concert, and the music was great. It was a wonderful diversion, and it changed my mood. We began to laugh and make light of our separate situations. Then, something totally mind-blowing happened! I told Ms. Gray that I would really like to move out of my neighborhood before the new school year would begin. Ms. Gray then told me that she owned a fully furnished three bedroom single ranch home in the suburbs just north of our city that she would like to rent to me, and I could take it right away.

She had just purchased a new home in a neighboring state, to qualify for a position as a professor in a nursing program in that state. She owned one home in the city I lived in, and the third home in the northern suburb close to our city. She was a single mother, with one married daughter. Ms. Gray had been praying for two weeks to figure out what to do quickly with her "northern" home, since it was so far away from all of her other activities. Whaaaa!! This was coming from someone whom I hardly knew, other than seeing her at work. Today was our first real conversation with one another!! Well, by the time I reached home that evening three hours later than usual; we had a handwritten 'rent to own' agreement for a house I had never seen. Within a month, I put my home up for sale, forfeiting any real profit that I could have made from it. I didn't care, I just wanted out!

I began working overtime like crazy so I would have enough to pay for us to move; plus to have money to get the kids a few new things to wear to the new schools they would be going to. Things were looking pretty tight, but I kept praying and had all of the people in our church praying for us. When the time came for us to move, near the end of the summer of 1984, Ms. Gray would not accept any security deposit from me to move into her house. She further insisted on paying the rental fee for the moving van!! The brothers from the church came to drive the van, and would accept nothing except a meal. Only God!

I could not believe my eyes!! The house was a beautiful gray stone single rancher, with a huge pine tree in the front yard, a carport, a nice size front yard and a "small park" for a back yard. There was enough land to build another house on it. The house was right down the road from a beautiful pond and tennis courts. There was a huge shopping mall about two miles in one direction and another smaller mall about two miles in the other direction. Ms.

Gray left the house fully furnished, including all three bedrooms, living room, kitchen, and laundry room. Forgive me for all of the details about the house, but I want you to understand the magnitude of the miracle which God wrought in the lives of me and my children. Every single thing that my family needed was provided for us, with the monthly rent being the same amount that I had been paying for mortgage in the city!!!!!!!!!!!!!!!

...Suburban Challenges...

Wonder of wonders! No one locked their houses or car doors or windows out here. No fear of break-ins here! The area was probably 95% Caucasian at that time, and my children were the only Black children in most of their classes. It was as if I was transported back in time to some of the areas where I grew up, in Rose Tree, N.Y. In spite of his being married to someone else, Ricardo came up for the first couple weekends we were there to cut the grass, and to help us get set up. He was already expressing regret for the choice he made, saying his wife had lied to him about some important things, and that she didn't even really want him to touch her sexually. The skirt chaser got shorted.

Talk about irony!! We laughed about it, but I did still feel a little twinge. Why did he have to do that? It seemed like every man that I had ever really trusted deeply with my heart, had walked on it – go figure!! I dealt with a couple real doozies!! Mom-Mom laughingly told me again and again that my "picker was off". That's all right; Ricardo was still my very best friend forever!! That new wife had better watch herself. Ha-ha!

Living in the suburbs did not come without its own set of problems; but nothing that made us regret having moved there. For one thing, most of our family and friends acted like we had moved to the moon; and as if we were trying to be better than other people. It got old really quickly to only visit when we were the ones who made the trip into the city, without any reciprocation. Only a select few dared to come the distance to visit us on rare occasions. So, my children had to adjust to not hanging outside on a porch with a close group of friends. Their social circle became more diverse, racially and economically, and the types of activities they did were quite different. Needless to say, my poor social life went as far south as it could go without being in the South Pole. Lawd!!

Much of the time was spent with our immediate family. There were times that I felt somewhat badly that we no longer had a house full of other children and friends, such as when we lived in the city. Nothing worthwhile comes without a cost, and in hindsight, I know that our move was the best thing for all of us, but it was a real sacrifice. I know it was God's intervention again at a major intersection in our lives, because all of my children went on to graduate high school, and each one has gone to college. To God be all the Glory!!

It was the spring of 1985, and Doretha and I began to prepare for her upcoming Prom and high school graduation. I could hardly believe that my third daughter was getting ready to graduate. Where had my life gone? We went shopping for a Prom gown, but she couldn't seem to find one she liked. A few days later, she came home with a magazine picture of a beautiful gown, which was tapered and with big ruffles around the shoulders. We spent a few fruitless days looking for one like it in the stores. Then, I had a moment of sheer insanity and allowed her to talk me into sewing the gown for her. In my bygone days, I had been a power sewing machine operator, and still custom made my own church suits and dresses.

I thought to myself, since I used to make all of our dress clothes and my own designer suits; surely one little old prom gown should be no problem. Hah! With picture in hand, we went to the fabric store and found a pattern which was close enough for me to modify it to match Doretha's picture. That's when the real problems began! My little "Miss Prissy" decides that she wants the gown to be white satin (yes, I said whiiiiiite satin). No problem! Nothing is too hard for my child! All I will say at this point and time is that the amount of time and effort it took (including covering and constantly cleaning every possible thing every day that touched that white satin) will never cross my path again, unless it is a wedding gown!! Actually speaking, Doretha's gown turned out fabulous, and she looked so much like a bride in it, that I cried for half of the night (such a Wuss!) Finally, another very proud graduation day! Wow!

...Get A Life...

After we had lived in the suburbs for a while, I was personally bored enough to picket the front of our house to say that "Yes, somebody besides kids really does live here too." Then, a dear friend of mine and her husband invited me to go out to a birthday party with them, being held at a West Indian Cricket club in the city. After I finished balking about it being in the city, as usual, and on the far side of the city from me at that, I agreed to go with them.

It was there that evening that I met a Jamaican gentleman, named "Tustee", which I would eventually come to marry almost a year later. He wasn't my Ricardo, who was Trinidadian, but at least he wasn't married. (Hah!) I had been sitting at a table talking to my friends and listening to the completely hypnotizing Reggae music, when Tustee asked me to dance. At first I said 'no', because I didn't know how to dance Reggae style; although I have always absolutely loved Afro-centric music, and loved to dance. My friend's husband, who was also Jamaican and like a brother to me, encouraged me to enjoy myself. So, I accepted the invitation to dance. That one dance set me on a course where I fell completely in love with the Jamaican music and culture. I became fully hypnotized by the accent, the foods and everything about the people in general. *At one point years later, while visiting the island of Jamaica, I phoned my Mom to ask her if she was sure that I was really her child and not adopted from a Jamaican family.*

I began dating Tustee, and he also began attending church with me and the kids on Sunday mornings. I knew that he drank socially and also smoked cigarettes and ganja (marijuana), but his rationale to me was that it was only because he had been out of church for a while. He promised that he would work on quitting, if I "helped" him. I didn't drink or smoke at that time, and I had been going to church every other Sunday when I didn't have to work. The biggest thing for me was that I was tired of being by myself, and I wanted to be right before God. Michael was with someone else; Ricardo had married someone else; and other guys that I had dated wanted me, but not my large 'ready-made' family. I was tired of straddling the fence, and did not want to get into another ungodly relationship with intimacy outside of marriage.

I decided that it didn't matter what else Tustee was doing, as long as he treated me right, didn't mind my kids and came to church regularly with us. I figured God could work out the rest. [Stoo-pid!!] I noticed that the kids didn't warm up to Tustee like they did with Ricardo, but I figured that was because Ricardo was still hanging around quite a bit. Of course, Ricardo and Tustee hated one another, but that was normal, I thought.

...Going To Get Married...

Tustee and I set our wedding date for October 6, 1985, and I assumed that by the time we would get married, everybody would love everybody. We went to pre-marital counseling with my Pastor. Of course, I had to tell Pastor a "little white lie" that I had met Tustee at my girlfriend's house. I didn't think he would take too kindly to one of his Deaconesses being in a social club, even though I wasn't drinking or smoking. After all, we were working on making it right.

We got through the couple months of counseling pretty good; although I had the feeling that at least half the time, Pastor did not understand one word Tustee was saying. He is from a rural area of Jamaica, and his accent was thicker than molasses in the winter. Somehow, we muddled through, even completing written assignments. We got all the way to the last session before Tustee almost blew it with Pastor; though I thought his answer was kind of flattering, myself! Pastor asked Tustee, "Why do you love her?"

I took a deep breath, thinking about all of the sun, moon and river promises that this brother had whispered to me. I must have blushed four shades redder because all of a sudden, you could hear a pin drop in the room. I stopped breathing, and the longer the silence went on, the further up in his chair Pastor looked like he was swelling. After what felt like a half-hour Tustee said with the thickest accent I had heard him speak with yet, *"Yaz, Pas-tah, me love 'er to da depths of me 'eart. All me dayz sinz me born, me pray Gawd gim-me one wo-mahn wid one cok-ah col-ah boddle body, and Gawd, 'e did 'ear me prayerz. Me baby iz da pure cok-ah col-ah boddle."* [emphasizing his point by making the coca-cola bottle shape with his hands].

Oh my! I looked at Pastor's face as the words of what Tustee said sunk through to his mind, and I could see the flames coming up out of his nostrils as he sat up on the edge of his chair. He glared at me, while speaking to Tustee in a booming voice, "Brother Tustee, do you have any other good reason why you love this sister?"

By this time, I'm starting to hear warning bells going off in my head and seeing flashing lights, which reminded me that I probably had not breathed since the first question. As I gasped for air as quietly as I could, Tustee caught the picture, and took my hand and said to Pastor, *"Yaz, Pas-tah, 'er is a good Christian woman."* I glanced out the side of my eye long enough to see the billows going down out of Pastor's chest, and the flare out of his nostrils. He leaned back in his chair, stared at me again and said, "Sister, are you sure that you are going to be happy, or are you just settling?" At this point, I'm thinking to myself, "Just let me out of here. My mind is already made up. God will take care of the rest." I said, "Yes, Pastor, it's what I want." Months later, I began to wonder why Pastor never asked me, "Why do you love Tustee?" I'm actually glad he didn't, I don't know if I could have answered him truthfully that day. I just wanted to be married and settled. Hopefully, love would come later.

A few months later, after a whirlwind period of preparation, we had the beautiful huge church wedding I had dreamed of my entire life; although it was not with the "man of my dreams", Michael. Life is so crazy! I think "Murphy's Law" worked overtime on the day of the wedding – resulting in the ceremony being over two hours late. In spite of all that, once everything and everyone was in place, it all went breathtakingly beautiful. At the end of that day, I was just happy to be married again, and full of great expectations that somehow God was going to turn this whole question mark into a wonderful exclamation point – like Va-va-va-voom!!

..Oops!...

Maybe I was in serious denial, or just plain nuts. Either way, we left that evening on our way driving towards a honeymoon spot about six hours away. After just two hours driving, we both were deliriously exhausted, and agreed to stop over at a hotel in Silver Springs, MD. As we were unloading the luggage to take it into the hotel, Tustee pulled out a shoebox from under his car seat. To my utter amazement, that crazy man had a whole shoebox full of "Ganja", otherwise known as cannabis, marijuana, reefer or whatever you want to call it. As for this "saved" woman, I called the shoebox with all of its contents, plus the bearer of the shoebox some very unsavory terms, for which I had to ask God's forgiveness. I screamed at him for about a good hour, in a whisper so that no one would call the hotel security because of loud voices. I couldn't believe this guy put me in jeopardy of going to jail for transporting an illegal drug across several state lines. Even Michael had never been so totally inconsiderate and irresponsible to involve me in his illicit mess!

I couldn't even sleep that night thinking about what could've happen if we had been stopped for some reason by the state troopers, and they found the shoebox plus more that he had in his suitcase. They would surely have charged us with drug dealing. The honeymoon was over, just like that. I refused to drive even one more mile with him on the highway, because I did not trust him. I told him this was going to be the honeymoon hotel. Once I calmed down, we did manage to do some sightseeing in the area. At the end of the week, we returned back to the real world of work and kids. The kids still didn't warm up to Tustee as quickly as I thought they would, and he quickly stopped trying to be a loving step-father.

...Not Again!!...

Much of the time after dinner, a power struggle took place between Tustee and the kids as to who was going to look at what on the big TV in the living room. Never mind that he and I had a smaller one in our bedroom. As it turned out, this remained the tone of the relationship between Tustee and the kids for the full duration of our "happily ever after" life, which lasted all of about one year and a half. Yes, that's right – about 18 months!! By that time, I learned that not only was my husband a "reefer addict", but also that he was still sexually involved with a married woman whom he had been seeing before we met. I learned that he smoked 'weed' all day like some people smoked cigarettes, and that he was not at work on all of the days that he was leaving home.

I was stunned, to say the least. How could I have married another man with a substance abuse problem, not to mention one who was also a womanizer! I felt like I had a 'garbage' magnet or something going on that kept drawing these "whorish" (excuse my expression) men to me. I went screaming and crying like a madwoman to Tustee's "God-father", an older man who was actually his father's long time friend from Jamaica. In the process of telling Rankine and his wife, Mommy, about the situation, Rankine began yelling at Tustee. "Man, how could you be so ungrateful to your wife, since she married you in spite of all your troubles you had with the law."

"Hooooooooooooooooold on little dog-gie! Did you just say 'troubles with the law'?" Let's just back wayyyyyyyyyyyyyyy the heck up!! My mind was racing like a freight train, and my mouth was hanging open almost down to my neck. Mommy was the first one to notice the look on my face, and she stopped her husband from yelling. She asked me whether I had known about Tustee being on probation. Long story, short – Tustee had come into this country legally as a temporary contract laborer to a citrus grower in Florida, but had run off illegally and come North with the assistance of a childhood friend. On top of that (as if anything more was needed), after Tustee had lived here in hiding for about six months, he was arrested while carrying a "package" for his friend which turned out to be a large amount of marijuana. Of course, Tustee swore to me "on [his] Mother" that he did not know what he was carrying, that he was just doing what he had been asked to do.

The truly astounding thing is that when he was arrested, the police never asked him for identification!! His friend paid the bail for him to be released; and in spite of going to court three times, Tustee was never asked to show identification. Talk about irony! He was ultimately released on eighteen months probation. Well, all of that had just happened six months prior to me meeting this man who it turned out *I knew really nothing about*!! He was still on probation for the entire time that we had dated and were preparing for marriage!!!!!!!!!!!!!!

What kind of madness is this! The longer I sat and listened, and the more I learned, the more livid I became. That was the first time that I learned that some men from other countries marry American women to make themselves eligible to get a "Green Card" (alien registration) from Immigration. Tustee needed to marry me (or some American) so he could stay here in the country, without fear of being deported. What a real life education that was for me all in one day. Tustee fell to his knees and admitted to Rankine and Mommy that he had never told me about either of his situations, and asked for my forgiveness. Right about that time, I would have loved to push him off the Empire State Building, much less forgive him.

What I really wanted to do was to leave his butt right there in their house, but realized that it was not their problem. Tustee and I drove back to the house in complete silence. When I reached home, I went to bed in the middle of the afternoon and cried myself to sleep in utter and complete bitterness. I woke up and realized that it was dark out, and all the kids had gone to bed. As I lay there, I realized that Tustee was standing in the doorway over my head, glaring at me and looking like he was half crazy. As I turned my back to him, he came to the bed and grabbed my arm; telling me that I was his wife and that he wanted me to do what wives are supposed to do with their husbands. As I sat up, I could hear myself almost growling at him that if he didn't take his hand off my arm, he was going to draw back a 'nub'. At this point, I was probably looking like a Tasmanian she-wolf or something, or at least that was how I was feeling. He drew back his hand and said something which blew me out of the water. "What must I do, sex one of your pickney?

"Waaaait a minute. Did I hear what I thought I heard?" I asked him what did he say, and he had the audacity (or stupidity) to repeat it again. For those who don't know what "pickney" means, it is a Jamaican term for children. I asked myself out loud, "Did this "N----" just ask me if he should have sex with one of my children?" By the time I answered myself, I was up out of the bed, half way across the room and throwing his clothes from the closet into the middle of the floor. I forgot all about it being night time, winter time, below freezing outside, dark, in the suburbs, and no buses running during the night for him to get back to the city. While I was throwing his clothes in the heap, he was reminding me of all the above, and crying like a banshee. Okay - the human part of me came back into focus, and just as I opened the front door to throw his stuff out the door, I felt a twinge of compassion. Long story short, the next morning on my way to work, I dropped Mr. Tustee off in the city at a relative's house that had a room for rent. We never lived together again.

Tustee had his Mother and family call me all the way from Jamaica to ask me to give him another chance. Hah! Because I had come to love his Mom and Dad, I told her for their sake I would not have his rump deported! She shared with me how they were struggling financially there in Jamaica, and how the money that Tustee sent was the main thing keeping them going. At least, that was one thing about him that I knew to be true – that he sent money home to them each payday.

After Tustee moved out, Ricardo began to phone me again. He stopped coming to the house shortly after Tustee and I were married, except to pick R.J. up for some weekend visits. His explanation was that he didn't want to create any unnecessary problems for me while the kids and I were adjusting to Tustee. When R.J. told Ricardo that Tustee was gone, Ricardo called and told me that he and his wife were not getting along either. He told me that he was very angry with me that I had not married him when he asked, and blamed me for both our "rotten" marriages. *Give me a break! Who was he kidding?* We had a major blowout argument, and I finally told him that as far as I was concerned, if he had kept his "parts" to himself in the first place, he and I might have been married to one another before that trifling Tustee or his crazy behind wife ever came along.

...Now What?...

In the year following all of the "Tustee drama", my whole world was thrown into complete upheaval by two major situations. First, I was fired from my job because of my unit manager. This, in spite of my previous multiple complaints to Human Resources. I had filed several complaints against the manager, for multiple incidents of biased treatment towards myself as well as towards African American children with whom we worked. I felt it was clearly racial discrimination, but HR didn't agree with me. They concluded that the conflict between me and the manager was a matter of different personality types, and that we "simply needed to learn how to work together." Finally, things came to a head, when the manager attempted to make me handle a young Black male in a manner which was clearly not appropriate; nor was it the normal written procedure for our unit. Since I was up to my "eye teeth" with her stuff, and I refused to play a part of mistreating this child, I refused to do what she gave me a direct order to do.

I walked off the unit and went directly to HR. While sitting there giving my verbal report to the representative, she informed me that I was terminated immediately!! My manager came in with a security guard, and I was escorted to pick up my personal belongings first; and then escorted to the front door!! What I was told was that I was given a directive which I should have followed, whether I agreed with it or not. Afterwards, I would have been able to file a complaint. *How completely ludicrous is that*!! Bottom line, I was terminated on the grounds of insubordination. By the grace and mercy of God, I managed to leave the building without physically assaulting the manager or the HR person – better yet, I managed to 'not' say out loud what I was thinking! In my mind, I had called them every obscene name I could think of, and had cut both of their hearts out! I felt like a flaming stick of dynamite ready to kill anyone who even looked at me.

Long story short, I filed a racial discrimination complaint with our State Labor Board, and after three long months of working part-time for an agency, I was awarded the decision in my favor. The hospital had to pay me every dime of my back pay; and offered me my job back. No way was I going back there to work! I figured they would put me back on the same unit with my prior manager. I would not be able to take care of my children from Death Row in prison for killing that woman, after gouging her eyes out first.

I realized that I actually needed to do something different in my career, so I decided to work at a residential school for mentally and physically challenged children. Hah! That was the beginning of a very short work experience. The Woods School was actually a cluster of buildings within a five mile or so radius, which housed children ranging from moderately to profoundly mentally and/or physically challenged. The locale of the school is in a rural area, and all of the buildings are beautiful to look at from the outside. The time of year was spring, and that was good because I was hired as the third shift Night Campus Nurse, which meant I would be outside much of the time. I was to go from building to building making routine rounds for medication administration; and was on call for emergencies, such as seizures, fevers or other medical crises during the night. It all sounded very "free" and romantic. Somehow or other, I must have had a brief episode of insanity or amnesia which caused me to forget that I was still afraid of the dark – especially the dark "outside" in strange places with lots of trees, bushes, living things, etc.

The two week orientation period went off without a hitch, because it was during the day and with a full complement of staff around. The actual problems didn't start until my night shift began. One of the first things I was informed I was responsible for was to "walk quietly" into buildings as I made my rounds, and to file an immediate written report on any staff member whom I found to be asleep. Not! This was not in the job description! These buildings were pretty much totally quiet at night and the staff was not allowed to watch TV. They could only listen to a radio with the volume almost on zero. For the first few nights, I was ready to go to sleep my own self every time I sat down for a few minutes to get a status report from the staff. Well, I learned to handle the "spying" challenge by making a lot of noise with my keys as I came into the buildings, and bumping into things as I entered. I never found anyone asleep. Ironically, this was the first complaint which I received from my supervisor after two weeks. During that time, there was only one major medical crisis, for which I had to go flying across to the other side of the campus. I ended up calling for EMT assistance. Strangely enough, it was not a resident, but one of the young college student staff members who had the incident. He had taken so many "No Doz" tablets with cups of coffee to stay awake, that he ended up having an uncontrolled grand mal seizure. Sorry – he ended up being fired anyhow. Bummer!

That incident rattled me a little, but after a couple days, I calmed down. Then, one night around 4:30 a.m., I received an urgent walkie talkie call from a staff member to come to the building where the very young, profoundly challenged children resided. It was difficult for me to even look at so many of these children because I wanted to cry just to see them; so I usually tried to do my rounds through there pretty quickly. Thus far, I had only treated them for routine medications, or aspirin suppositories for unrelenting fever. Well, on this particular night, the report came that a child was having grand mal seizures which were not responding to the regular medications. Of course, I was on the other side of the campus, so I put on my cape (imaginary) and went zooming over to the site. Oops! As I prepared to get out of my car, I saw the quick flash of something white moving through the bushes. Wait a minute! I turned the headlights on, and there between my car and the front door was a small herd of skunks – yes, you heard me right – skunks! Just then, the phone rang again, and the staff member was panicking because the child was still seizing, and it had been almost 5 minutes.

"I'mmmm coming!" I informed her, "Just lay the child in a safe position on her side with her face down towards the floor." I was so proud of myself that I could still think rationally, and had not driven away from the skunks yet, like a madwoman. "God, what do I do? Please don't let this child die, but if I get sprayed by these skunks, I certainly won't be able to go in the house without making everyone in there puke." (...me first, of course) Then I drove around to the back of the house, and guess what - the wild cousins to the "front yard" family were out back, as well. The staff person is calling me, screaming and crying by now, and I am freaking out my own self. Well – I had to do the unthinkable – I called and told the staff member to unlock the back door and get out of the way. Then, I took the alarm whistle which I wore around my neck at night, and jumped out of the car blowing the whistle like a maniac. The sudden loud noise startled the skunks so much; they all froze for a few seconds before raising that back tail. By the time they let loose, I dove through the back door like an old acrobat. Thank God, we were able to medicate and stabilize the child within a short amount of time. That was the beginning of the end of that job for me.

I must have been drunk or something when I took that position!! I was definitely having second thoughts, but decided to still try to stick it out, since it was only about 10 minutes from home. I lasted for another three nights! The nail was hammered into that coffin when I received a phone call in the middle of the night telling me that I should be on alert in case I was called to come up to the campsite of the school because a child "**_may_** get bitten by a snake." *Okay* – let me just get this straight – firstly, the camp is a part of the school that *I have not been told about.*

Secondly, the campsite is up in the woods about three miles off the main road. This was an area that I would routinely "turbo speed" past when driving along there at night because it was all trees and spooky. Thirdly, did you say "snake bite"? Because, if that is what you said, wouldn't there have to be a snake out there to make the bite?

I hung up the phone, prayed that God would take care of the children and whoever else was up at the camp, sat down and hand wrote my immediate resignation. *These people have got to be on dog food, sniffing airplane glue, drinking moonshine or something else to make them craaaazy;, if they think for one moment that I am going up some dark country road through snake country to treat a snake bite. And just who was going to come and find me and resuscitate me when the first snake crossed my path???*

Needless to say, I was back to job hunting the next day. Moving right along!! After a couple interviews, I was hired by one of the area Psychiatric Hospitals as a "floater". I floated to any unit which needed a nurse for the shift that I worked. Not particularly satisfied with floating, I was more than happy to have a "safe" job, inside and away from all kinds of creeping livestock. Plus, it was during the daylight hours. Oh Hallelujah!!

...Second Major Event...

While I was in the midst of my career crisis, I received a phone call from Ricardo asking me to meet him at his niece's house to talk about something important. Oh my God! I instantly knew in my gut that something major was wrong, but there was no way that I could be prepared to hear what he would tell me.

Ricardo told me that he had slipped on some soap in the bathroom at work a few days earlier, had hit his head and side on one of the sinks, and had been knocked unconscious. As a result, he had been taken to an area hospital, where x-rays had been taken of his ribs, chest and head. While looking at his chest x-rays, one of the doctors noticed some abnormalities, and had requested that Ricardo be seen by a pulmonary specialist. Ricardo had been admitted for some more diagnostic evaluations, and their findings were mind numbing – he was diagnosed with Multiple Myeloma, a form of bone cancer!! *My mind started racing a mile a minute – "What did you say!! This is not something to joke about! You're always trying to be a jokester, but this is not funny. I should slap your face for dragging me all this way to tell me something so absurd. If you wanted to see me, you could have just asked without going to such extremes!"*

Just as I was working up a real good tongue lashing to lay on him, I looked at him and saw tears running down his face. Then I knew in my heart this was no joke. I suddenly felt like someone had punched me in the belly. The feeling grew worse as I began to search my memory for what I knew of Multiple Myeloma from my nursing school days. My mind starting zooming, *"How did this happen? Are you going to die? What are the doctors going to do? How long do they think you've had it?"* I could hear a voice sounding like me, asking a barrage of questions, as I thought in my mind, "Wow! Whoever that is talking sounds just like me." It felt like my lips were shut tight, while I was hearing this "sound alike" voice talking. Then my heart was beating like a drum in my chest just before the room started spinning. Then I realized that Ricardo was hugging me tight, and I couldn't stop trembling so hard it felt like the floor had a vibrator in it. I finally talked myself into taking some deep breaths, and getting some control. According to Ricardo, the tests revealed the Multiple Myeloma was advanced, with the primary sites being in his ribs; with metastasis to several locations including his hip, legs and hips. He was told he would need immediate surgery to place a rod in one of his legs and hip. What he had been thinking was muscle spasms for several months, had actually been the demineralization of the affected bones. The doctors expressed amazement that his bones had not spontaneously shattered as he walked and jogged on them every morning.

    To make matters worse, Ricardo told me that he and his wife had separated a few weeks before. She was upset with him for being home from work for weeks complaining of unbearable "muscle spasms". She accused him of malingering just to avoid working, and had asked that he move out. He had moved in with his niece just the week earlier; and had only been back to work for one day when the mishap in the bathroom occurred. I had been so focused on my own issues that I had not realized it had been more than a month since Ricardo had been to visit the kids and me. Now, I felt soooooo guilty and selfish. How could I not have noticed that something was wrong with him, as close as we were? He was my very best friend, and I still had a real special love for him, womanizer or whatever.

    We went back to the house together and told the kids. R.J.'s best buddy, who lived right next door to us, had lost his father a few years earlier from the same condition. When we told the kids, R.J. remembered the name from talking to his friend; so there was no way to keep the seriousness of the situation from them. Our house became like a depressed cave for a few days, with no one wanting to leave Ricardo even to go to school or work. It felt like we needed to stand guard over him to protect him against this "intruder".

About a week later, Ricardo began a series of surgeries and grueling treatments to combat the illness. It was so hard to see him walking with a cane, and wincing when he walked. Somehow the fact that he was able to get up and walk gave us all a sense of hope. Because he was a man who lifted weights prior to being ill, and had been in excellent physical condition, he did not develop a look of "sickness" over the next year that followed; even as he went through a series of chemotherapy and radiation. Sure, there were times when he was unusually quiet, but then he would bounce back quickly to his normal jokester self. Many months later, as I thought back to those days, I realize that my kids and I didn't fully understand how sick he was, because he didn't look or act like it. He was "Ricardo", our tower of strength. He had always been there for us, in spite of everything. He and I talked about both of us getting a divorce and marrying each other. We decided that we really didn't want to take a chance on losing each other to someone else again. Once was enough.

Following months of treatment, the doctor's report came back, and the lesions were slowly starting to respond to the chemo and radiation. However, there was another alarming concern. There had been so much damage to his bones, that his calcium level dropped to a level which began to affect his heart. He was hospitalized several times within a couple weeks, but after receiving IV medications, seemed to regroup and was discharged.

I was particularly stressed one specific week in May, working several double shift days of 16 hours to make ends meet. During those days, I talked to Ricardo a couple times a day over the phone, and he was his usual jovial and flirtatious self. I came home one night late, and he called me near midnight, telling me what all he was going to do for me and the kids when he was done with all of his treatments. I jokingly fussed at him a little for being awake and on the phone so late. I asked him where the prison guard nurses were while he was flirting on the phone. He laughed and said he just wanted to hear my voice. Then, he became quiet and said, "Girl, I outran that old death one more time. He thought he had me for sure this time because my heart stopped twice today, but he couldn't hold me." Then he laughed, and we giggled for a few minutes. I told him, "Good night, I'll call you in the morning." He made a long drawn out kiss sound over the phone; and we played, "you hang up first – no, you hang up first" for a few minutes before we agreed to hang up together on the count of three.

That was my last time ever talking to my "best friend"; the man I thought I would surely live the rest of my life with. He didn't seem almost 18 years older than me. The next morning, on May 20, 1987, I tried to phone him before I left home early. I thought he was still asleep when he didn't answer. I was in the cafeteria at work at lunchtime, when I heard someone call my name. As I turned around, with my food tray in my hand, I saw the Nursing Director's secretary walking towards me with a pink message paper in her hand.

As I heard the words, "Your niece April called…," I raised my hand to say "No". As the word was coming out of my mouth, I heard her say, "Ricardo died this morning". The next sound I heard was a woman screaming off at a distance. I remember thinking, "Oh my God, why doesn't somebody help that poor woman, she sounds like she is in pain." As reality began to return, I realized it was me who was screaming, as I was standing in front of the elevator jumping up and down like a wounded child, and then saying, "No, No, No, No, No…" One of my co-workers grabbed me and pulled me to her, hugging me tight until I stopped screaming and was just whimpering like a wounded puppy, gasping for air. Even now, as I remember that day so clearly, I still remember experiencing the greatest pain and emptiness that I had ever felt up until that time.

Then, in one coherent moment, I remembered my son R.J. He was just twelve years old at the time, and extremely close to his Dad. I had to get home before he came in from school – God forbid that someone should call and say something to him before I could get home. I thought of going to the school to get him, but decided to just go home and be there to tell all of the kids as they came in from school. As each of my three youngest daughters came in from school one by one, I told them. We would start bawling and wailing all over again. By the time my son came in last, I was ready to just go somewhere and lie down and die my own self. It's amazing how differently males respond to things, versus females. As I told him, he sat there and stared at me for a few minutes. Then he stood up and went into his room and closed the door.

My heart was about to burst, but I didn't know what to do – screaming and crying I could handle; that was my "female" language! This "male" silence, I didn't know what to do with. I sat there in one spot for what seemed like hours, waiting and trying to figure out what to do. Suddenly, I heard the most gut wrenching sobs I had ever heard, and I realized the sound was coming from my son's room. All I could do was go and sit on the side of his bed, and pray while he cried it out. Somehow, the next few days are like a blur in my mind, although I do remember sleeping much of the time. I felt a kind of "tiredness" I had never experienced, and I didn't know what to do to get over it. I remember the girls taking care of things, and I don't remember if they went to school or not.

April called and gave us the information about the upcoming funeral service, and somehow we made it there – I vaguely remember driving there. The only thing I remember clearly about that day is that as the casket was being lowered, I looked up in time to see my son trying to jump into the grave. I yelled and one of Ricardo's brothers caught R.J. in mid-air, yelling, "I want to go with my Dad."

I don't remember how we got back home; I guess I drove. What I do have a keen memory of is my anger with Ricardo for dying and leaving me here. To make matters worse, he left me here alone with a son. After five female children, what the heck did I know about how to handle a boy? For a long time afterwards, my first thought when I woke up in the morning was, "I have to call Ricardo and tell him…" My second thought would be, "Oh God, Ricardo's not there anymore", and then a silent scream would go off in my heart all over again.

...Bitter and Sweet...

It was the spring of 1987, and a bittersweet time in our home as we prepared for Esther's upcoming Senior Prom and High School graduation. Again, she did us real proud. There was such a mixture of excitement and sadness in our home, that at times, I felt a little schizophrenic. Ricardo's loss ushered me into a very challenging period in my life, in which the very core of my faith in God was tested. There were many weeks and months when I was very angry and bitter with life, and subsequently with God. Nothing made sense to me, and I was just "sick and tired" of feeling "sick and tired."

My son's behavior changed drastically, so that he became an instant "problem student". He lost all of his desire to do schoolwork which he previously loved; and he began to seclude himself in his room away from his friends. I sought out professional counseling for him quickly, which did seem to help him a little. However, his lack of interest in school lasted right through until he graduated from high school. Time will not even permit me to tell in this book all of the methods and interventions I had to use to get him through high school to graduation a few years later, including threatening to kill him quite a few times.

After Ricardo's death, I no longer had the heart or courage to stay in the big single home in the suburbs any more. Tustee had a friend who had a duplex apartment house in the city, so I rented both apartments from him, and moved us back into the city. I figured it would be helpful to all of us to be back closer to our biological family, as well as to our church family and friends. Now, do you want to talk about culture shock? I had to retrain my brain to stop leaving my car doors unlocked; not to even mention how many items were stolen from the kids which they left outside on the steps. Then, there were also the issues of the "roughneck" boys who liked my daughters; the totally different school environment for R.J.; and the fish market across on the corner with a smell that caused the entire area to smell like stinking fish.

During this time, my oldest daughter was out in her own apartment; and my second and third daughters were in college, and staying on campus. As for me, I changed my job from the Psychiatric Hospital after about a year, and decided to try my hand as a Home Visiting Nurse for a while. At first, the flexibility of the hours, and not being bound indoors all day was very appealing. However, the glamour of all that began to wear off after a few months of completing mountains of mandatory paperwork every evening. You would think I had learned my lesson from that last "outdoors" job – but, "Ohhhh No", not Ms. Die-hard.

The job was pretty challenging at times, especially because many of the patients in the area I was assigned to lived in less than comfortable situations; with some that I would call even downright disgusting. Firstly, you have to remember that I am one of the most squeamish people you could ever meet. Secondly, couple that with the fact that I am really more of a 'suburbanite' at heart – and not really comfortable in crowded urban areas.

I was definitely not comfortable to have to carry mace for protection, or to carry my nursing supplies in a big pocketbook instead of a medical bag so I wouldn't be 'mugged' for the syringes I carried! I lasted for about a good eight months. During that time, I cried almost every night because of the things I saw. I was sent to change the dressings on one diabetic patient with an open ulcer on his leg that was almost big enough to put your hand into – Ugh! He lived alone, and was relying on a neighborhood kid to go to the store for him daily to buy him sandwiches – and they wondered why his sugar was out of control! Thank God, we were able to get him connected with a senior citizen food service for homebound people. I also took care of a husband and wife who were both my patients, he with cancer and she with uncontrolled diabetes with multiple complications. Each one was in a hospital bed, in separate adjoining rooms, in a house which was indescribably filthy. They would talk out loud to each other, through the walls. They loved to tell me how long they had been married, and how they had never spent one night away from each other. If one had to be hospitalized, the other would go and stay the night with them. They depended on a young adult son to assist them, but he would disappear for days at a time, leaving them laying in their own waste and unfed. After a few visits to see them, I had to report them to an adult abuse agency, who hospitalized them each, in rooms on the same floor. They both died soon after, without ever leaving the hospital again, leaving me heartsick and depressed for weeks.

There were so many other tragic cases, but the one that finally caused me to give up the job was when I was sent into a public housing development which was particularly known for heavy drug abuse and violence, day or night. The patient was a gunshot wound victim who needed his wound dressings changed daily – the problem was that the nurses were supposed to have a security guard to escort them to his home for protection. The "rent-a-cop" security guards failed to show up several times. The patient's dressings were unchanged because he couldn't do them himself, and his family was angry with him and uncooperative. On the day that I was assigned to go, it was overdue by 3-4 days. The security guard was supposed to meet me at the office, but again failed to show, claiming a mix-up with the time. While I was sitting at the office waiting for the guard the patient called about ten times or more in tears. I made a decision to go alone, which I did. Thanks to God's favor, I walked past a huge gang of boys with no problem. However, that was it for me. I was done with Home Visiting Nursing!!

...Trying To Find My Way...

The same time that I was trying to find my niche in my career; my personal life was chaotic. I had regained some of my confidence and faith in God again; deciding that He was "not the darkness", but the "light in the midst of the darkness." On the personal side, the problem by this time was that I was totally tired of being by myself, but was very untrusting of guys. I started going out on the weekends occasionally, with my sister and girlfriends. I came to realize that I really liked Caribbean and Reggae music, and would spend almost the entire evening on the dance floor, either with a partner or alone. We had a couple different West Indian or African clubs that we would visit, and I found that moving to the music made me feel happy and free. I drank occasionally, but it wasn't really my style; I preferred just dancing.

There was one major event which occurred during that time which shook my very foundation (or maybe just my ego). Tirzah told me she was going to have a baby. *Say whaaaaaaaaaaaat?? I am still trying to get used to having high school graduates for children, and now you want to tell me that I am going to be a grand... what???????????* I wanted to barf!! Well, I set her straight, right up front – "I am too young to be called Grand-mom, so the baby will just have to call me "Mom-Mom". Soon afterwards, my first little grand-daughter was born! Wow!! I fell in love with her, and decided that it was not the end of the world.

...Anything For You Babe...

Soon afterwards, a girlfriend and I were standing outside of an auto mechanic's shop, where I was having some work done on my car. I heard a car horn blowing, but as I turned to look, I realized I didn't know the guy. I turned back to talking to my friend. The horn continued blowing, and a couple minutes later, I heard the driver say, "Excuse me, can I speak to you for a minute." The mechanic looked outside, spoke to the guy as someone he knew, and told me the guy was talking to me.

I made it a habit to not speak to strangers, and especially to guys who blew their horns at women. As far as I was concerned, that was like the epitome of being 'Ghett-O', with a capital "G" and a separate "O" on the end for emphasis. On top of all that, he was driving a little Volkswagen Beetle car – not even a full-sized, "real" car. I am 5'7", and I figured that a man with a VW bug was probably only 5 feet maximum. As far as I was concerned, he definitely was about a foot too short, and probably broke on top of it. Certainly, he couldn't be of any help to me or my children, always foremost in my mind. All of this ran through my mind while I was still talking to my friend, with my back to the horn-blower. I purposely refused to look around, until my girlfriend said, "Oh my God, he's getting out of the car." As I turned to see if I needed to run into the shop, I watched in total amazement as the man started standing up to get out of the car. The thing that amazed me was that it seemed like it took him a good 4-5 minutes just to stand up straight. When he finally stood up fully, I could see he was one of the tallest men I had ever personally seen!! I later learned that he was 6'6".

Whaaaaaat? I was so floored watching him 'unfold' that I was still standing in the same spot, when I realized that he had crossed the street and was right in front of me, with his head back laughing. I was totally flustered, and before I could regroup, the mechanic came out to tell me that my car had to be left with him over the weekend. The dealer had to order a part, and the earliest possible time for me to get my car would hopefully be on Monday. It was Friday at that time. I told him that was not what I needed to hear, because I was supposed to take my son the next day up to an overnight camp in the Poconos, about 3 hours driving time. The mechanic had no loaners, and I had no extra money to rent a car. As I was saying all of this out loud, the "giant" said, "I can drive you and your son to where you need to go."

I laughed hysterically for about 5 minutes before I was able to pull myself together. Then, for some unexplainable reason, I asked him if he would really do that. I was desperate to get R.J. to camp, and hated to disappoint him. I asked the giant why he would do that for me, a complete stranger. He then said something that would often be repeated for a few years to come, "Anything for you, Babe." The "giant" introduced himself to me as Harley, and then told me that I was actually standing in front of his Mom's house. I was immediately fascinated by his Jamaican accent, which reminded me so much of Ricardo, not to mention that he definitely was not too hard on the eyes either. (smile)

Because I couldn't think of any immediate alternative, I accepted his offer, while trying to imagine how even he and I were going to get into that car, much less R.J. and his duffle bag. We exchanged numbers, the mechanic drove me home, and I prayed half of the night that the guy would really show up the next morning. Sure enough, I heard a car horn outside at the agreed time, but when I looked out of the window, I didn't see the "bug". I went back and sat down, until Harley rang the doorbell. I introduced him to R.J., and took a deep breath, thinking I was going to really look like a fool to my son, as I squeezed into the car; but it would be worth it to get him to camp. He was soooo excited to be going!

We all came out of the house, and as I was about to ask Harley where his "car" was, he put R.J.'s bags into a huge beautiful metallic green Lincoln Town Car parked in front of my house! I realized that was the car whose horn I heard earlier. Long story short, the VW had just been a 'loaner' from the dealer, while Harley's car was being serviced by the dealer the day before. I don't think my feet actually even touched the steps as I floated down, while trying not to start a Praise Dance on the front pavement. Needless to say, Harley and R.J. had great fun at my expense all the way to the Poconos, about my facial expression as I came down the front steps.

That was the beginning of the next phase in my life and in the lives of my children. Harley and I developed an almost inseparable relationship for the following five years. In no time, we became totally enmeshed in one another's lives; even though we each came into the relationship with a lot of baggage. For now, suffice it to say, to me Harley was like the positive traits of Michael and Ricardo combined, with the added bonus of being very kind, considerate and affectionate.

...Next!...

After leaving the Visiting Nurses, I decided that I needed a break from nursing for a bit. I decided to start two home-based businesses, a housecleaning service and a home-based day care. It didn't take long before both businesses were doing very well. I had a couple friends whom I hired to do the cleaning, and worked at it myself part-time also. The bulk of my time was spent with picking up, caring for and returning home my "little darlings" from the daycare (six total, with three in diapers). That is one point in my life when I can truly look back and say "I MUST HAVE LOST MY COMPLETE MIND!" First of all, I never should have agreed to be caretaker and transportation too. By the time I picked everyone up, arrived back home, carried five of them (1 at a time with belongings) up the 20 plus steps on the front of my house, and unwrapped snowsuits, blankets, etc., - my body felt like my day's work should be done.

Between feedings, burpings, poopings, messes, and catfights, I slept extremely well every night; only to get up the next day to do it all over again!! Well, that was the shortest-lived career path of my life. (screeeam) The proverbial straw that broke the camel's (mine) back was the day that I had PMS at turbo force. All but one of the babies had diarrhea and had puked and cried all day. By the end of the day, when Harley came in, he found me sitting in the middle of the living room floor bawling loudly, with all of the babies hanging off me and crying louder than me. After standing there staring at all of us incredulously for a few minutes, he said "This is it. If you don't give those babies back to their Momma's and give them a termination notice, I will have you admitted to the Psych Ward for your own sake." Not that he was my boss or anything, but that was one sure time that I heartily cooperated with him without putting up a fuss! As I dropped each snotty-nosed kid home, and told their parents they had one week to find an alternative, I felt layers of my brain cells returning to normal. Oh, Hallelujah!!

By this time, I still had a few regular commercial and residential customers for the cleaning business. However, I decided to pass those few customers on to someone else. I needed to get back to the "peace and quiet" of a regular full-time job, with normal hours. Shortly afterwards I found a professional nursing job that was not 'clinical', and required no direct patient or doctor contact. I was employed as a "Clinical Data Analyst", with a CRO (Clinical Research Organization). Our company did Data Management and Safety Analysis of patient data for large pharmaceutical companies. The salary was much less than the hospital or visiting nurses; but there was no "blood and yuck", no critters or gangsters, and best of all, there were no weekend hours required.

The year was 1988, which was a year of amazing events in our family. First of all, my first grandchild, a girl was born in February! Then, it was spring and coming up on the time for my baby girl's Senior Prom and high school graduation!! In addition to those things, Lisa was also my first child to be graduating from College. I was a doubly proud Mom all over again, plus now a Mom-Mom! Wow! I still had problems wrapping my mind around the fact that I had kids old enough to graduate from high school, much less college. Now, on top of that, I had a granddaughter? Where had all the years gone?

...Where's My Shotgun?...

Before I knew it, I had to change my job again. I loved that job, but had to go back into clinical nursing after two and a half years because of financial need, with Doretha and Rose in college at the same time. In hardly any time, I was back to working sixty to seventy hours a week again. I continued working in the hospital until each of my daughters graduated. During the few short years after Ricardo's death, my family and I moved three times – primarily because we had such a difficult time adjusting back into the city neighborhoods. Harley spent many of the nights with me, because he knew that I was uncomfortable. That's when he began to insist that I find a house to buy, and that he would do whatever it would take to make sure it was secure.

R.J.'s behavior had become more of a problem in school; not so much because of his acting out, but rather a lack motivation to complete his school work. I tried everything I knew from loss of privileges, to grounding, to holding his allowance. None of it seemed to faze him in the least. One day, I received a call at work to inform me that R.J. had been absent for quite a few days, on days that he should have been in school. I was livid! I went home early from work, only to have my neighbor meet me at the door to tell me that she had been seeing my son going back into the house often, after I had gone to work. As if that was not bad enough, he also had a girl that he was sneaking into the house with him!

I began to have flashbacks of the "beat down" episode I had with Tirzah several years prior. I went in the house and sat there waiting for R.J. to come in. Sure enough, he showed up at the right time as if he had been in school, and had a young lady with him. I asked her to leave, and confronted him about the days he had hookied from school. He sat there and stared at me, which made me want to jump on him and pull his eyebrows out one by one, before slapping him into a stupor.

I restrained myself as I thought of Ricardo's passing, and thinking maybe this was contributing to this boy acting out. Then I told him what the neighbor told me about him and the girl coming into the house during the day. Well! That got a spark out of him, as he sarcastically informed me that he was "in love" with the young lady, and he was old enough to date, "if I want to." I gritted my teeth together, as I envisioned myself pulling his tongue out; and as I remembered that I was still angry with Ricardo for dying and leaving me with a "boy child" alone (as if he had a choice). I reminded R.J. that he was only fifteen years old, and that dating was not allowed in our family until sixteen. He informed me that was 'girl stuff', and that he was a guy. Okay -now I'm starting to feel tingling in my fingers, as I have visions of myself punching him in his mouth.

I decided to change the subject. I asked him how old the girl was. He looked at me with a twisted smile on his face and said, "21". I know that I did not hear him correctly! Let me ask him again; "How old is the young lady?" This time, I was sure that I heard him clearly say, '21'. I asked him for her phone number, as visions of 'the she-devil' who was trying to pervert my baby boy danced in my head. At the same time, I was trying to remember if I still had any 'holy oil' from church left over anywhere in the house that I could pour on him. This was serious!!

After he whined about not having her number, and I threatened to break his neck and do him other bodily harm, he suddenly found it. I called her home, and learned that she was indeed 21, and a college student. Even more absurd, I learned that she still lived at home with her parents, and that her Dad was a Pastor. He explained to me that his daughter had been "wild and uncontrollable" for a long time and now that she was grown, there was nothing more he could do with her. I took a looong slooooooow deep breath so that I would not offend the man of the cloth, by the words that were on the tip of my tongue. Then, I explained to him that since he felt there was nothing he could do with his daughter, I would help him and his daughter. I explained that the next time his 'adult' daughter was seen with my fifteen year old 'minor' son, or if I even heard that someone saw the two of them together; she would spend some time in jail for contributing to the delinquency of a minor. "Good day, Sir." That was the last I ever saw or heard of her. Wow! I deserved a peace medal or something for how well behaved I was!!

...Does Anybody Here Speak "M-a-l-e"?...

The next few years were tumultuous to say the least (that's not saying, of course, that the earlier years had been a piece of cake either). R.J. grew more insolent, withdrawn and preoccupied with nothing that didn't have a music note attached to it. Throughout his young life, from the age of three years old, he had demonstrated a natural gift for playing drums. He was often asked to play at our church and also at other churches from time to time. He became a star on his band in Middle School because of his drum playing. During his last year in Middle School, he did barely enough work academically to not fail. I pulled him off the band as a way to discipline him, but then I watched him slip into a level of depression and detachment that unnerved me. Per the request of his music teacher, I allowed R.J. to travel with the school band to Canada for an international competition. Sure enough, they brought home a medal, with R.J.'s lead.

By then, R.J. was a full blown adolescent, and I had to pray every day for grace not to give him away to someone in Japan. He was insolent, belligerent, unkempt, disheveled, and 'without a clue' of the world around him. No amount of screaming, fussing, cajoling, threatening or allowance holding had one bit of impact on him. I even paid a heap of money to send him to the Sylvan Learning Center, which was supposed to be able to help him refocus his thinking on academics. The only thing that was refocused was the thousands of dollars out of my pocket, and into their cash register. The only time when R.J. would come "close" to paying attention was when he was playing music at church. Everyone there thought he was the best thing since sliced bread – but that's because they didn't have to live with him.

His sisters accused me of being the wicked witch of the north; and Lisa even went so far as to tell me she felt he would do better living with her. Everybody had an opinion of what I was doing wrong. One day when I had it up to my eyeballs, I called and asked Lisa if she was serious about him living with her. "Oh yeah, we'll do just fine. You don't have to worry; he and I understand each other." Hah! They lasted less than a month before she called me screaming like a madwoman in the phone about how "trifling and uncooperative he was." Not only that, but that he was not her son, and that she didn't have to live with his nastiness, so I should come to bring him home. I laughed and cried all the way to her house.

In the meantime, Harley was bugging me ceaselessly about him wanting me to own my own house. He absolutely tuned out my feelings that I was moving closer and closer to an "empty nest", and had no real desire to have a house of my own. In fact, I was just counting down the days that all of my children would be grown and gone, and I really wasn't interested in having to maintain a property. Harley was not trying to accept that, and bugged me to no end until finally I did start looking around in the area One thing I did not want to do was to transfer R.J. into another school district, since he only had two more years to go before he would graduate from high school. After a couple months, I found a vacant house not far from where we lived which caught my eye. The owner turned out to be a sick elderly man who agreed to sell it to me for a nominal amount of money, once I agreed to assume the delinquent taxes.

Harley was happier than a "pig in slop", because the house needed a lot of renovation; and he was a budding general contractor. He made the house his pet project – stripping all the walls, knocking out some walls, replacing all the electrical wiring and plumbing, installing new windows throughout, and then putting in an all new interior. We moved in together with R.J. and for a while, things went pretty smoothly. I resigned myself that

R.J. would somehow come through his adolescent years, and all I could do was pray that he would survive a mother who wanted to kill him half of the time. He and Harley had a neutral relationship; cordial but not really buddy-buddy. Things were pretty good between Harley and I. We spent a lot of time doing things together, and I began to think "just maybe", it would become permanent. By then, I was going to church less and less often and had begun to spend more time on the weekends hanging out with girlfriends. Harley was an amateur Reggae disc jockey, and I would often accompany him to various Jamaican nightclubs for parties and other events. During the few hours that I was on the dance floor, it seemed like I was away on a little mini-vacation away from the tension and stress of home, bills, and responsibilities. It didn't matter if I danced with someone or alone, just the movement of dancing to the music gave me a sense of freedom.

By the grace of God, and one million threats, we managed to get R.J. graduated out of high school. It was so awesome to see him go off on his Senior Prom, and go down the aisle for his graduation. I think my family screamed louder than anyone else in the place. I felt like I had survived a full-blown war. Lisa had moved out of state, down south during R.J.'s last school year, and they had made up with one another. The week after graduation, the two of them asked for permission for R.J. to come south with Lisa for the summer as a graduation gift. I consented, and for the first time in over twenty-five years, I felt like I could take a really deep breath, and exhale.

...Yet, Again...

A few months later, Harley proposed to me, and we began talking about marriage; but for some reason that I couldn't understand, I began to feel uneasy concerning him. There were only the two of us home now, and there should have been a sense of peace. However, it seemed that every little thing would end up in a disagreement between us. He had never stayed out all of the time we lived together, but all of a sudden, whenever we argued, he would storm out to go to his Mom's house.

Then, he began trying to convince me to have a child for him. I was dumbfounded! Harley had five children from previous relationships, and I had just finished raising my sixth child – what was wrong with that picture? Of course, I tried to show him how between the two of us, we already had more than enough children, and four of his children were still much younger than mine. Not to mention the fact that by that time, I had two grandchildren thanks to Tirzah and Esther. I wanted to go forward, not backwards. Hello! I was just starting to have visions of him and me taking some cruises, and travelling to some romantic places. The more I tried to show him how unrealistic it would be for us to have a child, the more he begged and tried to convince me. One other major point that I tried to help him understand is that I had already been a single parent for many years; how was I to know that he would be there until a child reached adulthood. I was feeling more and more confused, and he was becoming more and more insistent.

This power struggle went on for months with me getting increasingly uneasy in my heart. Harley began going out on the weekends alone, and R.J. decided to stay down south and take a job with a gospel singing group. I found myself alone more and more often. What was really bizarre is Harley's spell of hanging out alone was short lived, before he switched up and went back to his old pattern of spending all of his time with me. But, I began to have disturbing and vivid dreams, which provoked me to play detective. It's amazing how out of a myriad of numbers he had in his wallet because of the general contracting work he did; somehow I zoomed right in on a particular one. Things turned ugly really quickly. I didn't confront him, but I made the foolish choice of calling her. I lied and told her Harley and I were married, and she informed me that she was pregnant for him. I still didn't say anything to him.

The next day was my birthday, and we agreed to take the day off from work and spend it together. Astoundingly, Harley took me to a jeweler in Center City that day and bought me a beautiful engagement ring!! I began to think to myself that maybe I had imagined the entire phone call the day before, with the "girlfriend". We hung out all day, and had an absolutely fun and romantic day. We returned home laughing and talking, when his beeper rang. He checked the beeper and excused himself to go upstairs to make a call. I knew something was really wrong because of how long he stayed. About a half hour later, he came downstairs with some of his clothes packed in his suitcase, and told me he was leaving! The call had been from the woman, and he had the nerve to stand there and accuse me of being a sneak and a liar, and that he could no longer trust me! *Now, would you please tell me what kind of total insanity is that?*

My mind and mouth started going a million miles a minute: *"We live together – you get another woman pregnant – you propose to me and buy me an engagement ring -and then stand here and accuse me of being a sneak and a liar!! You told me you would always love me and be there for me no matter what. You promised!! We have over five years of living together, and you come down these steps in less than a half hour with your clothes (and my heart) packed in a couple suitcases. How could you??"*

By this time, I was in the kitchen throwing dishes at him, and finally I lost sight of how big he was, and ran up on him like he was my little boy, swinging like a madwoman!! He kept trying to back me up, but I was relentless – every hurt and wound that I had ever received from a man came up in my gut, and all I could scream over and over at the top of my lungs was, *"You told me you loved me and you promised, you promised."*

I remember being like an octopus, swinging both hands and feet at him, until he reached out and slapped me. The problem was his huge hand slapped me just as I was opening my mouth to scream at him again, and the way his hand hit my jaw, it unhinged my jaw! All of a sudden, it seemed like things were moving in slow motion, like a dream. In an instant when I went to try to speak, and I couldn't get my jaw to move, I tried to scream, but couldn't get a sound out. In a flash of a few seconds, I thought to myself that with all I had been through with guys in my life, I had never been physically abused until now!!

Harley looked at me and realized something was wrong and reached for me, and I started swinging again. Within a few seconds, by the mercy and grace of God, my jaw relocated itself again and then I tasted blood inside of my mouth. Then, I became hysterical, screaming at the top of my lungs. I started swinging at him again. Harley had tears in his eyes, and was pleading with me to just stop, and let him leave before I made him hurt me. *"Make you hurt me! You mean ripping my guts out is not enough."* Finally, he backed his way to the front door, and left, leaving all his clothes behind. I lay in the floor and cried myself to sleep. This was all too surreal. This level of pain in my heart was overwhelming to my mind, and I wasn't sure if I would actually be able to recover this time, without going really crazy.

...Post Traumatic Stress...

A couple days later, Harley came to get his things, accompanied by his Mom. I guess he wasn't sure how I would act. By then, I was too numb to react. *What was it about me that caused people who appear to really love me, to move away or to leave? Why can't I find someone who really means it when they say they love me? Why is it that when you've done all you can do, and you have given it your all and all, but it is still never good enough?*

As I went through that following week shut up in my house, only allowing one of my girl friends to call and check on me, a change took place in my heart. I decided to never again trust or care for another human being, no matter who they are. It would be several years before I allowed God's love to break through my wall of stone and anger. Ironically, within two weeks, Harley called and begged my forgiveness. He told me that he had not meant to get caught up with the woman, and that he didn't know her well. She had come to a club where he was D.J. one night, and he decided to have a little fling. He was angry with me because I refused to have a baby with him. Amazingly, he said that made him feel that I might walk out on him one day. Go figure!!

He said he had only gone out with her a few times, and that he broke it off and came back to make it work with me. Then, she called and told him she was pregnant, that it was definitely his, and she couldn't live without him. He had been trying to keep it a secret while trying to figure out what to do about her. He asked me to go for counseling with him to a Pastor and her husband, who we both knew. He wanted us to work things out, get married and move on with our lives. I agreed to try, and we went for several sessions. Things were not the same. Harley described the situation perfectly one day in a session when he said, "I don't know how to fix things, but it seems like something inside of her (me) is broken and can't be fixed."

The problem was that the "something" reached to the very core of my gut, and was called "trust". It wasn't easy to come by in the first place, and now that it had been so harshly broken, I didn't know how to get it back. It seemed they didn't know how to help me. In my heart of hearts, I still loved Harley, and on some level, I probably always will because during the time that things were good between us, I was assured in my heart that we truly had a genuine love for each other – we were truly happy for a good while. We tried to get back together a couple times after that, partly because we didn't know how to live without each other. We were truly soul-tied, if you know what that means.

One thing that came out of all that pain was that when I finally regrouped enough to start going out of the house again, I felt so empty inside that I knew I needed something more than partying and dancing could give me. I realized that when I went to the club and danced, it no longer held the same sense of joy and freedom for me. I tried to cover the pain by going out with different guys, but afterwards, I still felt empty; and then I would feel angry and bitter for days. I went through a period of time when I began to dress very provocatively, wearing tight, short clothes. I bought my first Chevy Camaro, and for the next several years would only drive flashy and fast sports cars. Although my natural hair was a nice length, I had a few extensions added. I woke up one morning mad, after spending the night with Harley.

I looked in the mirror and said to myself, "*I am sick of fake men, fake hair and fake everything else.*" I went into the closet, took R.J.'s hair clippers and shaved all the hair off my head except the long bangs in the front!! My hair was only about ½ inch long all over my head. Then I smathered it down with gel, put on some big hoop earrings and went to work, daring anybody to say anything negative about it. Would you believe that the hairstyle was a big hit, and I ended up wearing that style for about 5 years?

It was my way of saying, *"What you see is who I choose to be. Like it or lump it, I don't care what anyone thinks."* I remember when Tirzah was married in 1993; I wore a beautiful designer baby pink two piece skirt suit. The problem was that the skirt was so short that I couldn't sit down for the whole wedding and reception without covering up myself with some guy's jacket. Trust me; I was definitely not Popeye's girlfriend, "Olive Oil" either; if you get my drift. *Thank God for deliverance*!!

...Will Wonders Never Cease?...

R.J. came back to the city after a couple years away, and enrolled into one of the College of the Arts in our area. Can you imagine that? The guy that I had to drag through high school kicking and screaming actually returned to school on his own!! He made us proud one more time by graduating with honors; and reconnected with a church in our area, where he played the drums. As for me, the only time I was going to church during that time was if there was some kind of special program going on that my kids were involved with. I also decided by then to move out of my house and make it a family home. I couldn't stand being in there without Harley, and I wasn't comfortable to let him move back in. I would go out with him once in a while, but we were each doing our own thing separately, as well. The hurt was still too real for me to get past it.

I moved out into a two bedroom apartment not far from the house, and R.J and Esther moved into my home with my first grandson who was a couple years old by that time. I began to slowly come out of my anger and extreme hurt; and I began to start getting out more and more, especially on the weekends. As I began to feel better about myself and life in general, little by little, I would go out with my friends and socialize on Saturdays. There were actually a couple times while at the Jamaican club, and after drinking a couple glasses of Jamaican Rum Punch, where I would start singing church songs or praying out loud while crying. After a while, my girlfriends didn't want to hang out with me again – they said I was becoming a "fruitcake". I wasn't crazy! I was just totally a walking "wounded heart", and sick to my very soul with life. It was gut-wrenchingly sad that my life wasn't straightened out like I thought it would have been by then. Occasionally, I would find myself going to church on Sunday, but would sit in the back so no one would notice me.

I had dreamed of being happily married to Harley, with he and I doing things together, including church. I was not prepared to still be single and dating. I was totally miserable. I kept going to the club on the weekends after working all week, because I would be too lonely and unhappy to just go from home to work and back to home and back to work. I began reading my Bible again, and praying a little more often. Finally, Harley and I began talking a little more seriously about getting back together again. Only this time, I didn't feel that I could trust him unless he was willing to go to church with me. I felt that was the only way I could feel comfortable that he had a changed heart, and wouldn't do the same thing all over again.

According to him, the woman had a baby girl, and he felt sure that it was his child. However, he said he didn't love the woman and that he still really loved me. He claimed then, and still claims that he named the child after me – now, should I believe that or not? You decide!! One thing that truly concerned me was that Harley said the woman told him she would kill herself if he broke completely up with her. I truly didn't want to have anything like that on my conscience. I hated her for helping to wreck my life, but not enough to want her to die.

We spent New Year's Eve together that year. He called and asked me to get dressed in formal wear because he was taking me to a New Year's Eve Ball. We had a totally awesome time, and then we stayed over in a beautiful suite afterwards. We spent all the next day together watching football and talking about what we wanted to do with the rest of our lives. If only we could have blocked out the real world. Late in the evening of New Year's Day, his pager began to buzz repeatedly, time after time. Finally when he checked it, and called the number, it was the baby's grandmother calling to say the woman had run her car into a wall because he had been missing for two days. She was still pregnant at the time, but she and the baby were okay. He left the hotel, and asked me to wait until he came back. I couldn't bring myself to sit and wait while the baby's mother needed him. After that, I stayed away from him for a while, to give them time to work things out without any influence from me.

A couple months later, Harley called me and asked me to meet him to talk for a bit. He had something important he wanted to tell me. I steeled my heart, expecting him to tell me that he was either married or was getting married. I was not at all prepared for what he said. He asked me to pack my clothes and leave town with him; and to go some place to start a brand new life away from everyone we knew.

...Can't Live With/ Without Him...

At first I thought he was joking, and I giggled. Then I looked at his face and realized he was serious. We talked for a long time, but the bottom line was, I told him I couldn't leave my children, grandchildren and parents with no contact for a long time. I have no idea what he was planning, but I wasn't willing to go. Afterwards, we began to see each other less and less often. Either he or I would say it was over from time to time, but after a week or so, we would wind back up together for a bit. One time, he "jokingly" told me that I had some kind of "spell" on him because he felt like he was hypnotized and couldn't live without me.

I didn't know anything about 'soul ties' back then, but knew exactly what he meant. Whenever I tried to think of moving on in my life without him, I would have a panic attack and have trouble swallowing. I would literally have palpitations of the heart and feel like I was going to pass out. At one point we were so bound together, that when the first cell phones came out – yes, those really big ones – he was one of the first people I knew who bought two. There was one for me, and one for him, so he could call me every couple hours all day while we were at work. They looked like big old walkie talkies. The thing was so big; I had to sit it on the desk at work, because it wouldn't fit into my pocket. He would call and say just a few words, or sing Stevie Wonder's song, "I just called to say I love you." What a lovable giant klutz! Unfortunately, I loved him but couldn't bring myself to trust him.

Finally, he came to the apartment and spent a couple days with me. We talked again about what we wanted to do. He asked me again to marry him, and this time I said "Yes". We began to make plans to elope secretly to get married a couple days later. I began to feel uneasy, so I called two close church friends whom I knew would pray with me and tell me what was right to do. I really loved Harley, but did not want to make another mistake. I called the Pastor who had counseled Harley and me when all the confusion first started, and I told her we were going to get married. I expected her to be happy for us, but she voiced opposition, saying "How do you know that he has all of his business straightened out?" "Oh no", I thought to myself, "I really don't want to hear this." I hung up the phone with her, and she called the other sister friend, who called me and hit the roof.

I guess those two must have prayed some super duper prayers, because somehow or other, Harley and I never did what we said. There was always some reason or other why we couldn't go, until eventually, I changed my mind. I began to pray and ask God to fix my heart so that I would not be so lonely as to be willing to settle for someone who was not really the right person for me. My heart was so messed up, that I just couldn't think of being without him for the rest of my life. I felt like I would rather be dead. I began to pull back from other guys as well, and began to stay home more. I began inviting family and friends over to my apartment occasionally, and tried to find some other activities to do besides going out to the clubs. I really missed the camaraderie of partying and dancing on the dance floor with other people, but I wanted to get myself together.

I began to go to church more often, and began to feel better about myself. My biggest challenge was my extremely mixed feelings about Harley. Every day I would pray and ask God to change his heart, so that he would be interested in church along with me. It seemed like the more I prayed for that, the harder he began to party and go further away. He never discouraged me from going to church, but he definitely was not interested. He and his siblings had been forced to attend church as children in Jamaica, by his grandmother; and he wanted no parts of it now. That posed a big problem for me because I knew that ultimately, I would not really be able to trust him fully if I felt that he was not fully committed to doing what was right. To my understanding, the only thing that would make any human being do or not do certain things, would be an internal sense of right or wrong guided by their awareness of God. I mean, after all, him loving me had not prevented him from being unfaithful previously. I felt that there had to be a different type of change within the inside of him that would "check" him even if I wasn't around. As time went on, I tried everything that I could to coerce him, and to show him how wonderful our life together could be. He loved all of the extra attention, but felt that I was trying to control him; which in a way, I guess that I really was.

While all of this was going on, I was being more stressed on my job. I was working as the Charge Nurse of an extremely busy inner city Psychiatric Emergency Room with too many patients and too few staff members. I began to experience panic attacks, with problems swallowing, shortness of breath and palpitations of the heart. The more stressed I was at home and at work, they more frequent and severe the attacks would come on. The attending doctor on my job prescribed something to help reduce the anxiety. Hold it just one doggone minute!!! This is nuts!! Finally, I made a decision that something had to give, and it definitely was "not" going to be my mind. After all, I was a Psychiatric Nurse, not a Psychiatric patient.

I bit the bullet with all of my damaged inner strength, and broke it off with Harley. Say what!!! Of course, I had to take extra medications for a few days; and had to take some days off from work so that I could intermittently bawl and scream without them locking me up in isolation. By the end of the week, I could finally take a full deep breath without feeling like I was breathing through a broken straw. Hallelujah! I was going to live after all, even without Harley. I really involved myself with work, family, and going to church on my weekends off. I began to feel almost normal again.

...Blast From The Past...

One day when I came in from work, there was a voice message for me on the answer machine. I was absolutely floored because it was a young lady whom I had not seen or heard from in about ten years. She had a telephone company supervisor help her to find my name and number. I was informed that Mother Murdock, the woman who had prayed for Michael and me many, many years before was in a coma, and on life support. I rushed up to the hospital, and there were all of her children, none of whom I had seen for almost twenty years. We all cried, comforted and prayed with one another; and exchanged phone numbers. A few days later, Mother Murdock passed.

Soon afterwards, I received another surprise phone call; this time from Mother Murdock's son, Eric. He invited me to dinner and to a small circus taking place in the park. From there, we ended up dating, and were like two peas in a pod. I could hardly believe my ears; here was another guy who liked so many of the same things that I liked. Plus, the very best part was that he was a man who loved going to church and reading his bible. Awww shucks!! Things are about to change big time!! – or were they?

Eric and I would talk for hours about everything, and it seemed that we agreed about most things. He was coming out of a failed marriage, after finding his wife in bed with a friend. He shared with me that he had filed for divorce, and was waiting for it to finalize. We were even able to talk about the pain of being betrayed, and together we decided that neither one of us would do that to someone whom we really cared for. After about six months, Eric asked me to marry him, and I said, "Yes".

There was one primary concern that I had, which was the fact that Eric had a very young daughter, Jasmine. I soon learned that the daughter was not a problem, but her mother used Jasmine as a source of contention with Eric. The mother knew that he really loved his daughter, and that he would do anything that he could for the child.

There were a couple times when Eric called me and was very angry because his "ex' wife had come to his job on pay day asking him for extra money, even though they had a court agreement that child support payments would be made through the court. Eric had requested this arrangement so that he would have to have no contact with the mother. Eric and the child's mother had shared custody of Jasmine; and Eric's twin sister, Erica was to be the liaison for weekend visits. The child's mother lived not far from Erica, and was to leave Jasmine with Erica every other Friday, and was to pick her up on Sunday evenings. Somehow, there seemed to be a problem with the drop-off or the pick-up every few weeks or so. Eric asked me not to allow his ex-wife's issues to become my issues or to frustrate me. He assured me that the courts were going to make some changes soon, and that he was filing for full custody of Jasmine. After several discussions, and me pondering over it for a while, I agreed that it was okay with me if he had to do that. Jasmine was young, but thank God she was not still in diapers. (Ha-Ha)

Eric and I were very happy together and began making plans to have a decent sized wedding. Erica and her fiancée decided they wanted to have a double wedding and reception with Eric and me; which was fine with us. We were happily preparing for a New Year's Eve candlelight wedding for about 150 guests – the church was paid for, the bridesmaids' dresses were ordered, the reception supplies were purchased, etc., etc. Everything appeared to be going along well, until just before Thanksgiving. It was around that time that I noticed Eric seemed to be increasingly irritated with even the smallest of things. Then, he showed up late after work one Friday that we were supposed to go out, and I could tell he had been drinking. No matter how much I tried to get him to talk about what was bothering him, he just begged off from talking about it.

By the next day, he was very apologetic, but by now, I was definitely getting to be more than a little apprehensive. Then he seemed to work whatever it was out, and we were sailing clear again for a while. Finally, he broke down and told me that his "ex" wife had been calling his job every day, crying and asking him for another chance. He said that he really loved and was happy with me, and had no thought or intention of going back with her. He expressed concern about Jasmine. My conscience began to bother me, thinking that if he was not with me, perhaps he would have given her another chance. He assured me that this was not possible, and that he had caught her in the same kind of situation on more than one occasion, and had given her multiple chances. I began to really pray and ask God for clarity about the situation, and to show me what to do. That following Friday, Eric was missing after work again until late. This time, I knew in my heart that he was with his wife, and by the time he called me later that night with some excuse about a buddy, my decision was made to leave him alone. I told him that I was calling everything off, and he begged and pleaded with me not to make a final decision until we could talk face to face. I agreed to talk the next day when he came over. When I took one look at his face, I knew that he had slept with his 'ex' wife, and when I confronted him about it, he broke down and asked for my forgiveness.

He explained that she had called him again for some "emergency" with Jasmine, and that he had gone there, and one thing led to another. Long story short, it was over for me. After I made my final decision, he went back with her, but before the month was out, he found her in a compromising position again. Of course, he wanted to come back to me, but I was more than through!!

...Taking Care of Me...

I decided that I really truly needed to take some time out for my own sanity sake. At that point, I stopped seeing anyone at all for a long time. I began to be frustrated again with my job back in the clinical setting. I wanted to make some extra money, but not by working overtime in the hospital. I typed resumes for a couple co-workers. Then, the word began to spread that I was good at typesetting, including resumes, flyers and term papers. Little by little, my client list grew until I had the idea to start a home-based "typing" business on the side. Within a few months, I actually had enough business to cut my hospital hours down to part-time. I enjoyed working from home much better than working in the clinical setting.

I decided to take a leap of faith to start another business venture, this time a typing service. I leased a computer, and spend night and day for about a week, teaching myself from the online tutorials, how to use the applications. After a couple major boo-boo's, I was adequately "computer savvy". I pulled out a yellow page book and went down the title insurance company pages; and within one week, I had two commercial customers that I typed insurance policies for from home. I was totally candid with the manager of the first office, and told him that I had no idea of what I was doing! However, I told him that I would type his first two policies for free, if he gave me specific instructions about which forms to use, etc. He did - I did - and the rest, as they say, is history.

A couple days later, as I was driving near my home, I walked into a copy shop that was in my area, which had "typing" in the window as one of the services they offered. I went in and offered my typing services to them; and was told their typist had just walked out that morning! All I needed was a fax machine at home to receive their work. I went straight to the store and purchased one. In the weeks that followed, I began spending more time typing from home, while working less at the hospital. I had finally found something creative that I liked doing, and which I was good at. Wow!

At the end of three months, I had so much work, that I hired a friend to help out. Much of my work came in by word of mouth and by referrals from other businesses. At the end of six months, I quit my job at the hospital and opened up a retail print and copy shop in a small leased building near my home. I offered many of the services available at larger shops, such as Kinko's. Business was booming, and I had about 200 regular customers on my books. When I was preparing to open the shop, I was pondering over some equipment that I would need, and guess who showed up. Remember the one who told me years earlier, "Anything for you Babe." Well, let me remind you, it was my sweetie pie giant, "Harley". We kept in touch occasionally by phone, but no longer dated. When I told him that I was trying to get things set up to open the shop, he was right there, "Johnnie on the spot."

He and one of the brothers from the church painted and hung blinds, in preparation for the opening day. Then, Harley totally blew my mind by purchasing a commercial high speed copier for me! Wow! I could hardly believe it. He reiterated to me that he still loved me and would always do anything that he could to help me or my family. I was ecstatic over how God blessed me in such a quick time to get things in place for the business. On the other hand, I cried for several days afterwards, wondering why Harley and I could somehow never quite seem to get it all together. Even now, as I write this, I feel a twinge of sadness because he and I didn't make it; even though I am like 110% sure that we really cared deeply for each other. Who knows why??

Meanwhile, with all of the pros of my booming business, there were some 'cons' coming about as well, including me working harder and for more hours than when I was at the hospital. Instead of forty hours per week, I was working sixty to seventy hours again! Most of my customers did not want my friend to do their work; they insisted that they could tell the difference. I think I had just given them too much special attention when I first started out, and they were spoiled rotten! I wasn't even getting to church on most Sundays. In addition to these issues, I also had double the expenses now, between home and the business.

I found that to run a successful business, there is a lot of hard work and maintenance to be done. Whew! All I actually had wanted to do was to do some typing for people, to pick up extra money. I attended multiple training sessions sponsored by the Small Business Administration in our area, and made use of many free and low cost services which they offered. By the end of the second year, I decided that I was not in a season in my life when I wanted to work so hard that I had no time for a social life or family. I decided to close the business, and return to a regular "9 to 5" job with normal hours; with no one hounding you to get a job done even after the office closed.

...Which Way To Go?...

I decided that I would take a little time off before transitioning back into my nursing profession. It was early 1997, and I used that time to go and stay with my youngest daughter, who was living alone in a small town in New York State. The area was mountainous and absolutely gorgeous; and the few months that I stayed there with her were very restorative. Eventually, I decided it was time to return home, and get back to "real life". I realized that I really did not want to go back to work in a hospital setting. I decided to return to my previous job with the Clinical Research Organization, as a clinical data analyst. I worked in an office setting reviewing patient records for side effects to new or updated medications. There was no direct patient or physician contact, for which I was grateful; and best of all, I didn't work weekends or holidays.

This time around, I decided not to take another apartment right away, so I opted to rent a room in the home of a young lady who was a friend of my son. In actuality, I had the use of the entire house, and I began to settle in peacefully. I was finally able to have some social and family time again, and enjoyed going back to church. One Sunday after church, I went up to greet the Pastor. She hugged me as she always did, and this time she whispered in my ear, *"God is going to move you to the mountains."* I smiled and hugged her back, not having the faintest idea of what that meant. I thought about it for a few days, and then decided that she must have been talking figuratively, and that maybe I was going to start another business project, only this time bigger and better. I continued on with life as usual.

The only real challenge for me at that time was the 1 to 1 ½ hour commute to and from work every day. For this reason, I began to look in the area surrounding my job for an apartment. I noticed a flyer posted on the bulletin board at work by a female coworker, 'Sharon', who was looking for a tenant to share her townhouse. Moving to the small township where she lived would cut my commute about half the time and distance. That seemed like a "no brainer'. I followed Sharon home one day after work, and was really impressed by the beauty of the area as we travelled over some back roads. The house was a beautiful stone front twin townhouse in a fairly new development. I immediately fell in love with the surrounding area, the fireplace and her beautiful golden Cocker Spaniel named "Mags", short for "Sugar Magnolia". I wasn't sure that I would really like the area, so we agreed to a six month lease period. We came to an agreement the same day, she gave me a key, and within a month I moved to Marshfield.

In the meantime, as I began to bring boxes home from work to pack, another coworker asked me where I was moving to. I told her the name of the township and she said, "Oh, that's nice, you're moving to the country." I politely let her know that where I was moving to was not country, but the suburbs, and "don't get it twisted." First of all, I am city born and suburban bred; and secondly, I am afraid of everything living that is not human and walking on two legs. I assured her that I had already driven up to see the place, that it was not far from a neighboring city, and that the only animals I had seen near the house were dogs and cats.

Well!! That sweet darling coworker felt it was her duty to inform me that she had worked in Marshfield for a few years, and that the area was rural and country, not suburban! After a few rather tart comments from me, I started thinking that maybe I had better do a little more checking. I called a good friend of mine and asked her if she and her husband would take a ride with me the following Saturday to go back up to take another look at the house. I needed to reassure myself, and prove a point to Ms. Smarty-pants on the job.

...Country or Not?...

This time I had to use MapQuest to get directions directly from my friend's house in the city, since the first time I went, we started out from the job. MapQuest suggested the drive time to be about an hour, which seemed about right to me, since the house was not far from my job. I picked my friends up, and we laughed and talked, following the directions. At one point, the directions led us up a portion of highway near the job, and then unexpectedly to me, we had to go one exit on the turnpike.

I started feeling a little edgy, but since it was only to be one exit, I decided not to get all freaked out about it. Plus, according to MapQuest, the house address was only about 5 minutes from the exit we would be coming off of. Sure enough, we came off the turnpike, took a couple quick turns past a convenience store, some businesses and another housing development and were right there. Oh boy! I just couldn't wait to get to get back to work on Monday to rub my coworker's face in her "newsy" mis-information. Sharon wasn't home, but my friends and I went inside and took a full tour of the house, and they loved it as much as I did. We talked about how wonderful it was that God was blessing me to live closer to the job, and in such a nice area. We said a short prayer and prepared to leave. Then, my friend's husband suggested that we ride around to do a little sightseeing of the area, and find a bite to eat.

None of us knew where we were so we just decided to drive down one of the roads to take a look-see. It was an absolutely beautiful late September day. We rode for about five to six minutes outside of the development. To the complete surprise of all of us, we rode right past some farmhouses, with LIVE animals outside grazing!!!!!! Whaaaaaaaaaaaaaaaat! Right there in front of my eyes were sheep, goats, and horses! Not to mention, that smell!! Oh my God!! This is not even funny!! Okay, okay, okay – don't freak out completely – it is only 1 of the roads in the area!! Let's go back the same way we came as fast as we can. My friends thought the whole thing was hysterically funny, but trust me, I was not laughing at all.

Long story short – the housing development that I was preparing to move to the following week was smack dab in the middle of "farmland" in all four directions! Now, that was one of the few times in my life that I truly, truly, truly knew that God has a real sense of humor – and I definitely was not feeling it right then!!!!! As we were driving down the next road, a huge truck drove past us jammed pack full of humongous squealing pigs!! You have got to be kidding me!! Do I puke now or wait until later from the smell or from the sight of those huge creatures???????? (How many exclamation marks am I allowed to use to let you know that I was totally and completely freaked out by now!!!!!!!!!!!!!!!!!!!!!!!!!!!!!!?) Of course, my friend's husband felt the need to educate me right at that minute that the name on the side of that "pig truck" was a brand name of bacon and other pork products commonly sold in our supermarkets. *Thank you, brother, I really needed to know that right now as I see my life flashing before my eyes!*

To make matters even more hysterically worse, the last road that we drove down for about ten minutes proved to demonstrate to me that not only was I "in the country", but also that I was "in the mountains" because we were in the foothills of the Pocono Mountains!! Okay – somebody can pinch me good and hard to wake me up now!! Needless to say, I cried and prayed for the next day and a half, trying to figure out a way to get out of the lease. You have to understand the seriousness of this to a person who is squeamish about even a little thing like a housefly! I decided to put my foot down, and no matter what – I was not going to do it!!

Somehow, some way, I managed to drag myself to church the next day, and I told my Pastor what happened. She prayed with me and related that she felt like this opportunity was going to open up some major doors for me in my life, and that I should take courage and go for it. Soooooo, after wimping around and whining for a couple days, I decided that I was not going to chicken out.

...I Really Did It...

In October of 1997, I moved to Marshfield, and my life changed beyond my imagination again. To begin with, for the first time in my life, I was physically living away from everything and everyone familiar to me, including all of my family and friends. Sharon stayed away from home at her boyfriend's house about 80% of the time, and I was too far from the city to go visiting every day. I was also now living in a geographical area where the color of my skin was seldom seen; Sharon was Italian. Thus far, I had seen only one other African American in our complex at all. It was bad enough that I was only one of a miniscule number of Blacks working at my job. The challenge of that alone was stressful for someone who had real struggles with my self esteem. Now, here I was in the country and in the mountains – and just how did this happen????

In addition to all of that, winter was coming and I was really concerned that I wouldn't be able to get down to attend my own church each week. At least, I had found some small sense of belonging there, which has always been a real challenge for me. I have always felt somehow on the "periphery" of things and people; never quite a "real" part. I have come to peace with the idea that this is one of my "healed scars" from all of my life's experiences; and that it was something that I always had to work at. The good thing is that it no longer caused me to have serious bouts of depression.

After the first month of feeling totally isolated, I bit the bullet and visited a church not far from where I lived, after riding back and forth past it about *ten* times – it was soooo huge, and the number of people coming and going made me feel overwhelmed. I finally forced myself to go in, and much to my surprise was greeted warmly by most. Ironically, I was personally challenged to not succumb to my own sense of racial tension and prejudice. Once I addressed that within myself, I was able to interact comfortably with those who made themselves friendly towards me. All of this was definitely a proving ground for me, and no, not everyone received me with open arms. I actually had to have a verbal discussion with a couple people who were disrespectful towards me, but we all managed to iron things out.

For the first time in a long time, I was blessed to develop some truly meaningful relationships with people not of my complexion, and I learned just how ignorantly judgmental I had been. Trust me, that doesn't mean that everyone warmed up to me, and neither did I warm up to everyone else. However, I did have some major positive surprises. Within a couple months, I was actively involved with the Counseling Ministry, and also became a small group leader. After about a year, I was ordained as a Lay Pastor and was busily working in the church. Amazingly, although my initiation into Marshfield was rather unconventional, I grew to love the area in spite of all of the smells (yuck) and strangeness. In spite of my original six month "trial" lease, I ended up living there with Sharon and Mags for five years!! By that time, Sharon was engaged to be married. I moved to another small town, directly adjacent to Marshfield and actually spent another year there. Go figure!

One of the major areas in my life that I had begun to work on during the earlier stay with my daughter, was my desire for a more structured education of the Bible. I began to ponder the possibility of enrolling into a seminary, but didn't feel that I wanted a program that would be quite so intense. Instead I enrolled into a distance learning course through a well known School of Ministry, and was still in the process of completing that course when I moved to Marshfield. After I moved, I decided to pursue Biblical

Education more seriously. I completed the distance learning course, and then enrolled into an on campus class of the same School of Ministry, near where I lived. At the same time, I enrolled into a Pastoral Counseling Certification Program through another well known seminary, by Distance Learning. Call me crazy, but I became totally enmeshed with the two programs full-time, and I loved it!! I didn't get much sleep for a few years while living in Marshfield, and again had minimal social life, but I had found a major "love" of my life. I realized that my love for learning and teaching was an integral part of who I was, and I no longer had to be embarrassed because of it.

Wow! I began to develop a strengthening of my "selfness" – and I began to be in touch with the idea that I had a "right" to do something that made me feel good about myself. I had a right to learn about as many things as I wanted to, and to challenge myself to go beyond what other people felt I should and should not do. It was during this same period of my life that Michael kind of floated in and around my life, making contact from time to time, even though he was living with another woman again. There were even a couple times that we tried to talk about working things out again, but somehow we always ended up getting into a heated argument about the past. He still accused me of abandoning him for God, and I was still angry with him for leaving me alone to raise our children while he was busy drugging and whoring. Is there any way out of this quicksand?

As a part of the Peer Counseling Ministry at the church, I was encouraged to attend a specialty support group called "Divorce Care." Initially I resisted the idea, thinking to myself that Michael and I had been divorced so many years earlier, that surely I was over it. Plus, as far as my second "marriage" to Tustee was concerned, I knew that it was not even a real marriage at all, because I later learned he was already legally married to someone else. I figured that I had enough experiences over the years, that I didn't need "divorce counseling".

...Awakening...

In obedience to the recommendation of the Senior Pastor, I signed up, and began to attend the weekly group. The meeting consisted of watching a videotape about various issues such as emotional trauma, depression, anger, damaged self esteem, etc. The videotape would then be followed by a 45 minute group discussion. To my utter amazement, I came face to face with some very strong emotions in myself that I thought I had overcome years before.

Part of the message of the Divorce Care Program was to show couples who are married and contemplating divorce, what a healthy marriage is supposed to look like. Then each week, a different area of challenge was addressed that takes place within marriages, which can result in an erosion of the relationship. The program helped to identify problem areas, and also offered techniques of problem solving, or emotional healing in that specific area. The mindset is that even if a person's current marriage is irreconcilable; hopefully lessons would be learned to help avoid the same problems in a possible future marriage. In addition, there were several couples who decided to not divorce, but to work through the problems which had now been uncovered.

While attending the meetings, I personally had a very challenging time when coming face to face with some of the issues. For example, I had to realize and admit for the first time that Michael and I never really had a "healthy" marriage, and that we had never had a time when we were in a monogamous relationship. Throughout all of the time that we were together, he always had someone(s) outside. In spite of this, something in me had caused me to join myself to someone who was "emotionally unavailable", when I myself felt so "needy". The crazy thing is that I repeated the same pattern with other guys after Michael as well. I had to go through a real challenging time of self introspection to look at what it was about my own warped emotions that caused me to always seek after the "forbidden fruit" – the fruit that these guys seemed to offer, but which was really just an imitation of the real thing. Would I even know what "real" love, not just temporary passion or sympathy from a man looked like?

I had to come to grips with what it was in me that kept driving me to get into relationships with guys who would turn out to be unfaithful – and usually from the very beginning of the relationship. As I began to look back, I realized that in every single serious relationship (or what I thought was serious) I had been in, I would later realize I had been "victimized" because they had been unfaithful; and I had been "blind" (by choice or voluntarily, hard to tell) to it – me, the *grieving victim.*

Wow! This was a time of serious soul searching for me, and it changed my whole perspective about myself – because I realized that the key to my failed relationships was in me, *not the guys*. I also had a real revelation that I, myself had also been "emotionally unavailable" to my mates because I was too "needy". I was like a vacuum or a bottomless pit, always looking for a man to help me be filled. Yes, I did feel actual love at that time for the person "down in my heart". But now in hindsight I understood that my need to control (out of fear of rejection) and my voracious emotional hunger, completely overshadowed my ability to really express (freely release) my feelings of love.

...Choice...

"Love", like "Joy", is not just goose bumps and a "You take my breath away" sensation. True "Love" comes out of a ***choice*** to "care and to share, no matter what". The "feeling" of love comes and goes, but the choice is what has to stand! Then the feeling will return again and again. The same is true of true "Joy", it is a ***choice*** to recognize and appreciate (savor, like slowly rolling candy over your tongue) someone or something, while taking the time to stop and say, "Wow!" on the inside. Again, the "feeling" of joy comes and goes, but the decision to remain "satisfied" is what you have to choose to stand in, no matter what! Then the feeling will return again and again.

For example, in spite of the smells (yuck) and the creepy creatures in Marshfield – it was while there for the first time that I was quiet and alone within myself long enough to recognize even the small things that gave me joy. I learned that I actually enjoyed the country. I am a person who does enjoy the beauty of the sky, and the hundreds of different trees and flowers. I also enjoyed just riding or sitting in my car on the side of the road, looking up at the larger mountains in the distance.

I had never taken the time to take a deep breath and just feel the sensation of inner "joy" that comes from within, when feeling the warmth of the sun or smelling the air during a fresh rainfall. Thank God that while in the open environment of the country and mountains, away from the constant need to push, push, push – run, run, run, I began to heal from the inside out. The deep emptiness and longing for peace and contentment began to be filled, even without my understanding of how or when. That's where I learned to experience real "joy" just by being "me" where I was; and to savor the feeling on the inside of "Wow". Since then, I've learned more and more how to experience life, love and joy with positivity – I "choose" to do so.

My daughter and her husband sent me away for a few days to the shore last year for my birthday – it was an amazing experience for me! My bedroom had one entire wall which faced the ocean. I lay on the bed and watched the beautiful sunrises and sunsets over the ocean. I looked at the never ending beauty of the ocean for as far as the eye could see. I listened to the sounds of the waves and I "felt" the peace of God give me an astounding 'inner joy", just because I am – and because I was there. Wow!

More recently, I stayed overnight at a luxury hotel as a courtesy from a church where I was to speak the following morning. I was tired after travelling quite a distance from the wonderful seminary graduation of my youngest daughter; so for the first time "ever" in my entire life, I opted to use the room service which was also provided for me, to order a late dinner. As I was sitting there quietly eating the food, which somehow tasted amazingly delicious, I felt an inner sense of satisfaction and "joy". As the tears began to run down my face, I smiled from the inside out and said, "Thank you God." I have come to understand that it's not at all about the biggest or the best – that there is an "inner joy" that is reachable "just because". Because of ...? *Just because I choose to "recognize and appreciate" whatever or whoever, at any given time or place.* There is no possible way for me to record in this book my entire day to day journey during the season of my life that I have lived since Marshfield, because it would become an encyclopedia.

Let me sum it up by saying this – I no longer hold Michael or anyone else hostage in my heart or mind for "what they did to me". (Or, at least, on most days I don't). In their defense, let me say, "It is impossible to fill (satisfy) a *bottomless* pit". I was sooooooooooooo emotionally needy, the Grand Canyon pales in comparison. As I worked my way through the Divorce Care groups, I came to realize that for the rest of my life, with God's help, I will never "choose" to be a victim again. I still hope to be remarried at some point in my life, but this one thing I know for sure, we both will have to be emotionally healthy and available. I have learned that the true source of my "Joy" has to come from a source higher than a man – and then we as humans can share it with one another. (And the church said "*Amen*")

During those "healing" times in my life, and up to the present, I have come to realize and understand something – I DO HAVE REAL VALUE, and so do you. I deserve to love and be loved by a man who knows that I (and he) am precious enough, that no other supplement is needed. (You go girl!!) There is a saying that "Hindsight is always 20-20", meaning we can usually look back with clarity and realize how and why something happened. I have been out of the country and mountains for several years now, but I thank God every day for the opportunity that He gave me to "come aside" before I would "come apart", to find my life irrevocably devastated.

In 2001, I graduated from both the School of Ministry and the Pastoral Counseling programs, and since that time I have been called into the ministry to Pastor, and also to be the founder of a Bible Institute. Can you imagine that in the "real world" an emotionally crippled, sexually molested, wounded and broken, given up on, counted out, high school drop-out, single mother of six children and welfare recipient would ever become an emotionally healthy, happy, joyful and positive woman, with a zest for life and a love for people? This we know can only be by the Grace of God!

THE END

(or I should say, a new beginning)

Who Is September Summer?

She is a truly grateful woman whom God has awesomely blessed to achieve accomplishments beyond her wildest imagination. This, despite the challenges in her life which are chronicled in her books "While the Dew Is Still on the Roses" and "He Tells Me That I Am His Own"; "The Joy We Share As We Tarry There_

Well known by many for her depth of love for people, September has a quick sense of humor, a "down to earth" perspective, and a faith-based worldview. If asked to describe her primary life focus in one word, most people who know her would assure you, the word is **"Relationships"**. In addition to this, she strongly affirms that God is indeed "the center of her joy". You could say her modus operandi is "Positively Positive".

As an author, September has a way of sharing a story which causes the reader to "be present" in the events as they are laid out before you. Her writing style is said to be "conversational", seeming as if you are sitting in her living room having a personal visit with her. Hence, her readers have often commented that they have "laughed, cried, cussed, etc." while reading her books; not to mention, many are unwilling to stop reading until reaching the end.

Her books have quickly become a favorite among her readers of all ages and gender. Look forward with anticipation to see other excellent books from this prolific writer and sought after inspirational speaker.

She is the very proud mother of 6, and "Mom-Mom" of 14 grandchildren and 5 great-grands. Surely her "cup runneth over".... Who knew??? "

"All of the Glory and Honor belong to God"

www.ingramcontent.com/pod-product-compliance
Lightning Source LLC
LaVergne TN
LVHW051544070426
835507LV00021B/2406